ADVANCE PRAISE

"Buckle up for an unforgettable journey as Roslyn Bernstein's *The Girl Who Counted Numbers* plunges her intrepid heroine into the secrets of her uncle's wartime past. Against the backdrop of the Eichmann trial in Israel, one woman's quest evolves from finding a missing person to confronting her own identity, forged from the ashes of the Holocaust and the conflicts of politics and prejudice. A thrilling detective story, a moving love story, a timeless encounter with history."
 —Ann Kirschner, Author, *Sala's Gifts*

"All families must deal with the past in order to move forward, but for some families that is harder than for others. Roslyn Bernstein's beautiful new novel chronicles one family's difficult quest for peace. Moving, nuanced and inspiring, this gripping book rings achingly true."
 —Gish Jen, Author, *Thank You, Mr. Nixon*

"This is the deeply researched story of a quest for a homeland that rings of *justice and longing*. Roslyn Bernstein deals with how we remember, and how we confront our morally complicated histories A wonderful book for our times."
    —**Colum McCann, Author,** *Apeirogon*

"The author brings the troubled young nation of Israel alive on the page... This compelling, character-driven story will captivate even those with limited knowledge of Jewish history, the Nazis, or Eichmann and teach valuable lessons along the way... An engrossing mystery wrapped in a coming-of-age story and the heart-rending legacy of the Holocaust."
    — *Kirkus Reviews* **(starred review)**

THE GIRL WHO COUNTED NUMBERS

A NOVEL

ROSLYN BERNSTEIN

ISBN 9789493276383 (ebook)

ISBN 9789493276369 (paperback)

ISBN 9789493276376 (hardcover)

Publisher: Amsterdam Publishers, The Netherlands

info@amsterdampublishers.com

The Girl Who Counted Numbers is part of the series New Jewish Fiction

National Jewish Book Awards 2023 Finalist

Independent Press Award 2023 Distinguished Favorite

Copyright © Roslyn Bernstein, 2022

Cover photograph: "Untitled" by Liselotte Grschebina, ca. 1960, courtesy of The Israel Museum, Jerusalem. The photograph was chosen by the author because it evokes the time and place of the novel. Grschebina (1908-1994) was an Israeli photographer who emigrated from Germany to Tel Aviv, Israel, in 1934, when the Nazis came to power. She was influenced by the New Vision, a photography movement, which developed in the 1920s and was directly related to the principles of the Bauhaus.

All Rights Reserved. No part of this publication may be reproduced or transmitted in any form or by any means, electronic or mechanical, including photocopy, recording or any other information storage and retrieval system, without prior permission in writing from the publisher.

This is a work of fiction. Names, characters, and locations are products of the author's imagination. Any reference to historical events, real people, or real places are used fictitiously.

CONTENTS

Chapter 1	1
Chapter 2	18
Chapter 3	47
Chapter 4	82
Chapter 5	138
Chapter 6	178
Chapter 7	199
Chapter 8	231
Chapter 9	239
Chapter 10	260
Glossary	263
Acknowledgments	267
About the Author	269
Amsterdam Publishers Holocaust Library	271

1

For almost a week, Susan rehearsed what she was going to tell her father. There were at least two different scenarios. They would be seated in the breakfast nook, the *New York Times* obscuring their faces. She would interrupt the moment by saying, "Dad, I've made a decision," and he would lower his paper and stare at her, waiting for her to speak. They would be out for a walk on the beach on a Sunday afternoon, the sky gray, as if snow were about to fall. She would throw a stone in the water and watch it sink. He would throw a larger stone in the water, forming concentric ripples until it disappeared. Both scenarios frightened her.

He would not be happy. She was sure of that. She'd already agreed to his plan, the one that he'd worked out meticulously since she was 13, the year her mother died of cancer. She'd graduated high school early, six months ahead of her classmates, finishing with honors in all of her academic subjects and she had won a scholarship to the college of her choice in New England starting in the fall of 1961. It would be the beginning of a bright career, he assured her, each step carefully conceived. She would go on to become a doctor or a lawyer like her father, Yehudah. He often joked that he could already see her name, Susan Reich, on a brass plaque on his office door, smaller than his of course.

Lately, just thinking about the plan for her future gave her hives. Itchy red bumps appeared on both arms when she sat in the Café Figaro at the corner of Bleecker and MacDougal Streets, listening to a folk singer strum his guitar and flipping through a *Life* magazine story on Greenwich Village. She envied the young folks hanging out on the grass in Washington Square Park. *That could be me,* she thought, scratching the hives incessantly. All she had to do was tell her father no.

No, I will not be starting college in the fall. No, I will not do what you want me to do. Yes, it is time for me to go out on my own, take a road trip west, and maybe even share an apartment. She could see his face: his cheeks flushed, sweat pouring down his forehead. No words at first. Always a measured response. Nodding before he spoke. Listening to the judge. Listening to the opposition's lawyer. Then, pouncing.

She would have to pounce first but she didn't have the faintest idea how to do it. Rebellion was difficult. Since her mother died, she felt that she should be nurturing him. It couldn't be easy raising a teenage daughter alone. Her best friend Barbara told her to make a list. She stole a yellow legal pad from her father's desk drawer. On the first line, she wrote: "I am an adult." Then, she crossed it out and wrote: "Prove that you are an adult." She sat there squirming for half an hour, writing a word, then crossing it out, then writing another. "Adult" was too strong a word. Too assertive. "Grown-up" was better. Grown-up, crossed out. Too wishy-washy. She tried a third word, "mature." He would, she was sure, cross that one out, writing over it in a flourish: "immature."

Making a list proved harder than she expected. A list of her favorite novels was easy. She'd read through the three shelves of Russian novels in the local library, books none of her high school friends touched. Their tastes in reading were different. *The Scarlet Letter, Huckleberry Finn;* assigned in literature to all of the better writers. No one cared about Turgenev's *Fathers and Sons*, a book she'd read twice.

Or a list of her favorite poets. Definitely not Rudyard Kipling, whose poetry struck her as pompous. Her English teacher was not happy when Susan told him that. Not Edgar Allen Poe, whose rhymes annoyed her. "Quoth the Raven"? That was a ridiculous line. It made her laugh.

She loved William Butler Yeats, whose collected poems, in a hard-bound edition, she'd received as a prize for winning a high school poetry competition; and William Carlos Williams, whose striking lines were simple and piercing. She memorized *This Is Just to Say*, taping his poetic confession to her refrigerator door.

> *I have eaten*
> *the plums*
> *that were in*
> *the icebox*
>
> *and which*
> *you were probably*
> *saving*
> *for breakfast*
>
> *Forgive me*
> *they were delicious*
> *so sweet*
> *and so cold.*

She wished that she could speak to her father that way. She tore the paper off the pad, crumpled it up into a ball and aimed for the wastebasket. It landed on the floor two inches away. She would talk to him on Saturday morning. No matter what.

It was getting dark now. She'd promised Barbara she would go to their friend Lenore's party, not that she really wanted to be there.

High school was over for her, thank goodness. She'd never fit in. No steady boyfriend. No slumber parties. None of that silly, chummy stuff. "Hey you, nose in a book," that was the nickname her class president called out when she passed him by in the corridor. It made her smile. *Nose stuck in a book, what could be better*, she thought.

Barbara picked her up at 7:30 p.m., chattering nonstop the whole ride about which boys were going to be there. "Say something," she said to Susan after five minutes. "Are you listening?"

"Sort of," Susan said. "I tried to make a list but I couldn't. All I can think of is my showdown with my dad. He'll never agree to my not going straight on to college. He's stubborn."

"You are, too," Barbara said, "just in case you need to be reminded of that fact. Stubborn and smart, not a good combination! Your dad always thinks that he is right. Even my parents say so. I'm happy to go along with my parents' dreams for me. Why not? They sound pretty good. All the smart kids in our class are heading off to college and no one takes a year off. Why do you have to be different?"

That was a question she could not answer. Discussions with Barbara always ended this way. She despised controversy. How they'd become friends amazed Susan. Barbara was her polar opposite. Susan was the first one to argue, quick to tackle a teacher or a text. "Why was Karl Marx always depicted as an evil man?" she asked her history teacher, who had emigrated from Europe and who never stopped praising American democracy. From that day on, he rarely called on her, shuffling around her chair as if she wasn't there. Once, she remembered raising her hand in front of his face, only to have him turn his back on her.

They rode the rest of the way in silence. A light rain began to hit the windshield. Susan watched the drops streaming down the glass. *That's me*, she thought, looking at the first big drop to hit bottom, resisting but then being swooped sideways by the windshield wiper. *Me versus the rest of my world.*

The next morning, her father was sitting at the breakfast table with his newspaper in hand just as she expected. "There's a terrific story in today's paper on the job market for college grads," he said. "You are one lucky girl!" He was about to launch into his favorite tale about his arduous path as an immigrant. She knew it by heart.

The streets of America were paved with gold. The local library was a holy sanctuary. Late-night newspapers (retrieved from garbage cans) to master English. Potatoes boiled and fried for lunch and dinner.

Interrupting his familiar reverie wasn't easy.

"What if I don't go to college next year?" Susan burst out, collapsing into a chair. Her legs were trembling. "What if I take a year off? I have my whole life in front of me. Why not take a little time off?" There, she'd said it. She could feel her heart beating in her chest. Faster and faster. She shredded the paper napkin by her plate, leaving a pile of white pieces on the table.

He was organizing his thoughts, putting his argument together. The set of his jaw told her so. The slight flaring of his nostrils. The nod to himself. All familiar facial tics.

"You're being foolish," were the first words out of his mouth. "Foolishly foolish!" He loved alliteration. He spread cream cheese methodically over his bagel, not looking up as he spoke. "Who have you been speaking to? You're too smart to hang out with no-goodniks."

That was his favorite expression. You were good or no-good. Never in-between. "There's no gray in this world. Things were black or white." Then, he added, "Don't disappoint me. Don't cheat yourself." He was pouring himself another cup of coffee now, waiting for Susan to speak.

She had spoken to her high school adviser who, although sympathetic, was against the move. It was, she insisted, bad to lose time, to get off track. "Everything's going your way. You're not quite

18 and the whole world is looking rosy." That conversation hadn't helped a bit.

"Give me a break," Susan said, hoping that a personal appeal would move her father. "It's more like dark gray. Just give me time, a year off from college. All I'm asking for is time. Then I'll get back on *your* bandwagon."

"Your bandwagon, not mine," he said, shaking his head. "Why are you so stubborn?" Then, he picked up his *New York Times* and began reading again.

Two days later he brought the subject up again. He was holding a newspaper story that he'd ripped out of the *New York Telegram*. "I've found the perfect solution," he said, reading the headline aloud: "How American Jews Claim Their Jewish Heritage in Israel." Beneath the headline, there was a photo of a group of young people standing in front of the SS *Jerusalem II*, a ship that sailed from New York to Haifa for the Zim Lines.

"That could be you," he said, pointing to the picture. For the first time in a week, he was actually smiling. Her father had come up with a new plan, one that he approved of. "I'll send you to Israel," he said. "You can take a year off *there* instead of dropping out *here*."

Susan wrinkled her nose and clenched her teeth. "That's *not* what I had in mind," she said. "I'm not into the Jewish thing. I don't want to hurt you but right now I feel like I'm an atheist. I know that you sent me to Hebrew school and that I learned Hebrew. But that doesn't mean that I have to become a Zionist, like you."

He grimaced when she said the word Zionist. She knew he would. She could read his face: how dare she reject his beloved Israel, the Jewish homeland.

"If you love the country so much, why haven't you visited it?" After she spoke, she was sorry. His face changed, his skin sagging and his wrinkles deepening. All she could see was the light bouncing off his receding hairline.

He was suddenly somewhere else. A boy of 12, back in his

shtetl in Rozwadów, Poland, walking around the snowy paths of the town square. Chanukah candles flickering in the storefront windows. By his side, his older brother Yakov, his best buddy.

"I've thought of traveling there so many times. I imagined myself getting down on my knees and kissing the holy soil, the land of my fathers. Me, walking the cobblestone streets in Jerusalem. Two years ago, I bought tickets but I was a coward and cashed them in." He shook his head back and forth, interrupting himself. "Over the years, I've made a million excuses to myself. I was in the middle of a trial on an important accident case and I could not leave the country. I was needed to lead the fundraising effort at the synagogue. Without me, the shul would close.

"The truth was that I was afraid. For weeks, I had the same dream. I was sitting in an office in Jerusalem facing a man in a white short-sleeve shirt. 'This is for you,' he said, as he opened a folder and handed me a paper with an official seal. I cried when I saw the large black letters at the top. It said: *Death Certificate of Yakov Reich*.

"I screamed when I saw the paper. I argued with him. You don't know my brother, I said. If anyone could find a way to survive, it would be Yakov. When I woke in the morning, I noticed that I had torn off a piece of paper from the table next to my bed. It lay shredded on the floor.

"I tried so hard to find Yakov but it's been 40 years. No clues at all." He placed a green file on the table. "My correspondence," he said. "Back and forth to agencies in Europe and Israel." He pulled out one letter and read it aloud: "We are sorry to inform you that we have no record for Yakov Reich." Blunt, to the point, written by some functionary. A second letter was even more discouraging: "We have forwarded your letter of inquiry to every relevant agency in Israel and no one has any information on your brother Yakov Reich." Susan noticed that the letters were creased and the paper slightly yellow.

Her father sighed. "Somehow, I cannot convince myself to

travel to Israel without hope. Maybe a fresh outlook would help." He took out a large, white handkerchief and wiped his eyes. "Now, it's your turn. You can be my sleuth. If anyone can find out what happened to Yakov, you can."

The word sleuth caught her off guard. When she was ten, she loved Nancy Drew mystery stories and read them over and over again, dog-earring her favorite pages. Susan identified with Nancy. Both of them had lawyers for fathers. Carson Drew reminded Susan of her dad, with his hard-shell exterior concealing a mushy inner core.

Being a sleuth came naturally to Nancy who could speak French, play tennis, ride a horse, shoot a gun, do just about anything. She was a superhero, the girl who could conquer any obstacle. Susan hadn't the faintest idea how to shoot a gun and she had never really ridden a horse. Once, though, at a riding school, she sat on the saddle, as the instructor spoke. There was a loud boom and the horse started to move. Susan fell off and bruised an elbow.

Nancy was spunky. With her two sidekicks, her cousins Bess Marvin and George Fayne, nothing stopped her.

"I'm not Nancy Drew," Susan said, raising her chin and inadvertently biting on her lower lip. "You're expecting too much of me. Way too much!" She was angry now. Really angry. "It's *your* lost brother. You find him!" There, she'd said it. Bold. Disrespectful. Defiant. Obedient daughters did not talk that way. Her friends would never do this. Never!

He stood up and left the table, his newspaper falling to the floor.

During the next week, he avoided her. Not one "good morning." No eye contact. When she came to the table for breakfast, he picked up his plate and mug and put them in the kitchen sink. On Thursday, she found a brochure from the Zim Shipping Line on the dining table. On the cover was a photo of the

SS *Jerusalem II*, inside, photos of the cabins and the polished, wood-paneled dining room.

Not a very subtle hint. It was his plan; not hers. She would just refuse to go.

All week, she couldn't get the thought of the trip to Israel out of her head.

She drew a black line down a sheet of paper making two columns, con and pro.

Con: a *horrible* idea. A ridiculous idea. She was not going to say yes. She had already gotten into trouble in her Global Studies class by asking her teacher why their textbook only had three sentences on the 1947-1949 War of Independence. For years, Susan's obsession with numbers meant that she counted everything she saw: shoppers on line at the checkout in the supermarket, soda cans stacked on the shelves in the local deli, and white daisies blooming in her neighbor's garden.

There were 27 words celebrating the creation of the State of Israel with two black-and-white photos, one of an olive grove, its trees heavy with fruit, and the other of a narrow, cobblestone street in Jerusalem. Not one word on the displacement of Arabs. It was definitely not a subject that she could bring up with her father.

Moving to Israel, that was definitely not her thing. She wanted to move to Greenwich Village. She wanted to hang out in a coffeehouse and listen to cool jazz. She would grow her hair down to her waist, and patch her jeans in embarrassing places. She would learn to play a guitar. She would meet a guy in Washington Square Park and go home with him. The cons were pouring out of her. By the time she finished her entry, she had filled three columns.

Pro: a *good* idea. A smart idea. She already spoke Hebrew and she would have no trouble making friends. So far, Boston was the farthest city that she'd ever visited. Israel was much more exotic: the gritty port city of Haifa, the thick-walled stone buildings of Jerusalem keeping out the afternoon heat, the art deco homes in Tel Aviv with their circular windows and geometric lines, the barren landscape of the Dead Sea and the Negev. She would work in the fields of a kibbutz where she would meet a handsome sabra. She would be a brilliant sleuth, sniffing out Yakov's story, hitting dead ends, poring over old records, and tracking down flimsy leads. She would be better, much better than Nancy Drew.

She struggled to fill the pro column, constantly crossing things out. She did speak Hebrew but she certainly wasn't fluent. She would be devoured by mosquitos working in the fields. She was not the right type of girl for the handsome sabra. She was much too brainy and opinionated. Of one thing she was certain: she was definitely not a Zionist.

Not one decent night of sleep all week. Up, working on her list at two in the morning. Revising her list before the sun rose. Frustrated, she tore two sheets of paper out of the notebook and began again. The cons still outweighed the pros but the idea of traveling to Israel was growing on her. Maybe it was his idea but it was definitely an escape. She took out the gold Jewish star that her father had given her several years back for Chanukah that she had hidden in the back of her dresser drawer and put it on for the first time. At first, it felt cold, but after a few minutes, it felt warm, almost a part of her.

At the end of the week, she was still paralyzed, worn out by the back and forth. She reached into her box of treasures and took out her lucky coin, the silver half dollar that she'd won at the school bazaar. Heads: she would go. Tails: she would stay. Her hand shook as she threw the coin in the air. Heads. Benjamin Franklin was staring up at her. *Go*, he was saying. *Be adventurous, cross the ocean. I did.* She went over to her nightstand, picked up the Zim brochure and walked into the kitchen. She placed it in the fruit bowl in the center of the table, and clipped a note to it. Just three words: "Count me in."

Two days later, her father arrived home with a large black metal trunk, its heavy brass fittings clanging as he pulled it up the front steps. "I found it in a second-hand shop near my office," he said. "Couldn't resist!" The trunk was beat up, scratched on every side, with hundreds of dents and pockmarks as if someone had used it for target practice. "No holes," her father said, rubbing his hand over one side, "I checked it myself."

As an immigrant, he had mastered the art of saving pennies. He priced the airplane ticket to Tel Aviv on El Al and learned that it was exactly double the price of a Tourist Class Level D cabin on the SS *Jerusalem II*, which he promptly bought for her.

"I came over by ship," he told her, recounting how the SS *Rotterdam* ran smack into a storm halfway across the Atlantic. "We were in steerage class, no portholes, no air, so we slept outside on the deck, unless the waves were too rough. Your cabin is positively luxurious next to the space we slept in, my mother and sisters and me, all huddled together on one lumpy mattress."

Susan started to protest. "You know how seasick I get when we go fishing," she said. As she spoke the words, the taste of vomit filled her mouth. Their ocean outings always resulted in her throwing up all over herself. She came home green and reeking of her own putrid vomit. He never got sick and he insisted that it was mind over matter. "If you concentrate," he said, "you will never feel sick. That's the secret to life: never allow negative thoughts in. Deny the waves. Deny the rocking of the ship. Stay calm."

"It's not psychosomatic," she said, feeling angry. "There's nothing psychosomatic about feeling seasick. There's nothing psychosomatic about vomiting." She was yelling at him now, her voice shrill and loud. He stood there, like a stone monument, his eyes unblinking. There was no convincing him to return the ticket; she could see that from the look on his face. Rigid. No emotion. He would never concede.

Whether she liked it or not, she would have to endure a long sea voyage, her stomach rolling in unison with the endless waves, tortuous days and nights until they finally caught sight of the first land, the Rock of Gibraltar. She had agreed to go to Israel but now she was getting cold feet about the long journey. She doubled her pillow over to prop her head up and lie down on her bed, immediately beginning to argue with him. "Dad. I said yes but I should have said no," she whispered, pretending that he was standing next to her bedside. He did not respond. She tried another tack. "Don't you love me? Do you want me to get sick, fall overboard, and drown?" No matter how extreme her question, he was silent. A deal was a deal with her father, like a legal contract that had been officially notarized. No backing out.

Finally, in desperation, she gave up. Tossing and turning from side to side, she fell asleep. When she woke in the morning, she remembered a piece of her dream. She had been arguing with someone in Hebrew but she did not know who he was and what they were fighting about.

On the day the ship sailed, her father accompanied the porter to her cabin. Her trunk was already there, occupying most of the floor space. There was a narrow single bed, built into one wall, adjacent to a shelf with a night light. There was a tiny sink with a mirror and a toilet big enough for one small person. On one wall, there was a print by a contemporary Israeli artist, a field of olive trees in fractured sunlight.

"Looks cozy, doesn't it?" her father said. Susan did not answer. The walls were closing in on her. She was shrinking, becoming smaller and smaller until she felt paralyzed. Her legs and arms unable to move.

A loud bell rang and then there was a long whistle, followed by an announcement: "We will be departing in ten minutes," the voice said, first in Hebrew and then in English. "All family and friends should say their goodbyes now."

"Write often," her father said, as he kissed her goodbye. "I'll miss you." Susan walked him back up to the main deck. She wanted to tell her father that she was scared. But he did not give her a chance to speak. "You can do this," he said. "I'm counting on you. You're brave and you're smart." There was no time for tears.

The bell rang again and her father walked down the gangplank. He turned and waved, his hands pivoting back and forth in the air. Overhead, seagulls flapped their wings as they swooped up and down in the sky. Two tugboats escorted the ship out of the harbor. Within a short while, they passed the Statue of Liberty and were out to sea.

Susan had barely slept the night before and she lay down on her bed exhausted. Within seconds, she dozed off. When she awoke, it was six o'clock, time for dinner. She pumped the little faucet in the sink several times to get enough water to wash her face and found the stairway to the dining room on level A. Just inside the doorway of the wainscoted hall, the staff had set up a sideboard on which folded seating cards had been placed. Susan was at table 16 in the corner. As it turned out, she was the last to arrive. Already seated and chatting were David and Daniel, two college roommates from Chicago who were heading out on a work-study program to harvest vegetables and pick cotton on an agricultural kibbutz up north, and Flora and Sandra, two sisters from Boston who were on their way to their cousin's wedding in Tel Aviv. The girls looked very much alike, their hair piled high on their heads, their lipstick bright red. They were busy talking about who had the better manicure when Susan sat down. Susan stared at her own nails, short, cut straight across, and unpolished.

The meal was simple, a choice of cold tomato juice with a wedge of lemon or chicken broth, followed by roast chicken or Salisbury steak. Oh, how she hated that mound of ground meat shaped into an oval and slathered with mushroom gravy that her father served at least once a week. She would cut it into even chunks and pretend to eat it, leaving a grid of them on her plate.

There was a basket of soft white rolls in the center of the table but no butter because the food was kosher.

She was halfway through her tomato juice when Flora asked

her why she was traveling to Israel. It was a friendly question although it caught Susan a little off guard. She had been asking herself that question over and over again ever since she gave in and agreed to go on the trip. Was she just doing her father's bidding? Was she really interested in finding her lost uncle? Did she care even a little bit about his Jewish obsession, his Zionism?

Most of the time, her answers were negative. No, she was not just trying to please her dad. No, she did not care what had happened to her Uncle Yakov. No, she was secretly an atheist. There was, she said to herself, no all-embracing God hovering in heaven, protecting the Jews, his chosen people. The idea of a chosen people was pretty elitist, anyway. What made the Jews any better than the Catholics who lived next door?

Once Susan had gone to Sunday Mass with her next-door neighbor Dorothy. The sunshine pouring in through the stained-glass windows soothed her and the priest's chanting was melodic. It was so unlike the davening of her rabbi on the bimah, his voice harsh and his chanting always off-key. There were moments when she wanted to put her fingers in her ears to block out the sound.

"My father sent me on a quest," she said, watching all four of her tablemates wrinkle their brows at the word "quest." "I'm to see if I can find out what happened to his older brother Yakov who hasn't been seen for forty years. The big question is, did he survive the Holocaust?" After barely looking up, three of them returned to their food.

Only Daniel seemed to be listening. "My immediate family survived because they came to America," he said, "but those who stayed were lost, shipped to the death camps. Guess I can say that I'm lucky. You, too!"

He mumbled a little Hebrew prayer under his breath. Susan had no idea what he was saying but when he finished, she said, "Amen." That's what you did when someone said a prayer, you said Amen. At least, she knew that.

Flora and Sandy spent the rest of the meal talking about the dresses that they'd bought for the wedding. They were unhappy that they had to wear green as bridesmaids. "Not my best color," Flora said. "Not mine, either," Sandy agreed. "Green makes my skin look green."

The sisters reminded Susan of the girls in her senior class who spent lunch hour in the cafeteria obsessing over their prom dresses. Off-the-shoulder, strapless, organza, silk and taffeta. Cinched waistlines, pencil skirts, or for those who wanted to conceal a few extra pounds, full ruffled flounces.

Such a waste of time, she thought. She'd much rather be curled up with a Russian novel, where she could hardly pronounce the characters' names. Once, when she went to check out Ivan Turgenev's *Virgin Soil*, she noticed that the last person had done so 20 years earlier.

Yes, she was different. Out of sync with her generation. Much too serious.

Daniel was the only one at the table who knew any Hebrew. Like Susan, he was planning to take an intensive language course at an ulpan, a language school for immigrants in Jerusalem. David was sure that he could manage in English. The girls had no interest in learning Hebrew. "French was too hard for me," Flora said. "Why should I tax myself with another language?"

Most dinners, the girls chatted with one another, barely acknowledging Susan's presence.

Daniel and Susan did talk, mostly about the Holocaust. He'd been following the news accounts on the Eichmann trial, which was to begin just after they arrived. Susan told him about her father's obsession with the trial. Every minor mention was torn out of the newspaper and underlined in black ink.

In her home, scraps of paper were piled everywhere, on the table in the entrance hall, on the coffee table and in the narrow breakfast nook, where you had to climb around a person to find an empty seat. Just overwhelming. Susan crumpled up several of the scraps. "Too depressing," she said, as she threw them in the garbage.

When her father wasn't looking, though, Susan retrieved and read the notes, returning them to their stations as if untouched. *Not my obsession*, Susan kept telling herself. Still, she wondered how she could search for Uncle Yakov without having to dig into the drama of the Holocaust. It would consume her, the murders, the bodies piled in ditches that the people had dug before they were shot, the families crowded into carts and freight cars, layered in clothing against the cold, children clutching a tiny toy—a finger puppet of a clown, still smiling, a hand-carved wooden top.

Susan threw up for two days after they hit 15-foot swells. Even the stewards were green. Following her waiter's advice, she put on a heavy sweater and went upstairs to sleep in a canvas deckchair, sucking in the salt air and trying her very best not to look directly at the waves which induced vertigo.

By the time the ship entered the harbor in Haifa, the sea was calm. She stood on the deck and looked at the houses dotting the slopes of Mt. Carmel, the ones that her father had shown her in a photo book on *Eretz Yisrael*. "Paradise," he'd said.

After collecting her trunk, she hailed a collective cab, the last person to squeeze in. They were heading to Jerusalem, a three-hour drive. When she gave the driver the address of her apartment, he thanked her. "Your Hebrew's great," said an American girl next to her. "I can only say two words, shalom and *todah*."

"I'm not fluent," Susan said. "I've decided to go to an ulpan so that I can learn to speak like a sabra. Sometimes, when I reach for a word, nothing comes out."

Susan dozed off, only to be awakened by the voice of the driver who called their attention to the remains of tanks from the War of Independence prominently placed along the highway. They were rusted relics, planted there by Israeli patriots to remind citizens and visitors of the historic battle for their homeland. "It's green and beautiful now," he said, "but I fought in the war and it was ugly. I have a bullet in my leg to prove it."

Susan translated his remarks for her neighbor who didn't seem particularly interested.

She was busy applying purple eyeshadow. "Doesn't it make me look exotic?" she asked Susan. "Just like the Jewish girls from Morocco. I've seen their photos in *Life*."

Susan nodded. Speaking was too much effort. Then, she closed her eyes for the rest of the ride. She tried to imagine Uncle Yakov's face but all she could see was her father's blue eyes. So blue that the sky seemed pale, even white.

Why did I ever agree to this? Why am I here? Before she could come up with an answer, the driver pulled up to her apartment in Rehavia, owned by the small pension across the street, dumped her trunk on the sidewalk, and mumbled, "Your new home." Then, he took off down the street, his exhaust pipe clanging as it hit the pavement.

She hadn't thought of it as her home. An adventure, perhaps, completely free of the yoke of family. Staying up all night drinking wine, hiking in the desert, exploring the stone passageways in the Old City, most of all, finding a real boyfriend. Someone dark and handsome and definitely exotic. How could she ever confess that to her father? And, of course, there was her official assignment, her new job, sealed with a handshake from her father: find out what happened to Uncle Yakov.

2

Susan sat doodling the letters of Yakov's name as they read the charges. Then, she drew his face or at least what she imagined his face would look like. Ears standing out just a little more than they should, bridge of his nose high, nostrils chiseled, straight hair, parted carefully on the left side, eyebrows arched gracefully above penetrating wide-set eyes. A face not unlike her father's. Yakov Reich would be about 55 years old, if he were alive.

The man on the TV screen looked so fragile. Dressed in a dark suit, a white shirt, and a gray tie with a discrete pattern, he stood up when the three judges in black robes entered the chamber. Then, he sat down on a small folding chair in the bullet-proof glass box, a military police guard on either side of him.

The picture became blurry and, for a few moments, the screen went dark. The audience sat quietly, patiently, awaiting its return. It came back in fits and starts, a bit of white, then black again, static, then a few words in Hebrew, silence, then a deep voice in German: *Sie können sich hinsetzen und Sie können Ihre Kopfhörer entfernen.* You may sit down and remove your headphones.

The accused listened as one of the judges read the 15-count

indictment. He fidgeted, rubbing his right index finger back and forth across his left thumb. His face had no expression. Susan fidgeted, too. In the newspaper photos her father had shown her, he was a grainy presence. She would sit on the floor in the living room staring at this small man who had killed so many people. "Study his face," her father said. She stared and stared but she only saw an ordinary man, someone she would pass on the street without a second glance: a man in a dark suit and a white shirt, swinging a leather briefcase as he walked the streets of Lower Manhattan.

Back home, Susan always woke without an alarm clock, falling out of the same dream, a knock on the front door, a messenger in a khaki suit, cap tilted over his eyes, handing her a telegram from Western Union: black letters on tan paper: *Running Out of Time. Stop. Help Me. Stop.*

She'd been having the dream for months, ever since she finished reading *Night* by Elie Wiesel. Inside the front cover, there was a note written in black ink in his strange, old-fashioned handwriting. "After you finish this book, you will never be the same. Dad."

He was right, of course. All she could think about was Eliezer, trapped in a battle to survive: loyal to his father, sharing his ration of bread and his thin soup, and yet, wanting to consume his father's share for himself. Eliezer, who struggled to believe in a merciful God and blamed God for hanging his people on gallows and for gassing them in showers. When Susan came to the final pages of *Night*, she screamed out loud: "I don't believe in God. See what happened to these pious Jews who kissed their *tzitzis* and bobbed up and down in prayer. Nothing good came of religion!"

That was not the change her father had wanted. "You've misread the book," he said. "Eliezer suffers but he remains a man of faith, a devoted Jew, who knows that only by recounting history will the memories of his parents and his sister and of the millions who died, be preserved." He flipped through the pages in an effort to find the right passages.

There was no point arguing with him. She decided to return the book to her father's bookcase, the one with the glass doors and the key, placing it next to the three-volume set of Carl Sandberg's *Lincoln*. A man who overcame suffering and rose from poverty to greatness.

Her father's Lincoln speeches were almost as frequent as his Holocaust lectures. Over and over again, words of praise for his idol, Lincoln, the president of *all* the people! A poor immigrant who began his life in America in a tenement building on Catherine Street in New York City, her father knew plenty about poverty. "I've spoiled you and it's my fault," he would say, shaking a finger at himself.

He could recite the Gettysburg Address by heart and he tried to get Susan to memorize it, too, often stopping in the middle of a sentence so that she could fill in a word. "Conceived in liberty," he repeated, "what do you think that means?" Susan never quite gave him the answer he wanted. "Born free?"

"Not really," her father said.

Every Sunday morning, her father would take out the family portrait he brought from Europe and place it as a centerpiece on the breakfast table between the plate of bagels and bialys and the bowl of cream cheese. Their ritual even extended to the food. Susan placed a sesame and a poppy seed bagel on two plates, positioning cream cheese and butter in the center of the glass table. Her dad insisted that there were two butter knives, one reserved for the cream cheese. The rigid design made Susan laugh. She much preferred wiping the cream cheese off the knife with a paper napkin before using it again for butter.

No matter how often he showed her the picture of his family, there was new information. His mother was sitting on a chair in a room with an Oriental rug and brocade curtains, surrounded by her brood. She was wearing a dark shirtwaist and a black wig, parted severely down the middle. Around her neck she wore a small, gold heart on a twisted chain. Next to her, on the left, was Susan's father, the youngest child, then perhaps seven or eight, his hand grasping his mother's. "I squeezed her fingers tight that day," her father told her. "I was afraid of the camera." To her right were his sisters, one standing, a strand of pearls looped twice around her neck, the other sitting on a wooden chair, an open book in her lap. Their Shabbos shoes were buffed, catching the photographer's light.

The picture must have been taken in 1915 or 1916, four or five years before they left Poland for America. They were dressed in their best clothing, their posture impeccable and their gaze impenetrable. Strange, that even in this formal family portrait, Yakov was absent. "Where's Yakov?" Susan asked. Her father didn't know. It was up to her to find out.

Susan looked around and counted six people she recognized from the café, crammed into a stuffy meeting hall in the Ratisbon Monastery, a couple of blocks from the Beit Ha'am building in Jerusalem, watching the opening day of the Adolf Eichmann trial on closed-circuit TV. Meyer Reinert, the owner of the café, who lived with his wife Giti in a small apartment in the German-Jewish neighborhood of Rehavia, sat in front of her, periodically wiping his forehead with a large, white handkerchief.

She knew their story. They immigrated to Palestine in 1938, two days after Kristallnacht, leaving their cultured and comfortable life in Vienna after their shop window had been shattered and their café destroyed. Meyer's café was located a few blocks from the Vienna State Opera on Opernring and was a popular destination for upper-class Jews who stopped in before the performance. He knew them all by their first names. One of them, Werner, arranged for their safe passage to Jerusalem.

Now, he was sweating profusely as he studied Eichmann's every movement. The accused stood, answering the prosecutor's questions with "*Jawohl. Jawohl*, I am Otto Adolf Eichmann. *Jawohl*, I was born on March 19, 1906, in Solingen, Germany. *Jawohl*, my father was Adolf Karl Eichmann."

"He doesn't look nervous," whispered Ruth, the waitress in the café who was sitting next to Meyer. "He looks perfectly calm."

Susan sat behind them. She'd met Ruth one week after arriving in Jerusalem. A city map in hand, she'd wandered up and down Ben Yehuda Street, stopping for coffee at a crowded café, which had the look of an old Left Bank establishment. People sat at their tables smoking, with black coffee and newspapers in Hebrew, English, German, and Yiddish. In the glass case against the wall, Linzer tarts dusted with powdered sugar were piled high on blue china plates.

Ruth took her order, placing a small paper napkin folded in a triangle on the table. The coarseness of the paper felt like the toilet tissue in her rented apartment. Relatives told her to travel with her own stash of soft, two-ply American toilet paper. She'd lined up a dozen rolls on the rug when she was packing, but left them abandoned in a heap at the last minute. "That's for wimps," she told herself.

She'd filled her black metal camp trunk with a year's worth of clothing and her prize possession, an Olympia typewriter. There had been a big debate about bringing the West German-made typewriter to Israel. Her father was convinced the authorities would confiscate it. He'd bought it for her thinking it was Dutch, only to discover, to his dismay, that it was German.

In the end, Susan didn't listen. She packed the Olympia with its shiny gray case in the trunk, locking it securely and placing the tiny, chrome-plated key on her key ring. If there was a problem, she would deal with it.

Ruth had settled in Israel in 1948 when she was 24 years old. She told Susan that she'd spent two years in Mauthausen before she was liberated, and then another two years in a displaced person camp before arriving in Jerusalem. "My parents and my two sisters died in the concentration camps," she said. That was all the history she was willing to tell Susan.

Susan knew better than to ask for more. Ruth's English was

excellent and she was happy to accompany Susan on long walks around the city, always reaching into her green bag to give a few coins to the beggars who stopped them along the way. "Survivors have to give," she said as they walked the cobblestone pathways of the Old City.

Now, they sat glued to the monitor, watching the opening of the trial. Giti sat to the left of her husband. Susan could hear her tapping her foot incessantly. Shlomo, who owned a men's clothing store on Ramban Street, sat next to Giti, "52475" tattooed on his left forearm. Three men with numbers on their arms occupied the remaining seats in the row. One was taking notes. "I saw him once in Auschwitz," he said aloud. "He was inspecting the kitchen and I was on duty peeling potatoes. He asked me how many potatoes I peeled every day. I had no idea but I told him one thousand."

There was a loud shush from the back of the hall. Eichmann spoke to one of the guards who left the cage and returned with a glass of water. "They should poison him," Meyer said, loud enough for Susan to hear. "They should put cyanide in his water."

"Not a good idea," a man she did not recognize answered. "We need to hear him testify. We need to testify against him. After we have heard him confess, we can commit *retzach*. Only *after* the trial, is it OK to torture and murder him."

More shushing from folks trying to hear. More comments from the audience.

Susan was trying not to stare at the numbers on one man's arm, which seemed to move as he spoke. In New York, survivors covered their numbers—at least the ones she knew did. In her small Orthodox synagogue, there were two survivors. Both wore long sleeves all the time, even in the heat of summer. Susan sat behind one of them in the women's section. Every five minutes she would scratch her arm, rubbing hard at the fabric sleeve. Indelible ink; impossible to erase.

In Israel, the survivors' arms were exposed. When she looked into their eyes, there was one message: who said that the Jews went to their slaughter like sheep? Who said we were all cowards? See our numbers. Pay attention, the Nazis did not destroy us all.

Susan had seen their pictures at home, in newspapers, magazines, and books. There were two copies of the *Diary of Anne Frank* in her father's library, one carefully covered in plastic, the other heavily marked up with commentary in his old-fashioned European hand. The flourish of swirled s's, looped l's and crossed t's, in black ink. "How sad," he wrote at the bottom of one page. "I was fortunate," he wrote in a margin. "I left Poland in 1920." The first American edition was published in 1952, when Susan was nine years old.

On her tenth birthday, her father gave her a copy of Anne's book. The inscription read: "Be Proud That You Are a Jew. Love, Dad."

Susan read the diary, finishing it in what seemed like hours, and then reread it. Anne was trapped: "I long to ride a bike, dance, whistle, look at the world, feel young and know that I'm free and yet I can't let it show," she'd written. Susan rode her bike freely and pirouetted around the living room but she did not feel free. Like Anne, she wrote daily entries in her red leather diary. "I am a Jewish girl who lives on the wrong side of town," Susan wrote. "It would be better if I celebrated Christmas."

She hid the gold Jewish star that her father had given her. His memories of Eastern Europe were few since he came to America as a young boy of 12. He'd lived in a brick house in a Polish shtetl. His father and his oldest brother had come to America first, leaving his mother, his sisters, his brother and him to fend for themselves. They sold cigarettes and whiskey to the soldiers. Susan remembered her grandmother's tough gaze, eyes that pierced, a straight spine. This was a woman who made sure her family survived, no matter what it took. When she decided to leave, she could not persuade her son Yakov to travel with them. He remained behind, working in a neighbor's store.

They arrived at Ellis Island, Susan's father's height and blue eyes noted clearly on the ship's manifest. They forged a new life on the Lower East Side of Manhattan where her husband was a tailor and the children worked odd jobs during the day and went to school at night. Like so many immigrant families, the youngest child was the one who made it out of poverty. That was the case with her father who sold ladies' shoes, often selling women stylish models that were a size too small at their request. He became a lawyer.

Through hard work and intelligence, he'd made his way into the middle class. Although he left Europe before the Holocaust, he carried the shtetl in his heart and he mourned the loss of his brother. They'd been best buddies. Though he'd sent letters to all of the agencies, no one had news of him. There was no record of his having escaped or of his having been liberated. Yakov—his older brother who looked like his twin—vanished forever.

He spoke of Yakov so often that Susan could see the two brothers playing tag in the forests around their small shtetl, sharing their lunch, bread slathered with chicken schmaltz, whispering secrets to one another in cheder while the rebbe wrote on the blackboard. They met in the forest after school and picked up the bootleg cigarettes that they hawked to the soldiers. She would never have been brave enough to do that. "Weren't you afraid that you would get caught?" she asked her father. A one-word answer: "No."

But Yakov stayed and her father left for America. He remembered hugging him goodbye, his long, skinny arms encircling Yakov's narrow frame. Their hearts beating in unison. They held onto each other but, her father said, Yakov let go first. "He was always the brave one, able to jump across the slippery rocks on the river, motioning that I should follow him." The story always ended with a sigh.

Her father commuted to work daily, wearing a dark suit and a white shirt. Although he had no accent, he treasured his memories of Yiddish. If you stood close to him, you could hear him humming a few lines of the Yiddish lullaby *Rozhinkes mit Mandlen*.

Susan remembered him trying to teach her the melody when she was five or six years old. He had such a beautiful voice; she had none. Still, he would sit her on his knee and repeat the beloved words over and over again.

> In dem Beis-Hamikdosh
> In a vinkyl cheyder
> Zitst di almone, bas-tsion, aleyn
> Ihr ben yochidle yideln vigt zi keseider
> Un zingt im tzum shlofn a ledeleh sheyn.
> Ai-lu-lu
>
> (*In the Temple,*
> *in a corner of a room,*
> *Sits the widowed daughter of Zion,*
> *alone.*
> *She rocks her only son, Yidele to sleep*
> *With a sweet lullaby. Ai-lu-lu*)

Sometimes, not knowing how to respond, she giggled. Sometimes, she had tears in her eyes. The song was so sad. Sometimes, she had questions. Did *vinkyl* mean tickle? No, he answered, it meant a corner. The song was more than a lullaby, her father said. It was the song of the Jewish people, scattered throughout the world. In Poland. In Europe. In America. In Israel.

On the steps outside the synagogue, she could hear his sweet tenor voice carrying the melody for the congregation. He read the Yiddish *Forverts*, and spoke Yiddish to his eldest brother who arrived every Sunday morning for a private visit. Susan sat on the floor behind the striped couch catching a bit of their conversation when they spoke in English. Her uncle had to sneak out of his house to visit his brother. "She doesn't want me to visit you," he said. "We're poor shtetl Jews from Rozwadów and she's descended from Jewish aristocracy. Her father and uncles were famous Torah scholars and rebbes. She married beneath her class and she never stops reminding me of that." Susan waited to hear her father's answer but most often he was silent. Once she heard him say, "You cannot leave her." A cowardly answer! *Leave her!* Susan mouthed to herself.

Every day, her father brought home newspapers with stories circled in ink. There were profiles of Holocaust survivors who'd opened up their own businesses in New York. It was as if he knew them personally. "Look at him," her father would say, handing Susan a clipping about a Hungarian Jew who'd landed in the States without a dollar and now ran a company that employed 20 workers. "I'm nothing special," the man told the reporter. "I just was lucky."

"Not just lucky," her father told her, tears in his eyes, "he was smart and determined." He loved that word, determined. Smart was not enough, he told her.

Susan felt the pressure. Her father wanted her to do well in school, succeed in a career and, most of all, to be a good Jew. Susan was not sure what that meant, especially growing up in an Irish Catholic neighborhood. She often wrote about the struggle in her diary.

"Today, I helped Mary Catherine decorate her family Christmas tree. I stood on a stepladder and placed the glass angel on the top of the tree. When we were finished hanging the blue lights, we flicked the switch and sang *O Christmas Tree*. I pretended to know the words and moved my lips. It felt good."

Susan stared at her handwriting. It was round and girlish, written in blue ink with her refillable Parker Pen. She'd received the fountain pen for Chanukah and she kept it in the white satin-lined gift box that it arrived in, always careful to wipe off fingerprints before she put it away. From May 16, 1956:

Yesterday I went to see a matinee performance of The Diary of Anne Frank at the Cort Theater in New York City. Although I'd seen The King and I two years earlier, this was my first serious play. I sat in Row G of the orchestra, next to my aunt who first married a gambler and then a Jewish businessman and who had no children. Hers is the only home I have ever visited that has a Murphy bed.

Great-Aunt Harriet loves the Broadway Theater and she invites me to come to shows with her. I can smell her Chanel No. 5 perfume. She is a tiny woman who loves jewelry. She wears two ruby rings, one on each pinkie finger and a matching ruby brooch shaped like a cornucopia on her jacket lapel. Her hair is combed to the side and held by a jeweled barrette. In her alligator pocketbook she carries a lace handkerchief and lemon drops, which she gives me at the slightest cough.

I loved the play. Susan Strasberg was Anne, not quite as I imagined her physically, though. Her blouse, with ruffled sleeves, was tucked into her skirt and her dark, brown hair cascaded down to her shoulders. She was hiding out, a prisoner, and I spent two hours rooting for her. I knew the ending, of course, but I wanted her to live.

After the play, they'd stood by the stage door, waiting for the actors. Susan Strasberg never appeared but Joseph Schildkraut, who played Anne's father Otto, did and he signed Susan's program. She saved the souvenir in the back of the diary.

Now, five years later, Susan was living in a ground-floor apartment with roommates on Rehavia Street in Jerusalem witnessing the survivors in person.

Her roommates didn't seem to be aware of the survivors. They were three American girls all in Israel for different reasons. Carol, with ash-blonde hair, was the only Jew that Susan had ever met from North Dakota. She'd been engaged to a non-Jewish fellow at home and he'd broken it off. Her parents sent her to Israel for one reason: to find a Jewish husband. Naomi was from Chicago, a Zionist whose parents wanted her to experience life on a kibbutz. She was only in Jerusalem for a month and was then heading north to work on a kibbutz near Haifa. Charlotte was their southern belle, a Jewish girl from Charleston, whose father had arrived there as a peddler and turned his small clothing store into Kaufmann's, a major department store on the main street. She came with a large trunk full of stylish print dresses and high-heeled sandals. Charlotte spent her mornings applying makeup and her afternoons in a watercolor workshop, painting scenes of Jerusalem. "I never know who I'm going to meet," she explained to Susan, as she applied mauve lip liner.

The survivors' faces were fuller and their backs straighter than Susan imagined. Their skin was tanned by the Middle Eastern sun. But the sadness in their eyes and the numbers on their arms remained.

On her first Sunday morning in Jerusalem, she walked to King George Street and took the city bus to the German Colony, getting off at the stop nearest to Ulpan Etzion. Susan had received a form letter from the director asking her to come in for a Hebrew language test. They were trying to determine which class to put her in, the highest being Yod, the tenth letter in the Hebrew alphabet.

The school was crowded. Someone tapped her on the shoulder. It was David, her tablemate from the ship. "Settling in?" he said. "What an adjustment!" Susan didn't get a chance to ask him what he meant. Instead, they exchanged addresses and parted.

The lobby was filled with immigrants, most from Algeria, Morocco and Yemen. Their skin was much darker than the skin of the survivors. Susan didn't hear anyone else speaking English.

The test was easy. There were 100 fill-in-the-blank questions that she raced through and two passages to translate. The first was from *Haaretz*, a news story on the latest immigration figures, just released by the Israeli government. Next to the story was a chart with the number of immigrants from each country. The second was a passage on kibbutzniks near Afula who were successfully growing cotton. It was a patriotic piece, describing the battle that they had waged against mosquitoes and malaria, undoubtedly included in the exam to inspire new immigrants. There was no mention of the tensions with their Arab neighbors. Susan finished the test quickly and then watched the woman to her right struggling to answer questions. She kept on erasing her answers and she tapped her worn sandals incessantly on the stone floor.

Two days later, an envelope arrived with the news that Susan had been placed in level Yod. It was not a surprise. Although she'd also studied French and German, Hebrew was the only foreign language she could speak without translating word for word from English. It was because of the year she spent in a yeshiva in Brooklyn when she was four years old. It was a tired old building with peeling paint, one block from her home. All she really remembered about it was that the linoleum floors smelled of Lysol and wet mops stood on each side of the front door greeting the students every morning. There was no mistaking the emphasis in the curriculum: mornings were given over to Hebrew; English was demoted to the afternoons, just before naptime. Maybe that was the reason her mother had complained to her father that Susan's English sounded funny. Foreign, she said. She wanted to remove her from the school but her father stayed his ground. "It's good for her soul," he'd said.

The guard in the supermarket had an Uzi slung over his shoulder. He inspected her bag, asking her where she was from and why she'd come to Israel. Noticing the numbers on his arm, Susan said nothing about the Holocaust. Instead, she spoke about her Zionism. She was, she explained, trying to discover what it meant to be Jewish.

He laughed. "I can give you the answer," he said. "Suffering. That's what it means to be Jewish." He dumped everything out of her handbag looking for explosives. Her lipstick rolled to the floor. He took out a small brown packet of letters that her father had written to the agencies and put it on the table. Her father had given them to her the day before she left. "You will find out what happened to him," her father said.

She'd read the letters over and over again. The same facts, told and retold. The same answers. No, they did not have a record of any Yakov Reich. No, there were no records in the town hall. No, there were no neighbors who remembered the Reich family or their brick house. No, he was not listed on any official lists.

There was a folded newspaper clipping, recently arrived from America, with a photo of the stone Beit Ha'am building, site of the Eichmann trial. It looked like a fortress with hardly any openings from the side view on Bezalel Street. There was a diagram of the external courtyard where booths had been constructed to search people prior to their entrance to the courtroom. Above the headline, her father had written: "You should go!"

The guard picked up the clipping. "It's down the street," he said. "Very crowded. You can see the trial nearby on closed-circuit TV. I went yesterday." He motioned to her that she should throw everything back in her purse. She didn't tell him that she'd already been there.

She stared at him for a minute. There was no expression on his face. No smile and no sadness. The face, Susan thought, of someone who'd learned to conceal his emotions, the face of someone who'd taught himself to become a blank slate when a Nazi officer passed down the line making selections, workers for the brick factory to the right, prisoners for the gas chambers to the left.

Susan bought a loaf of bread and a package of *gevinah levinah*, the most popular white cheese. She loved the way the curds fell apart. It was dry and a bit sour, unlike the creamy cottage cheese in markets in New York. She threw her purchases into her mesh bag and made her way to the ulpan. On the street, she began counting. Counting the cracks in the concrete sidewalk. Counting the people bowing after the last act of a play before they disappeared behind the curtain. Counting two more people with numbers on their arms. She was now up to ten.

When she entered the classroom, it was almost full. "Shalom," the teacher greeted her. "Shalom," Susan said, slipping into a wooden seat at the back of the room. The teacher was explaining that the class would only be taught in Hebrew—no other languages were allowed. Then, she went around the room, asking the students what their native language was. She listened to their answers in *Marokayit* and French. Susan was the last one to speak and the only person who said English.

"These days," Esther explained, "those of you coming from lands where Arabic is spoken are technically Mizrahi Jews. But here in Israel, all non-European Jewish immigrants are lumped together and called Sephardim, along with the Jews from Spain and Portugal."

The Arabic and French speakers helped one another, translating difficult Hebrew words into their mother tongues. Susan was on her own. Two seats in front of her, Susan saw a woman she recognized. Her name was Rachel and she was a cleaning maid for the apartment that Susan was sharing with three other girls. Susan had spoken to her just the other morning.

Rachel was from Rabat and she had been in Israel for one year. Her hair was black and thick, and she kept it pinned out of her face. Her eyes were almost black and her skin was very dark. She wore a bright turquoise blouse and a bold print skirt, with swirls of pink, yellow, and blue. In her ears were tiny pearl earrings. Susan imagined that they'd been there since she was an infant.

The Moroccans were a tightly knit group, always gathered together to share food. Most of the women cleaned houses; the men were laborers on construction sites. Just down the street from Susan's apartment, she could see the men at work on a three-story apartment building, their hands stained gray with concrete dust, sweat rolling down their faces as they lifted blocks of heavy stone. "Shalom *motek*," one of them whistled at her every morning as she passed by. He was dressed in a yellow T-shirt. His muscles bulged in the sunlight.

He was handsome and definitely not a young man her father would welcome into the family. *A common laborer*, she thought. *He'd probably dropped out of school.* A white bandana was tied around his head. She ignored his greeting. On the third day, she nodded as she passed by. On the fourth day, she gave in. "Shalom," she said.

Susan woke early to do her homework, translating a news story in the immigrant edition of *Haaretz* on Moroccan adjustment to life in Israel. She understood why the teacher had chosen the assignment.

With the occasional help of a Hebrew-English dictionary, she also read a longer piece on Moroccan immigration in the regular edition of the paper. Only three months earlier, still at a time when the immigration of Moroccan Jews to Israel was not permitted by Morocco, the ship *Egoz* had set sail from the port of Al Hoceima. According to the news report, there were 44 Jews aboard. The ship had been leased by the Mossad a year earlier and it had made eleven successful voyages, transporting some 40 to 50 Jews at a time from Morocco to Gibraltar, where they would then continue on to Israel. But the twelfth voyage was unsuccessful and the ship sank. A day after the tragedy, 12 corpses were collected from the sea.

The deaths resulted in an agreement that allowed for the Jews' departure from Morocco if they paid a ransom fee and if they took a route that passed through a third country. So began the "legal" Jewish exodus from Morocco. The Hebrew date of the ship's sinking, 23 Tevet, the story said, was a key one in the story of the immigration of North African Jewry.

Now, here they were, in the ulpan classroom, discussing their homework: a story that reported that thousands of Moroccan Jews who'd immigrated to Israel were living the good life. Big apartments with sunlight streaming in the windows. Plentiful hot water and abundant food. Green and black olives soaking in oil, fish freshly caught from the Mediterranean Sea, ripe cucumbers and tomatoes still on the vine, and fragrant melons in shades of green, orange, and red.

"What do you think of this article?" the teacher asked, speaking slowly in carefully enunciated Hebrew. "Please say your name when you answer."

The first hand up was that of a fellow with curly hair and a handsome face. "Andre," he said, adding that he was from Casablanca. Andre didn't like the story. "What do these Ashkenazis, these people who write the official newspaper, know about our life?" Susan saw that many heads in the room were nodding in agreement. "Our life was hard there but it is hardly better in Israel. Here, we are looked down upon by the Zionists. We are second-class citizens."

He spoke about the landlord who barely gave him heat and about only getting hot water once a week, just before Shabbos. "The halls are dirty and the garbage cans are never emptied. Our homes stink of rotten fish. He thinks that we are"—he paused, looking for the right Hebrew word—"inferior. *Pachot!*"

Pachot—less—that was impossible in the Promised Land, the land of milk and honey!

His classmates wrote the word down in their notebooks. Susan noticed that the woman next to her underlined the word three times.

Esther, their teacher, didn't look happy. She was a German Jew whose family had managed to get out of Europe in the early 1930s, along with the family jewels, the monogrammed silver, furniture, a piano, and other household belongings, packed in big wooden containers nicknamed lifts. German Jews who could prove they were bringing in 1,000 British pounds could get an immigration visa from the British.

Esther lived in Rehavia in a beige stucco art deco house, its garden overgrown with bougainvillea. Susan liked to walk through that neighborhood in the evening. The families were eating dinner in their formal dining rooms, white linen tablecloths illuminated by blazing crystal chandeliers.

The teacher called on another woman with dark skin who sat in the first row. The woman stood up and faced the class. She was fidgeting with her fringed shawl, tugging on the twisted white strings as if they were *tzitzis*. "Shalom," she said. "My name is Marie. My friends call me Maya. I do not like to speak in public. I clean houses," she said. "I always dreamed of becoming a teacher. But it will never happen. Moroccans here are like the black people in America." Susan noticed that as she said the word black, she brushed her cheek with her hand. "We are at the bottom of everything," she said. Before she sat down, she reached into her pocket and took out a handkerchief to wipe away her tears.

Susan had read about the Freedom Riders. But she was struggling with her own identity. What did it mean to be Jewish? Why had the Jews been slaughtered in the Holocaust? Why had they marched into the cattle cars without kicking and screaming and punching with all their might? What could they have done to save themselves?

That last question was one Susan often discussed with her father. He insisted that the Jews had done their best. There was just no way to deal with the German power structure. Susan wasn't so certain. When she was a kid, her father had taught her to fight back. The only way to deal with a bully, he said, was to stand your ground. Never show them that you are afraid. They were the only Jewish family on the street. Everyone else was Irish. They were tough kids who would spit in your face for no reason. Or hit you with a rock. Once, Susan came home with a bloody nose. "What did you do to defend yourself?" her father asked. "Nothing," she said.

But still, she never understood his insistence that Eastern European Jews had done their best against the Nazis. There was no arguing with him. "My brother Yakov," he said, "would never have given in. He would have punched and kicked and screamed as they dragged him into the gas chambers." In her father's top dresser drawer, he kept the worn photograph of the family that he treasured. She would slip into his bedroom, stand on her tippy-toes, and carefully open the white tissue paper. There was her grandmother, surrounded by three of her children. On the left stood her father, in a buttoned-up jacket with a wide collar and laced-up boots. His hair was shaved, like a soldier in basic training. It was several years before they embarked on their long, steerage-class voyage to Ellis Island. They were not smiling and all of them seemed to be looking far off into the distance, beyond the camera. Even then, their eyes were set on America, the *Goldene Medina.*

She'd come to Israel to find out for herself. There were always victims, underdogs whose skin was too dark or whose hair was too curly, or whose noses were too hooked. Jews in Europe. Blacks in America. North African Jews in Israel.

Esther Wolff's face was pale. She was struggling to regain control of her classroom. She picked up a piece of chalk and wrote several words in Hebrew on the blackboard: "spacious apartment," "living wage," and "vacation." They were drawn from the first line in the story. Susan had already written a translation in English on her copy: "Moroccans who live in Israel are blessed with spacious apartments, substantial living wages, and three-week annual vacations."

"*Non, Vrai, Lo nachon,*" a voice rang out in French and Hebrew, without waiting to be called on. "*Petit non Gadol* apartments. Ten of us live in two rooms," an older woman called out. "We sleep in one bedroom." Then, she repeated the Hebrew word for spacious and they all laughed.

All of a sudden the quiet immigrants began to heckle the teacher. "What do you call a living wage?" Mordechai asked her. He looked angry. "Is it what you earn or what we earn?"

Esther Wolff did not answer.

Susan sat still and did not speak. They would resent her chiming in, she thought. An American girl with her own rented apartment, how could she comprehend their suffering? Translating political propaganda always backfired.

During their mid-morning break in the cafeteria, the Moroccans huddled together, occupying two long tables. They brought their own food. Hummus, pita bread, diced tomatoes, chickpeas, cucumber salad, and sautéed eggplant, each slice the same size, perfectly arranged like a fan. The dishes were placed precisely in a line down the middle of the table.

Susan was about to leave when Rachel approached her. "Please eat with us," she said. The invitation took her by surprise. They were such a tight group. She couldn't imagine them opening the door to an outsider, especially one who was American and Ashkenazi. She remembered sitting alone in the high school cafeteria while the popular girls gossiped at the next table. It was just as well that they'd left her out. They were usually talking about a Friday night dance that she couldn't attend.

Susan picked up her bag and her lunch and moved to the Moroccans' table, adding her food to theirs. It looked pathetic next to their homemade offerings. Two sliced hard-boiled eggs and a container of chopped salad topped with cubes of white cheese. Rachel handed her a plate of eggplant with a large helping of hummus.

They were speaking in *Marokayit* and French. Occasionally, Rachel leaned over and translated their words. "They're not happy with this class," Rachel said. "That story on the happy life Moroccans lead in Israel made them furious." Susan could only nod. She was afraid to weigh in too strongly. How could she, a young woman so used to her creature comforts, comment on their plight?

For a moment, her mind wandered to the hand-crocheted afghan, striped in shades of green that covered her bed. Her first cousin Anna had given it to her just before she left for Israel. It was destined, Anna said, for the Holy Land, a place that she had never visited. Anna's mother kept a kosher home, a remnant of their immigrant upbringing. Beyond that, there was little in the way of observance: lighting the candles on Chanukah, fasting on Yom Kippur, and eating matzo on Passover. Their families celebrated the Seder together, 14 of them squeezed around a table that seated ten.

Susan always sat between Anna and her brother, Herbert, exchanging gossip about their parents. Anna's mother was bossy and demanding. Midnight curfew did not mean 12:01 a.m. Anna spent a week on house arrest once when she returned home a half-hour late. Susan's father was much more lenient. He had his old-fashioned ways, but he caved on the matter of curfew. Once when she arrived home 15 minutes late, she found him standing just inside the front door. He was pointing to his watch with his left hand. "You didn't quite make it on time," he said, with a smile.

As it turned out, the afghan from Anna was a godsend, providing a layer of warmth that made up for the thin blanket and the drafty apartment. Susan listened as the Moroccans complained about their lack of heat and hot water. The stone buildings in Jerusalem were cold and damp. In many, there were splotches of black mold, a sure sign that moisture was leaching into the walls.

"Where are you from?" Ezra asked Susan. She'd noticed him earlier in the back of the classroom, the cute construction worker who had called out to her on the street. Now, here he was sitting across from her at the ulpan lunch table. During the class, she observed that he never looked up at the teacher, instead he sat scribbling in his notebook. He had dark, deep-set eyes and thick curly black hair. His fingers were thin. They were, she thought, the delicate hands of an artist.

"I'm from a little town near New York City," she said. "Just arrived. How long have you been in Israel?" He told her that he'd been there for eight months, arriving with some knowledge of Hebrew and moving up through four classes as he mastered the language. In Morocco, he was a potter, known for his intricate glazes and original designs. "I had a small shop where I sold plates and vases, many decorated with snakes and vines that curled under a deep purple glaze. The snakes' fangs shimmered on the ceramic surface, moving ominously. Now, I'm a construction worker, pouring concrete seven or eight hours a day, building apartment houses, sheathed in beige and reddish limestone that the city officials mandate for all buildings in Jerusalem." Day after day, he toiled on the new residences that were being constructed up and down the hills of the city. "I've given up trying to wash the cement from under my fingernails," he said. Susan could see a smear of cement dust on his neck. It was moving up and down as his vein pulsed.

When they returned to the classroom, the teacher had changed the subject. The lesson was grammar and the topic was reflexive verbs. Esther went around the room calling on them to conjugate: I wash myself. He washes himself. She washes herself. I am ashamed. He is ashamed. They are ashamed. In Hebrew, the verb changes were tricky. Susan was struck by Esther's choice of verbs. *How insensitive of her*, she thought. Had she selected them because the students were immigrants who were unclean and lacking in confidence? When it came to Susan's turn to conjugate the verb to wash in the past tense, she made a mistake. Ezra called out the correct answer.

He winked at her. She smiled back, a smile so slight that her prominent front teeth didn't show.

Ezra was handsome in a rugged way: a straight nose, dark brows that curved over almost black eyes, a full head of wavy black hair. She felt a magnetic attraction to him, like the positive and negative poles of two magnets. Clunk. Bang. Impossible to pull apart. She'd done that experiment in physics class. People were different, of course, she told herself. Or were they? If she really fell for someone, would she be able to detach, rip herself away?

The boy she'd been dating at home was pale, bookish, and thin. He wore blue button-down shirts that he rolled to his elbows. Not a serious boyfriend, Susan told herself. She was just biding time until she found the right guy. They'd been dating for two months and there was definitely not much chemistry. When he kissed her, she found her mind wandering to scenes from the movie *Gone with the*

Wind. She'd watched the movie three times. Dashing Rhett Butler, effortlessly sweeping Scarlett off her feet. Feisty Scarlett, her eyes wide, lower lip pouting. There were none of the Scarlett-Rhett sparks with Bob.

He surprised her one Saturday night, at the drive-in movie, when he reached into his pocket and produced a condom, swinging it slowly before her eyes. She was still a virgin. All of the good girls at school were virgins, too. The few who boasted that they'd done it were definitely sluts. Susan secretly admired them. What was wrong with her? She was proud to be different, independent. She was tired of being a young girl and desperate to be a grown-up. So what if she didn't love him. What did love have to do with sex? She started to make a list but tore the page out of her notebook.

Her father didn't talk about sex. Her father left a book about it on her dressing table, with a note: "All you need to know." The black-and-white drawings looked like the anatomy of a frog in her biology textbook. There were arrows in all directions leading to names she could hardly pronounce. There were footnotes at the bottom of the page. All very scientific and sedate. Cut and dry. Her parents were discreet, always closing their bedroom door firmly, an announcement to stay away.

She didn't love Bob. She knew that already. Too ordinary. Nothing sexy about him. Much too respectable. Should she do it? Should she not do it? He had a condom. No worry about getting pregnant. She wasn't a slut. But she definitely wanted to get it over with, to break with her conservative friends and be rebellious, to *grow up*. She was tired of being a dutiful daughter. Finally, she decided. *Who wants to be a virgin anyway?* She didn't.

That was her last thought before they slid into the back seat of the car. The beam from a flashlight hit the hood of their car but thankfully the person moved on. Two people were arguing not too far away, their voices fading as they walked off. She shifted from side to side, trying to find a comfortable position. Eventually, she ended up on her back. His hands trembled as he slipped on the condom. She closed her eyes. She didn't want to look at his face. He was definitely not the love of her life, the man she willingly gave up her virginity to. Nothing about it smacked of romance.

Within seconds, it was over. Short, a little painful, and hardly memorable. He pulled up his pants, moved back to the driver's seat of the car, and left her alone in the back seat.

She never told her conservative friends. She never even wrote about it in her red diary. It happened but it was not recorded, except in her brain. It was as if she had crossed off one more thing on her to-do list. She was no longer a virgin. That was good. The whole thing reminded her of a long novel that she'd read by Samuel Richardson, *Clarissa Harlow*. No one else had ever heard of it and even the local librarian told her that the book was out of fashion.

But the description of the sex scene there was just like her experience in the back seat of Bob's car. Richardson had written: "The deed was done." No emotion.

Ezra, ah, he was definitely not Bob. She could tell that already.

After class, Susan walked to the bus stop with Ezra. He was in a hurry, on his way to a late shift at the construction site. On his back was a torn knapsack, one buckle broken. "See you tomorrow," he said, lightly touching her hand. She didn't pull her hand back. There was something about the warmth of his fingers, not sweaty, but a cool warmth. He smiled and walked down the hill, a gray figure receding into the landscape.

Susan heard the radio blasting from the bookstore near the bus stop. The announcer was summarizing the morning's testimony at the Eichmann trial. He was speaking quickly but Susan could understand most of what he said. Three Holocaust survivors had taken the stand that morning describing their ordeal. One had lost control, screaming uncontrollably at Eichmann, "You bastard. You bastard."

Susan repeated the word "bastard" to herself. Her voice, soft, almost in a whisper. What would she have done if she'd been trapped in a camp? Follow orders? Never. She imagined herself throwing a pot of scalding water at one of the guards. "Take that, you bastard," she screamed at him as she ran away.

The Moroccans were struggling with their new life in Israel. Mopping floors and cleaning toilets. They lived in damp, unheated apartments, where there was no hot water. They had no time to listen to the trial on the radio. They were not obsessed with the Holocaust like the folks in the café on Ben Yehuda Street. They were consumed by the task at hand: making new lives.

Susan didn't fit into either group. She'd never gone to sleep hungry. She'd never shivered in bed, clinging to a thin sheet instead of a blanket. Breakfast was always on the table and her clean laundry was always folded in a pile, waiting for her to sort and place in her dresser drawers. Always, there was one unmatched sock, sitting on the top of the pile. Susan identified with that sock. Her friends at school all had buddies. They spent their time poring over fashion magazines and they chose to dress alike, buying matching print tops and skirts. Susan bought vintage blouses from a thrift shop that reeked of mildew, washing everything three times in a determined effort to rid the piece of the smell. For years, her favorite outfit was a green corduroy jumper, trimmed with red rickrack, made by her grandmother. She was an old-fashioned girl who spent most of her free time in the local library, reading Russian novels.

The other girls had ponytails. But Susan's hair was braided into two pigtails by her grandmother who fastened the ends with tiny golden barrettes. It was a struggle to conquer the thick, frizzy curls, to tug them into submission. Her grandmother's fingers were strong from years of handling bolts of fabric on her industrial sewing machine. "Stop! You're hurting me," Susan remembered crying out, howling when her hair got caught in the teeth of the comb.

When Susan arrived at the café, Ruth was taking a break. She sat in a corner smoking; the radio from the trial was blasting. The announcer was interpreting the morning's session. "It was quite an emotional few hours," he said, "especially the testimony of Cypa

A. who survived Theresienstadt." He recounted her story in vivid detail. Cypa had arrived at the camp in 1943, when she was 12 years old. A gifted art student from Prague, she and her parents, a composer and a writer, were incarcerated in the camp, which the Nazis advertised as a model Jewish settlement. Cypa testified that life there was far from model. Everything was an act, a camouflage. When there were visitors, she slept in a bunk bed with two warm blankets. When the visitors were gone, three girls slept in one bed with a dirty sheet. "Under the beautiful watercolor, soft pinks and greens and blues, lurked black splotches of terror."

Cypa sang in the choir that entertained the Red Cross when they visited in 1944. "I do not sing now," Cypa told the audience in the courtroom. "My voice dried up, the sweet sound became hoarse and sour. That was my last performance." The next day she said, her parents were deported to Auschwitz where they were killed. Cypa survived, arriving in Israel in 1946.

One day after her testimony, the newspaper ran a photo of Cypa from 1946. Her face was worn and she was not smiling and the light reflected on her thick, black glasses. Susan stared at the picture. They were exactly the same age. It was hard to imagine Cypa standing on the stage in Theresienstadt singing her heart out. In the front row, a contingent of honored guests from the Danish Red Cross. They were clapping enthusiastically, whispering to one another. Behind the curtains stood the Nazi officers who were monitoring the performance. "We were told to ignore questions that were asked directly of us," Cypa testified.

Susan sat down next to Ruth. "There was no choir at Mauthausen," Ruth said softly. "Even if there was one, I don't sing," she added. Her words surprised Susan. They were full of emotion, not the usual cool Ruth who did not speak about her past. "I sang in my high school choir," Susan said. For a moment, she hesitated then she began singing the lyrics to *Singing in the Rain* softly. Her voice cracked and a scratchy sound came out. She winced. She tried a second time; then stopped. "They needed altos," she said.

Meyer turned the volume up and the announcer's voice filled the café. He spoke about the second person who had testified that morning, Hirsch R., a textile merchant from Lvov, the only survivor from a large family. Before the war in 1939, the city of Lvov was home to a large number of Jews, Hirsch said. When Lvov and the rest of eastern Galicia was annexed by the Soviet Union, the Jewish population swelled, its ranks filled with refugees fleeing eastward from the Nazi-occupied west part of Poland. Ironically, only those residents who escaped to the USSR survived the Holocaust.

The Germans entered the Soviet zone in June of 1941. By December, all Jews were ordered to move to a ghetto in the northern part of the city. Hirsch testified that his family moved into the overcrowded ghetto, his brother and three sisters sharing a bedroom with their parents while he slept in the parlor with his wife and two children. Shortly thereafter, the Germans initiated a series of deportations, as 15,000 Jews were deported to the Belzec extermination camp.

Hirsch's family survived the initial deportation. He was spared because he was useful to the Nazis. "I supervised workers in a factory which was making shirts for German soldiers. But, from day to day, I lived in fear. I trembled every time a new deportation was announced. One day," his voice wavered for a minute, "I returned home to find the apartment ransacked and everyone gone. My neighbors told me that they were taken to the Janowska labor camp. I ran to my supervisor at the factory and pleaded with him to help me save my family but his only response was, 'Keep quiet or else I will make sure that they are killed.'"

They could hear Hirsch crying on the witness stand. After a few seconds he blew his nose loudly, and then continued his testimony. "I never saw them again. When the ghetto was liberated by the Soviet Red Army on July 26, 1944, only a few hundred Jews remained in the city. I will never understand why I was one of them."

A spectator could be heard interrupting the proceedings. He shouted in Yiddish: "Murderers! Goebbels, Goering, Eichmann—let them all burn. Sixteen members of my family, all dead."

Ruth stood up and shut off the radio. "Losing three is just as bad as 16," she said, twisting the dish towel in her hands. "It's about people, not arithmetic." Her face was red. "I wish people would just stop counting."

Susan clenched her fingers into a fist as Ruth spoke. Her fingernails dug into the palms of her hands leaving eight red arcs. She was guilty of counting. On the winding streets of Jerusalem, in the shops, she counted the number of people she saw with numbers on their arms. Just yesterday, she'd reached 99—a woman in a flowered dress in the supermarket. Her groceries were lined up meticulously: six eggs, two containers of cottage cheese, two apples, two tomatoes, and two cucumbers. When she reached into her mesh bag for her wallet, Susan saw the numbers on her left arm.

She just couldn't stop herself from counting. Ruth was right. She was the girl who counted numbers. It was an obsession. Everyone had a different accounting. Fifteen to 20 million deaths. Five to six million Jews. One million children under 18 years of age. Her father told her once that he'd met a fellow in New York who worked for the United Jewish Appeal. His job was to compute the numbers. "The numbers bounce up and down," he told her dad. "They're never accurate."

Now, here she was in Jerusalem, recording her own tally. The numbers were small but each new sighting was a hopeful sign. She kept a notebook with her entries: "Slightly stooped woman on Ben Yehuda Street, carrying two shopping bags. Pale man with a beard, sitting at an outside table at the Atara Café, smoking a cigarette. Crossing guard with a red sash by the kindergarten on Ramban."

They didn't know each other. But she knew them. They were all bound together in her book, men and women who'd somehow managed to escape death because they were tall or healthy or because they could do something useful like build cabinets or sew uniforms, or cut hair. Or maybe, because on the day of the deportation, they just happened to be sick in the infirmary or on a work detail digging trenches.

At night, dybbuks kept disturbing her sleep—angry, sad, laughing, crying, screaming, and dancing through her dreams. Waking her in a sweat, with fierce leg cramps, she remembered her nightmare. "Did I tell you about the time we assembled in a field?" the crossing guard asked her. "It was Yom Kippur Eve, the time when we say the prayer *Unesaneh Tokef*," which describes all mankind as passing under God's rod. "A Nazi soldier called a tall boy to him and nailed a strip of wood to a post, marking his height. We knew what was coming. The shorter boys would be sent to death. Thank God, I was tall." She found herself unconsciously stretching her limbs in her dream as he shouted in her ear. Forcing herself to grow taller.

3

On Friday morning, Susan went shopping in the Machane Yehuda Shuk, winding her way through the stalls in search of the best olive vendor. At one stall, just in front of her, a woman was buying green olives. She was so close that Susan could read the numbers on her arm. The woman was the hundredth survivor Susan had seen.

There was a three-inch tear in the back of her short-sleeve blue cotton blouse and deep scratches in the black leather pocketbook that hung from her shoulder. Her hair was twisted into a bun. She gestured to the man to stop after he'd placed six or seven olives on the brown paper that rested on the scale. *Dai*, she said. *Enough.*

Dai. That was the word Susan heard everywhere in 1961. *Dai* heat. *Dai* talk. *Dai* remembering. *Dai* suffering. It was a word with an edge, meaning not just enough but *too much*. She was surrounded by people who had suffered too much. People who had broken stones in work gangs. People who had lost the right to vote. People who were rounded up and squeezed into ghettos, six people in a narrow, dirty room. People who hid out in cesspools, living with the stench, even in their dreams. People who were forbidden to immigrate to Israel. Husbands without wives, children without parents and grandparents. Remnants, from here, from there.

There was a brother who stumbled upon his sister in a Hebrew language class at the ulpan. A mother, weak and frail in a nursing home, whose nurse turned out to be her own daughter, the baby she thought dead. How difficult could it be to find Yakov?

She'd memorized his story. When her dad and his family left for America in 1920, Yakov stayed behind in the shtetl of Rozwadów. When the Nazis arrived, no one knew what happened to him. Perhaps he was sent to a camp, Auschwitz or Mauthausen. Perhaps he escaped east, like some of his friends. Her father had spent four decades writing letters but the trail was cold. Now, at the very moment that the Eichmann trial was beginning in Jerusalem, stirring up fierce memories of the Holocaust, her father had sent her to Israel to find out what had happened to him.

He was not up to the trip himself, he told her. Yes, he was obsessed with the Holocaust, reading everything he could get his hands on. The books were piled on his desk at home. The local librarian was under orders to send him a notice when a new Holocaust title came in. But the thought of actually searching for Yakov was beyond him. "I have too many obligations at home and at work to go on an indeterminate adventure," he said. "I've written too many letters and I have no answers. Now it's your turn." Clearly, this was an excuse. He said that he wanted her to dig into her Jewish roots but she knew that the real truth was larger. Her father was afraid. He wasn't a coward but somehow, he feared unearthing bad news about his beloved brother. And, there was an even bigger reason. He definitely did not want her to hang out in Greenwich Village, in torn jeans, learning to play a guitar with a bunch of hippies. "You have better things to do with your life," he told her.

He'd found no record of Yakov anywhere and the family assumed that he'd died. All that remained of him were her father's memories and a small, smooth stone. "Don't lose it," he said, handing her the stone and several photos of the stone to give away, just before she left New York. The stone was warm, even a little moist from his touch. She had watched him finger it lovingly, rubbing the middle round and round in a circle with his thumb, waiting patiently for a genie to appear, waiting patiently for the answer to his question: what had happened to his brother?

Her dad had striking, blue eyes and she knew the two brothers looked alike, at least her father said they did. Susan stared at the photo of her father that she kept in her wallet. He was thin and tall, with a serious face and a hint of a smile. He was posing on the steps of the Supreme Court building in Washington, D.C. On the back of the photo, he'd written, "Touring the Capital—Celebrating passing the bar exam." This was a young man who was determined to succeed. Although he had been placed in the third grade when he arrived at age 12, because of his math skills, within a year, he was promoted to a class with students his own age. He practiced speaking English in front of a mirror, enunciating each syllable. Before she left, he hugged her tightly. "All I want is for you to find out the truth."

But there was no time for Yakov now. Ezra invited her to Shabbos dinner with the Moroccans. When he asked her to join them, she felt her heartbeat speed up, as if she'd just run a mile. Strange, for two days in a row, he'd been in her dreams. Once, dressed as a fireman, he broke the glass on her bedroom window and rescued her through a wall of flames. "Hug me tightly," he said, as they climbed down the shaky ladder. His body smelled of perspiration. On the next night, they were walking through the Casbah in Casablanca, his arm wrapped around her waist. "Smell the bougainvillea," he said. "Sweet like you."

"Expect a great meal," Ezra said, encouraging her to accept the invitation. "Just bring a little something to share." His voice was like velvet. Smooth and soft. But his words made her feel anxious. She'd never liked to cook, choosing instead to eat whatever was put on the table.

In her house, that usually meant broiled shoulder steak, always tough, puckered baked potatoes, overcooked and mushy green peas, from a tin can, although her father had replaced them with bright green, fresh frozen peas that were packaged in a white cardboard container. Each pea was covered with a frosty coating. According to *Family Circle* magazine, this was the balanced meal of the 1950s, a chunk of protein with salt as the only spice. On special occasions, there was a glass bowl filled with wedges of iceberg lettuce and tomatoes.

Solid, basic food that built strong bones and made American children grow tall. Her father believed in this diet. If you cleaned your plate, the reward was canned peaches in a sugary syrup for dessert. She liked them although they left a coating on her lips and had a bitter, metallic aftertaste. That metallic residue was what Susan remembered most about the food of her childhood. Tiny meatballs and ravioli in tin cans. Pineapple rings in tin cans. Campbell's Chicken Noodle Soup in a red-and-white-labeled can, with tiny cubes of chicken in a gummy yellow stock. Even Susan knew how to make it. You added one can of water, heated it to a boil, and presto—you had soup.

There were no other spices that she could remember. She'd never seen an avocado until she came to Israel and she hadn't the faintest idea how you could tell when one was ripe. The only olives that were served in her house were soggy black ones that came in a can packed in water.

Olive trees were everywhere in Israel, up and down the hills, thriving in the rocky soil. Their gnarled trunks dotted the landscape. Some trees, she read, were over 1,000 years old and, amazingly, they still bore fruit. No one in this country ate olives from a can. Even babies knew how to eat olives, spitting out the pits without choking.

Susan pointed to some green olives and without hesitation the man handed her one to taste. Its flesh was firm and it tasted of salty brine and the blazing Middle Eastern sun that turned your skin a dark brown. "A quarter kilo," she told him, and then, thinking that there would be a big crowd, she changed her order to a half kilo. She would bring the olives as an offering.

The market was crowded and she had to push her way through the winding alleys, careful not to brush against the Hasidim who rushed past on last-minute errands. Most of them avoided looking at her tanned arms but a few strayed, their eyes fixed on her bare flesh and her uncovered head. A woman's hair was enticing and her dark hair, especially curly in the humid Jerusalem climate, was a trap, like the sticky flypaper that hung from the ceilings in the Jerusalem apartments, which had no screens. Golden brown ribbons of paper coated with scented glue that drew in flying insects. Susan was bait, forbidden fruit.

An Orthodox man was not to look at women, in the synagogue or on the street. Women were to dress to prevent the men from being tempted. Susan laughed to herself when she thought that God had made these rules because men could not control themselves.

Married women who could not afford real hair wore glossy synthetic wigs, reminiscent of Barbie dolls' hair, shiny and thick. Young religious girls were taught to tame their curls, to pull their hair back into neat bobs. Their mothers hid their bodies under long, loose skirts, hemlines trailing in the dusty streets of the city. Their long-sleeve blouses were buttoned up to their necks and they wore thick beige cotton stockings, even in the Jerusalem heat. Just the sight of the stockings made Susan break out in red, itchy hives. Blotches of pink and red that spread across her face and neck. She knew that she shouldn't scratch them but she did anyway.

So much effort to conceal the flesh, Susan thought. Just this morning, a young Hasid, his tzitzis flying, had brushed against her. Intentionally, she thought. For a moment, their arms touched, sweaty skin against sweaty skin. Susan was sure that he lingered too long, savoring the forbidden contact. His neck turned red and his ears, too. She could not see the features on his face but she could hear his breathing and it was heavy. Her breathing sped up, too.

She imagined his sheltered life in the dormitory of a boy's yeshiva. Three boys shared a bare room with each assigned two drawers in a bureau. The closet held white shirts on hangers, black pants and black silk jackets. Three hat boxes held their tall black hats. There was a shelf for religious books and a nightstand for an alarm clock.

There was the morning ritual of wetting and curling their long peyos, twisting the hairs around their fingers. The exacting regimen of dressing. Even shoes had to be worn and tied according to the *Shulchan Aruch*. The right shoe was always to be put on first. When tying shoes, the left shoe was to be *tied* first. Susan had read that the custom was based on the belief that the right foot is more important than the left. Therefore, it should not remain uncovered when the left is covered. Shoes should be tied from the left to match the tying of tefillin since knotted tefillin were worn on the left arm. A tangle of do's and don'ts. Susan stamped her foot. No, she would never agree to all of those rules.

There was a custom, a law for everything, including when it was safe to sleep with your wife. Some Haredi women wore a pin on their lapel to let their husbands know that they had visited the mikveh and were free from menstrual blood. Not one drop of blood was to touch the men or their souls would be forever tainted.

Susan arrived in Shmuel HaNavi 15 minutes before Shabbos. It was an old neighborhood, dating back to 1927 when a rich textile merchant built a three-story house at the eastern end of the street. According to the guidebook, he built his home facing the Sheikh Jarrah neighborhood in Jordan, because he wanted to expand the northern boundary of Jewish Jerusalem.

During the War of 1948, poor families who lived there were the victims of sniper fire from Sheik Jarrah. Afterwards, in the 1950s, the State of Israel built housing in the area for new immigrants. They erected no-frills tenement buildings with external concrete walls three times the normal thickness to withstand shelling.

Jewish immigrants from North Africa filled the buildings, which were soon overcrowded. The area quickly became a slum, the streets strewn with garbage. When immigrants arrived from Morocco, they found their way to Shmuel HaNavi, hoping to ease their dislocation by finding kinsmen whose dark skin and thick black hair resembled their own. They could whisper in *Marokayit* and French. They could dress as they had in Casablanca. The men wore colorful embroidered kippahs in synagogue and they prayed with books according to their own tradition. On Pesach, unlike the Ashkenazim, they ate rice at the Seder table.

The Moroccans lived in one of these old tenements. She climbed up the dark and dirty stairway, littered with sticky ice cream wrappers, to a modest two-bedroom apartment on the fourth floor. There were 12 living there in a space meant for four or five. Every room was used as a bedroom, with bedding rolled up or hidden away in a corner during meals. Often, young newlyweds moved into apartments with tiny bedrooms that just fit their twin beds, a kitchen that could hold a table large enough for two dinner plates, and two worn folding chairs, scavenged from a dumpster. There was a tiny bathroom where you stepped out of the shower and fell over the toilet seat. Married children could not entertain family. They usually ate their Shabbos meals at their parents' apartments or at the homes of somewhat more established relatives whose parlors could accommodate long folding tables.

Susan knocked on the door and a woman opened it. Her head was covered with a red and blue paisley scarf, twisted artfully like a frozen custard cone, folded fabric twirling upward. She wore blue eyeshadow and deep mauve lipstick. Susan guessed that she was in her early thirties.

"Shalom," she said in French-accented Hebrew that reminded Susan of Ezra. "You must be Ezra's friend. I'm his first cousin,

Batya. Welcome to our home." She leaned down and kissed Susan on both cheeks. "Ezra should be here any minute," she said.

Two long tables were set up for Shabbos and the family had already gathered. Three siblings—Ezra's mother and her sister and brother—and their offspring, 14 children ranging in age from Batya, the eldest at 37, to Chani, her daughter, who'd just celebrated her first birthday. Three of Batya's first cousins were also expecting babies soon. They all kissed her on both cheeks, warm, wet kisses from women who smelled of floral perfume and from men who broke the rules about kissing women who were not related to them.

The men had kind eyes, like Ezra's, large eyes that looked like pools of melted chocolate, and they all had the same dark unibrow that arched over their strong, straight noses. Theirs was definitely not the profile that Susan saw in the green leather-bound collection of the etchings of great rebbes in her father's library. She remembered sitting on one of his uncomfortable office chairs, its green imitation leather tufted by brass tacks, tracing their features with her left index finger.

Ezra arrived with a large bag of sunflower seeds. Unlike his cousins who were dressed in white, he was wearing a pale blue Shabbos shirt, embroidered with white doves. When Susan blinked her eyes, they were flying over the fabric, their wings outstretched. Doves who were, perhaps, descendants from those who flew over the Second Temple, the one destroyed by the Romans. Doves who lived in the caves south of Jerusalem. White and pure doves hovering over the Holy Land. Doves sent out by Noah to see if the waters had abated, arriving back the second time with an olive branch in their mouths.

It's the shirt that an artist would wear, Susan thought, unable to take her eyes off of him. Ezra walked over to three children sitting on a green sofa at the back of the room. He knelt down on the floor and hugged each of them, tousling their hair as he whispered something.

The little girl smiled and the taller of the two boys shook his hand. Then, hand in hand, all four of them walked over to Susan. "These are my new, little friends," Ezra said, "just arrived from Casablanca." The kids were shy and at first, they turned their faces away. He said something to them in French, and then continued speaking to Susan in Hebrew.

"They're part of Operation Mural," he said. "Have you heard about it? Kids who've been rescued and sent to Israel with their parents' permission but without their parents." She'd read a story about the rescue in the *Jerusalem Post*. Since emigration was restricted by the Moroccan government, the whole operation had to be secret, with Jewish children, allegedly on vacation in Switzerland, flown to Israel instead of returning home to Casablanca.

The idea of a child landing in Israel without the comfort of a mother or father seemed cruel to Susan. She often felt homesick for the smell of her bedroom, the handmade lavender sachets stuck in the corners of her dresser drawers. She'd stitched them in the shape of hearts when she was eight, filling the lace cavities with purple lavender from the garden. But her stitches were uneven and the hearts ripped apart, leaving a trail of silver buds in her underwear.

These kids looked forlorn. Their faces were scrubbed and their dark, thick hair neatly combed. Despite the attention, there was no mistaking the sadness in their eyes. Henri blinked constantly. Susan thought that it was to stop himself from crying. Some memory, perhaps, of his mother handing him sweet slices of carrots with her delicate fingers. Now, here he was at a table with strangers.

Susan wanted to talk to him but she wondered how much Hebrew he knew. Thankfully, Henri spoke first. "Shalom," he said. He paused and took a deep breath. "My name is Henri. I only speak a little Hebrew." Susan remembered that it was the first complete sentence that she ever spoke in Hebrew as well. The most important sentence, her teacher at the time had told her. Once someone understood that you were a beginner, they would only use basic words. It set the ground rules for the conversation. Not too sophisticated. Basic words like "house" and "street," "day" and "night," "left" and "right."

"How old are you?" Susan asked, making sure that she used the masculine gender. He would not know the difference but others at the table might. He held up eight fingers, struggling to keep the three on his right hand together vertically. "Bigger than eight," he said. "I'll be nine Chanukah."

His fingernails were bitten down to the skin. The nail on his right index finger, clearly his favorite, looked ragged, and the fingertip was bloody and raw. Henri lowered his hands quickly, his cheeks reddening with embarrassment.

Poor kid, adrift in Jerusalem where layers of concrete dust day after day stained the fingers of the Moroccan workers. He would probably grow up to be one of them, his dreams of Casablanca fading. One day, he would not remember the softness of his mother's kiss.

The grown-ups passed the bottles around the table. They were drinking too much, drowning their sorrow in cheap wine.

"They promised us apartments but we wait endlessly," a man with a thick, dark beard said.

"It's to give us hope," answered Ezra sarcastically. He winked at Susan as he spoke.

"Without hope we would all just pack up our bags and return home," a woman to his left said.

Everyone smiled since they all knew that such a return was impossible.

The discussion turned to jobs. It was so hard to earn a living in Israel. Teachers could no longer be teachers, at least not until they mastered Hebrew.

"I thought that I could teach French," Batya said, "but there were so many French-speaking Europeans that I couldn't find work. They speak German and French and English and Hebrew. It's impossible to compete with them."

Rachel cleaned houses. "Not bad work," she said, "if you're lucky enough to have a decent employer." Just last month she'd worked for a mean woman with a German accent in Rehavia, who inspected every piece of polished silver for a smidgeon of tarnish. "Nothing was good enough for her," Rachel said. "I tried and tried but she was never satisfied. One day she accused me of stealing a silver dish. That did it. I told her that I was not a thief and I quit." Rachel reached for a glass of wine, which she downed in one gulp.

Ezra jumped into the conversation. "I used to be my own boss," he said. "Now, I follow orders or else I'll lose my job!" He popped an olive into his mouth, deftly spitting out the pit and dropping it into a green ceramic bowl. He passed the olives to Susan, a hint that she should speak. All eyes were focused on her.

"I've been in school for the past few years," Susan said. "But I've always worked summers, typing and filing letters in a law office, and plugging in phone lines on a switchboard at a resort hotel." She scanned their faces trying to figure out if they understood her, then made a pulling gesture with both hands.

"I've had some miserable bosses. One of them was a woman who was almost two meters tall. Her hair was dyed blonde and she had a nose like a bird of prey, ending in a sharp point. Just looking at her made me tremble. If you made a mistake, dropped a dish in the dining room, spilled a glass of water in the office, she would scream."

She looked around the table to see if the Moroccans understood her Hebrew. They were nodding in agreement. "Once, I was talking on the phone and I disconnected her. It was just a tiny mistake, one careless tug of the cord and the call went dead. I sat there shaking as I listened to the buzz of the empty line. A half-hour later, she stormed into the office, wearing a kitchen apron that was stained with blood from butchering. Her pale skin was flushed bright pink and she was biting her lower lip to keep it from trembling. She was still carrying a carving knife and I thought that she was going to stab me." While Susan was speaking, Ezra picked up a small paring knife and twirled it in the air.

A woman interrupted the conversation. "We don't get good jobs because they think we haven't suffered enough. We didn't survive their Holocaust. What do they know? We survived our own suffering, didn't we?" After she spoke in Hebrew, she spoke in *Marokayit*. There was murmuring back and forth. They whispered to one another, remembering old wounds and antisemitic slights. Jobs they hadn't gotten; schools that wouldn't admit them.

The man next to the woman sighed, then he reached over and clasped her hand. They were wearing gold wedding bands with matching motifs of twisted olive leaves. "All we hear on the radio is news of the Eichmann trial. They never say one word about us," he said.

"Oh yes, they do," Ezra chimed in. "They write stories about the way we throw rotten garbage out the window and how we reek of body odor. Everyone else is building the Zionist homeland. We are the lowest caste, the untouchables, groveling in the land of milk and honey."

Jews in North Africa had their own trials, he told Susan. "Don't believe everything you read in books," the librarian told him when he checked out two French history books on discrimination against Jews in Algeria, Morocco, and Tunisia, France's three North African colonies. France fell rapidly after the German invasion in May 1940 and French General Philippe Petain was given control over the southern part of the country and the colonies by Germany. "I'm reading about the harsh laws imposed by the Vichy government," Ezra said. As it turned out, Algerian Jews had suffered the most. They were more integrated into society and many were professionals. They could not hold public offices and they lost rights to citizenship. They were not deported to the camps but they were victims, nevertheless.

"Moroccans were businessmen and they suffered, too," Ezra said. Hard-hit by economic laws that restricted business and manufacturing, Moroccans who'd managed to improve their lot and moved into European urban neighborhoods were coerced to move back into the mellahs, the traditional Jewish quarters. Poor folks, like his family, were already living there and they were definitely not being educated in the universities. "We suffered," Ezra said, "in our own way."

His words startled Susan. She had not seen this side of him. He'd experienced his own personal Holocaust. She'd heard him talking in school but there his voice was modulated. "This is definitely not the Promised Land," Ezra said, as he poured himself another glass of wine. Then, swallowing hard, he added, "It's tough here. They treat us only a little better than the Arabs."

There was silence around the table. No one had the energy to talk. No one was willing to argue with him, to defend the Zionist homeland, to wave the blue and white flag with the Star of David set dead center. Susan watched their lips, pinched together, their eyes cast downward, avoiding contact. They'd grown up in a land where being Jewish was a liability. The idea was not to call attention to yourself.

Batya changed the subject. "I love the eggplant. It's so spicy!" she said. "Who made it?" Michal raised her hand. "It's my mother's recipe," she said. "She used to make it every Shabbat." Michal choked up and then cleared her throat. "I miss her so much," she said. "I haven't seen her for nearly two years now and each day is lonelier than the one before. She's stuck there and I'm stuck here. So, I cook her eggplant and I pretend that we are eating it together. We have imaginary conversations, too. She asks me about my grand new life in Israel. I lie to her. What's so grand about it? All I do here is clean toilets."

This was hardly the Shabbos peace that Susan expected. Listening to their talk, she felt nauseated—a sickening feeling that rose up from her gut and left a sour taste in her mouth. Batya's words about cleaning toilets made Susan sweat. She closed her eyes and could see the ring of scum crusted on the toilet basin in her apartment; the congealed drops of urine dotting its rim. Only the cleaning woman used the toilet brush provided by her landlord, which stood in a stained plastic base on the stone floor. On Tuesdays, Susan always left an Israeli lira on the hall table for Rachel as a tip.

It was getting late now and they were ending the Shabbos meal with songs, *negunim* that were not familiar to Susan. These were melodies that were chanted by the faithful in synagogues in Fez, in Marrakesh, and in Casablanca. Even the children sang along.

The table was cleared and folded neatly in one corner of the room. There were goodbye kisses on both cheeks. Susan saw the women unrolling the bedding, about to transform the dining room back to a bedroom. There were four narrow mats lying on the floor, side by side. *Not very comfortable*, Susan thought, as she stared at the thin pads, which could hardly be called mattresses.

Susan hesitated as she was leaving, looking in Ezra's direction. Her eyes met his. Was her attraction to him obvious to those around them? She was never this bold in America. At school parties, she stood in the shadows watching the couples embrace on the dance floor. Now, here she was flirting with Ezra, silently saying: "Don't be shy. I like you."

Somehow, she felt as if her father was standing in the corner of the room. He was shaking his head at her, back and forth, his lips pursed. On his face she saw his "I raised you right" expression. In his eyes she saw: "Don't disappoint me now that you're thousands of miles away from home."

All of her friends thought that she was crazy. Why would she want to leave her pink bedroom, with its gray-and-pink-checked comforter and her stuffed animals sleeping in a row? Her walls covered with lines from her favorite poets. Oh, how she loved Robert Frost. "The woods are lovely, dark and deep, but I have promises to keep, and miles to go before I sleep, and miles to go before I sleep." She told Barbara, "I have miles to go before I sleep."

"You'll be home in two months max," Barbara said as she kissed her goodbye at the pier.

"Don't be so sure," Susan whispered.

Ezra left with Susan, offering to accompany her on the long walk back to Rehavia. The streets were dark and empty. Buses and cars were not running. When she looked up, Susan could see Shabbos tables covered in white cloths, illuminated by flickering candles. Men and women were *benching*, their heads bobbing up and down as they said their after-dinner prayers.

"I guess I'm not in a very thankful mood," Ezra said, gazing at them with her. "I try to be thankful but it's hard." For a second, his left arm brushed against her. An accident, she thought, but hoped otherwise. His touch was an electric buzz. Her heart thumped out of control. This man was dangerous. All he had to do was kiss her and she feared that she would jump into bed with him. She didn't dare look at his face.

"Definitely not easy here," Susan said. "When I see what people deal with in Israel, I feel guilty about my New York City life. I never struggled for anything back home. I woke up in the morning and breakfast was on the table. Clean, pressed clothes were stacked neatly in my dresser drawers."

He nodded as she spoke. She could see that his eyebrows were arched quizzically.

They walked in silence for forty minutes, making a right turn into Rehavia. Unlike Shmuel HaNavi, which was bare of trees and littered with Popsicle papers, Rehavia was green, with well-tended gardens and impressive art deco homes. The only Moroccans in Rehavia were gardeners, maids, babysitters, and handymen.

When she approached her apartment, she recognized the chef from the pension across the street, his tall, slightly stooped figure leaning against a stucco wall of the building. He was smoking a cigarette, despite the fact that it was Shabbos, gazing up at the Jerusalem sky, still dressed in his apron. The lights in the pension's dining hall were dim and the tables were empty. He'd probably just finished washing up.

They'd spoken twice. His name was Gerhard and he was a refugee from Austria where he told her he'd learned to cook in a DP camp. She'd asked him for directions to the ulpan one morning and they'd exchanged a few words. He lived in a room on the ground floor of the pension with his cat. He asked her about New York City. "I always wanted to visit there and see the skyscrapers," he said, adding that he didn't think he ever would.

On another evening, she returned from school to find him standing outside on a smoking break. She could hear the voice of the announcer on the pension's old-fashioned radio, reporting on the day's testimony at the trial. "Lots of commotion there today," Gerhard said. "I can't listen to the trial when I'm holding a carving knife. Who knows what I would do?"

Susan imagined him swinging his knife wildly in the air as Nazi soldiers jumped out of his way. His forehead was sweaty and his face set in a grimace. The soldiers slumped backwards, afraid.

Gerhard didn't seem to expect an answer but Susan replied anyway. "I can't stop myself from listening. I'm afraid to miss even one little detail." The word *detail* caught in her throat, like a piece of chicken cartilage that scratched on its way down when inadvertently swallowed. Her words surprised her. Until she spoke them, she hadn't admitted to herself just how much pressure she felt to find Uncle Yakov. Every tiny fact at the trial might be a clue. Someone might have seen him, talked to him, known him. Her father's obsession had become her own.

Susan stared at Gerhard's skinny arms and wondered if he had numbers on them. His whole appearance reminded her of Ichabod Crane in Washington Irving's *The Legend of Sleepy Hollow*, a tall, lanky fellow with a small head, large ears, and a long neck—much like a scarecrow, a teacher who carried all of his worldly possessions tied in one large cotton handkerchief.

They'd reached her building now and Ezra leaned forward, she thought to kiss her. But he stopped himself, reaching for her hand instead. His fingers felt soft to Susan despite his construction job. For a moment, she was not sure how she wanted to respond. She looked up at his intense eyes and his wide forehead and, without hesitating, she kissed him on the cheek, then on his lips. It was a long kiss. She started to count but, fighting her compulsion, she stopped. Both of them stood very still. Around them, they heard the sounds of neighborhood cats yowling in the darkness. When she first heard them, Susan thought they were babies crying.

The entry to her apartment was down a narrow alley. The cats lay stretched out on the concrete, just under her bedroom window. Closing the heavy wooden shutters did little to muffle their plaintive sound. For the first few nights, Susan could hardly sleep. Then, like the sound of crickets in the country, she got used to their wailing.

For a moment, she panicked. What was she doing? Leading a man she hardly knew to her bedroom? Crazy! Dangerous! She leaned over and gave him a long kiss. Then, a second. "It's late," she said, "and I don't want to wake my roommates." They stood there clinging to each other. She wanted him to come in. She stared into his eyes. Deep, thoughtful, passionate. She tugged on his hands. Come in.

He leaned forward and kissed her again. Then, he surprised her. He shivered and stepped back. "I'll see you in school," he said, as he walked quickly back to the street.

Once, when Susan was on a sixth-grade school trip to Washington, D.C., she'd gone to the café car on the train to buy a drink. She was returning to her seat with a full cup of orange juice when the train sped up for no reason. The cup slipped from her hand and landed in the aisle, splashing a businessman in a suit who was sitting nearby. He grimaced at her, took out a monogrammed white handkerchief, and began mopping up the mess.

She'd moved too fast, letting her emotions spill to the ground. He saw that. He felt that. She put her key in the front door and tiptoed in. Light shone from under one of the other bedroom doors but no one stirred. She undressed and fell asleep. Her last thought was of Ezra walking under the stars.

She woke to the sounds of pots and pans clanging in the pension kitchen across the street. She was lying in bed thinking about Ezra when she heard a crash and the tinkle of broken glass. She recognized Gerhard's voice, with his heavy German accent, calling for help. "Someone bring me a broom and a dustpan. *Maher, Maher,*" he cried, "Hurry."

He was up early, preparing breakfast for the guests, many of them reporters at the trial. Susan had seen them returning one evening, in a pack. Notebooks were stuffed in their back pants pockets. Most of them were men.

The trial consumed the city. Susan read everything about it, every scrap of news in the papers. She listened to every report on the radio. The reporters spent the day at Beit Ha'am, a stone building on Bezalel Street, surrounded by a ten-foot-high fence of steel mesh. There were floodlights on the roof and border police with rifles and submachine guns stationed around the building. Courtroom seating was limited with the majority of the seats, nearly 500, given to the press. There was even an in-house restaurant, the Menora Club, catered by the Army, who wanted to make sure that nothing dangerous would be smuggled into the facility.

There were only 20 seats in the courtroom for the public. Since there was no regular television system in Israel, most Israelis who wanted to see the trial had to watch it on closed-circuit television, which they could see nearby in an overflow hall with several hundred seats.

The guard there already recognized Susan, he'd let her in twice.

Her bedroom smelled of rosemary. Ezra had twisted off a branch on their walk home and Susan had placed it on the nightstand by her bed. It had a strong, distinctive odor, like pine.

With its dark-green spiky leaves and sturdy wooden stems, the plant was native to the Mediterranean, flourishing in every garden and on every hillside. Tough, resistant rosemary, just like the sabras, defying the hot Middle Eastern sun.

She twirled the sprig and thought of Ezra. One minute, he'd reached for her hand; the next, they were kissing. More than a kiss, really. He had wrapped his arms around her and held her so close that she could hardly breathe. One second more, maybe a minute, and he would have landed in her bed, tangled in the floral quilt. But he pulled away first. Letting her float free. She had never felt this way before. She wanted him to stay with her, but he'd stepped back as if to say, let's slow it down.

At home, she would never have allowed herself to have these thoughts. Just thinking them would have filled her with remorse. Losing one's virginity was easy. Taking a lover would have been impossible. There would have been excuses, lies, and elaborate explanations, saying she was in one place when she actually was in another. She would have had to face her father without breaking down and crying. Not an easy task. "You're lying," he would say, his voice angry. "Where were you?"

In Jerusalem, though, she didn't have to explain her behavior to anyone. There were no prying eyes. No neighbors who would rat on her. She was an independent American girl living on her own. None of her silly high school friends were nearby to gossip about her behavior. There were no neighbors watching her every move.

There was no hot water and Susan jumped into the shower, shivering before the ice-cold water even touched her skin. Then, she wrapped herself in a rag that her landlord called a towel. It was rust-stained, with fraying edges, and it was coarse from drying in the hot Jerusalem sun. She rubbed the rough fabric against her back, watching flakes of peeling skin loosen and fall to the floor.

She stared in the bathroom mirror. There was a crack in the glass that ran right down the bridge of her nose. On one side, when she squinted, she saw an American girl, with a prominent Jewish nose and thick, dark Jewish hair in tight curls; on the other, a suntanned sabra in jeans and sandals, hair pulled back into a ponytail. They were having an argument. "Who do you think you want to sleep with? This Moroccan? You hardly know him," the girl on the left mouthed off. "What would your father say?"

"Shut up," the girl on the right said. "It's none of his damn business."

Susan touched her hair. Her fingers caught in a knot as she tried to pull them through. "Comb your bedhead," her father used to say, as she was about to run off to school. But she never did.

Susan and Ruth had made plans to meet at the Windmill, only a short walk from Rehavia. Erected in 1857 by Moshe Montefiore, an Anglo-Jewish philanthropist, the Windmill stood just above Yemin Moshe, the first suburb to be built outside the Old City's walls. Montefiore was a visionary and a pragmatist, who built a printing press, a textile factory and the flour mill so the Jews who subsisted mainly on charity could earn a living. The guidebook said that the Windmill was the fulfillment of an ancient adage: "Where there is no flour, there is no Torah."

The stone houses near the Windmill, Mishkenot Sha'ananim, were completed in the 1860s but Jews had always been reluctant to move in. Even though the housing was better than the overcrowded conditions in the Old City, the area was deemed far too dangerous. After the 1948 Arab-Israeli War, it bordered on no-man's-land and was close to the armistice line with Jordan. People feared sniper attacks and the neighborhood became very run-down.

Susan loved to go there for the view and the breeze and the walk past the King David Hotel and the YMCA building. No one stopped her when she entered the lobby of the YMCA, its limestone exterior still pockmarked with bullet holes from the war. Not a single Hasid to be seen. There were no peyos and no tzitzis. A woman wearing a large cross walked toward Susan, making a left turn just before she reached her to enter a small elevator. Susan noticed that gold cross earrings dangled from her ears. A priest hurried by carrying a large leather-bound Bible and a black suitcase.

Susan sat on one of the wooden benches and looked up at the 17th-century painted ceiling. The guidebook said that it had been purchased in Damascus, dismantled, and transported to Jerusalem. The floor was a mosaic replica of the sixth-century Madaba Map, with Jerusalem at its center. Everywhere, there were arches and columns and windows representing Byzantine, Romanesque, Gothic and neo-Moorish architecture—reminders of Jerusalem's Jewish, Christian, and Islamic heritage.

But the tourist pamphlet that Susan had been given by the Jewish Agency upon her arrival spoke only of its Jewish past and the relief figure on the 50-meter-high tower of the six-winged seraph in the prophet Isaiah's vision. Her father, who played golf on Shabbos and who ate Chinese food on Christmas, loved the text: "The Lord of Everything is holy, holy, holy! His glory fills the whole Earth."

"It's hard to reconcile the Lord's glory on Earth with the survivors on the streets of Jerusalem," Susan wrote her father one week after she arrived. He'd quoted the Biblical passage in his first letter, which definitely disturbed her. Before she began to write, she debated just how much she would tell him. "They seem so worn, so defeated. Not spiritual at all," she wrote. There was no doubt about it. He would hate those words.

Ruth was waiting for her by the Windmill, a map of Jerusalem in hand. She'd planned their walk carefully, each stop marked with a red dot. This was their second walk together and Susan already knew what to expect. There were to be no surprises, no left turns instead of rights, no detours taken on a whim. This woman had survived the camps for a reason.

Not that she talked about it. Susan tried to get her to speak although asking questions didn't work. "Such a hard life," Susan remarked as they passed a woman with numbers on her arm, pushing a small shopping cart of groceries uphill.

Survivor Number 127: thin woman, about five foot tall, wearing a frayed black skirt and a striped, white blouse. Her face is heavily lined and her back is curved. Every few seconds, she stops to mop her brow with a large white handkerchief. She has a bad limp.

"They probably broke her leg in the camps," Susan said out loud. "I bet that she lives alone without any family." Ruth remained silent. Then, she gestured for them to cross the street, heading in the direction of Kiryat Shmuel. She opened her notebook and began to read: "It's an old neighborhood, founded in 1926 to honor Rabbi Samuel Salant, the Ashkenazi Chief Rabbi of Jerusalem from 1878 to 1909."

"You won't believe it," Ruth said, smiling. "The land was purchased to honor the Rabbi's 90th birthday and it stipulated that people who were given loans to build there had to be 18 years old and to live their life 'in accordance with the Torah, both the written and orally transmitted.'"

As she read her notes, a Hasid walked in the opposite direction, his peyos swinging. "He's probably a descendant of one of the founders," Susan quipped. There were no cars on the street because it was Shabbos and no stores were open. When they turned the corner, though, there was a coffee shop with several customers on an outdoor patio. It was Shabbos but there was a cloud of smoke circling their heads.

"Let's have a coffee," Susan said, pointing to an empty table in the corner. Someone had left a newspaper there and an ashtray full of cigarette butts. Ruth reached into her bag for her cigarettes. "Been smoking since I was a teenager," Ruth said. She inhaled deeply, closing her eyes as she did. In Israel, everyone smoked.

Susan didn't smoke. It was almost impossible to do so at home because her mother walked around with a wet sponge cleaning out ashtrays immediately after smokers finished their cigarettes. The smell was awful, like the pungent odor at the town dump, where flocks of seagulls circled overhead in search of treasures. Once, at the dump, Susan found a Class of 1956 ring in the pile of garbage.

The inscription read, "To Betty, With Love Forever, Hal." *Forever*, Susan thought. *That was not a very long time.*

They ordered two espressos. Susan wanted to talk about Ezra, but she hesitated. "I had Shabbos dinner with some Moroccans," she told Ruth. "One of them, Ezra, is in my ulpan class. He's very cute!" She waited for Ruth to respond. Ruth's face remained blank. "His family lives in Shmuel HaNavi. Have you ever been there?"

"Never," Ruth said. "The only Moroccan I know is the fellow in the *shuk* who sells me olives," she said. "We lead separate lives," Ruth said, shaking her head for emphasis. "What do *they* know about Europe?"

It was a movement that she made often, a slight lowering of her head, a shift from side to side, her eyes almost shut, her lips opening and closing in silent speech. She looked like she was in a trance.

Ruth was on her second cigarette now. She exhaled, then took a sip of espresso. For a moment, Susan remained quiet. Then, feeling brave, she asked, "What can you tell me about your life in Europe?" She wanted to be more specific, but she stopped herself. Ruth stared past her; her face whiter than it had been moments earlier. The blood had drained away, leaving pale, almost brittle skin. It looked like it could peel off in a single layer. Underneath, Susan imagined an angry, bloody scar.

"We survivors divide up into two distinct groups," Ruth began. "Those who want to talk and those who don't. Four years of my life were filled with pain. I listen to the survivors testifying at the trial and it reminds me that I was not alone. But I can't, I don't like talking about it. Europe, as I remember it, was full of snow and barbed wire, cities with bustling Jewish quarters and little towns where people spoke German, Polish, and Russian on the streets and Yiddish at home.

"When I was a child," Ruth said, "I dreamed of becoming a ballet dancer. I had a bronze bust of Anna Pavlova on the dresser in my room. It stood on a marble base that had been dropped and glued back together. I kissed her every night. I kissed her so often that my saliva wore off the patina on her nose, leaving a golden shine on its tip. I dreamed of twirling in a pink tutu, my satin ballet shoes thumping rhythmically against the wooden floor. I was destined for the corps de ballet in Paris or Moscow or America. I never thought that I would end up in a camp." She reached for a coffee stirrer and began to twirl the stick ferociously in the dark blue espresso cup.

Susan had her own memories of ballet classes. She studied twice a week in a mirrored studio an hour from her home. The teacher had a French name and a long ponytail. Her hands were bony and her body thin. She used a pointer, touching her students when their legs needed lifting or repositioning. Susan remembered holding on to the barre as Madame pushed her right leg higher in the air. She teetered and tottered, struggling to keep her balance. Once, she sat on the floor, her head and back against the wall, waiting for the spinning to stop.

Madame had a French accent and everything seemed to start with the letter z. "Zat's right," she said. She rarely praised Susan although she always said *"parfaite"* to Michele, a blonde girl with a dancer's short trunk and long legs who was her favorite.

Like Ruth, Susan loved ballet but she was forced to drop out when she discovered that she could not do the spot turns without getting violently dizzy. Look at an object across the room and spin in that direction, Madame said, but it never helped Susan. The wooden floor shifted, as if an earthquake had occurred, and the wall mirrors spun in flashing circles. "Help me! Help me!" Susan screamed as she collapsed on the floor.

In desperation she quit, her dreams of a career as a dancer replaced by a new dream of becoming a nuclear physicist after reading an orange-covered biography of Marie Curie. A career in science proved to be even shorter lived. Her moment of glory was winning second prize at the regional science fair for a project demonstrating how plants use carbon dioxide and water during photosynthesis. For the first two weeks, the plants turned yellow and the leaves began to drop off. Only after her father put his finger in the soil and told her that it was too wet, did the plants recover and begin to turn green again. "It's like raising children," her dad said. "Too much attention is not good." He didn't believe that girls were destined to become scientists. When she presented her findings in the gymnasium of the local high school, most people walked by quickly. One girl stopped to take the handout that Susan had prepared. "Nice poster!" she said, pointing to the chart that Susan's father had made.

At the next table in the café, a survivor sat down, her back to them, the numbers on her arm clearly visible. The sunlight bounced off the numbers and they seemed to fly in the air, circling her head like a halo. Susan blinked and they landed back on her arm, engraved in her skin.

Survivor Number 128: woman in a green plaid blouse, wearing thick black eyeglasses. Around her neck, a paisley scarf. Very sad face.

"How did you end up in Mauthausen?" Susan asked, hopeful that Ruth would open up to her. "Were you sent there with your family?" The questions were tumbling out. "How did you get caught? Where were you living? Did someone rat on you? Did you try to escape?" Each question triggering another. Her hands were hot. Her skin tingled.

Ruth turned to face her and began to speak. "There were four families living in our apartment building in Kazimierz, the Jewish section of Krakow. We had a one-bedroom flat on the top floor." She lit up her third cigarette and paused. "My two sisters and I slept in the tiny bedroom, our parents in the parlor. One day, our first-floor neighbors were gone. Their lights were out. Their window shades were down. No one knew what had happened to them.

"The rumor was that the Gestapo had knocked on their door and taken them away in the middle of the night. No one was sure where. For days, we hid in our rooms, waiting until it was dark to go out on the streets. We had an arrangement with the shopkeepers. My job was to get bread from the bakery and milk from the dairy by knocking four times on their back doors; my younger sisters were sent to the vegetable store for potatoes. That's what we lived on.

"A week later, the Blausteins and the Bernheims were gone, too. We were the only people left in the building. During the night, I walked through their empty apartments. My friend Shula's flowered nightgown lay on top of her mattress. One of her drawings lay on the wooden floor. It was a picture of a man in a Nazi uniform. There was a jagged scar running down one cheek and a gun slung over his shoulder. I folded the drawing, hid it in my pocket, and carried it back to my room."

Ruth's eyes were half-closed again and her head started to tilt downward. The pain was unbearable. Susan felt it, too, suddenly cringing with a sticking pain in her side. It was just like the pain she felt when she tried to race around the track in gym. She took a deep breath and held it until the count of ten, a technique that sometimes worked.

Ruth paused to wipe away tears and she began nodding, almost involuntarily. She seemed to be agreeing with some imaginary person. She seemed to be talking to someone else. *Perhaps*, Susan thought, *it was a few words to her best friend whom she would never see again. Perhaps it was, "I love you."*

"They rounded us up the next day," she continued, "and marched us into a gray van with no windows and two wooden benches. There were four other people we did not know inside. My mother was crying. My father was silent. My two sisters held each other's hands. Sascha, who was only seven, sat on my lap."

"Did they say anything to you? Did they tell you where you were going?" Susan asked. She thought about all of those black-and-white photos of families boarding trains, children clinging to parents. No one was smiling.

Once, her father brought home a book on the Holocaust with photos of the trains unloading at Auschwitz. The people were carrying worn leather suitcases, held together by frayed straps with broken buckles. Susan thought them much too small. She could never fit her treasured dolls in one of them. Raggedy Ann and Andy, the twin mop heads that still sat propped up on her pillow, would have had to accompany her on her journey. And her rubber duck collection would have had to be crammed inside, too; 20 ducklings who floated in the bubbles, responding to her squeezes.

Susan was reminded of their annual trips to the Ringling Brothers, Barnum & Bailey Circus, where her grandfather erupted in laughter when a stream of clowns and animals, including a giraffe, climbed out of a little blue Volkswagen Beetle parked on the ring floor. Susan blushed when she remembered that three years later her father revealed the secret. There was a trapdoor in the floor under the car, leading to a staircase and a room below.

The people loaded onto the cattle cars were stuck. There were no trapdoors leading anywhere. When the metal doors slammed shut, there was no sunlight and little air. Hundreds of them were pushed and shoved into the cold car. In one photo, Susan saw a young woman of about 20 standing by the still-open door. She was dressed in layers of clothing—a blouse, a sweater, a jacket—all hanging somewhat askew on her narrow shoulders. Her cheeks were hollow. Her eyes stared straight in front of her. Her lips were pursed.

In the van, Ruth's family was driven to the railroad station where they were packed into cattle cars. "My mother held my hand and her hand was trembling. We knew it was bad. But we didn't know where we were going. It was so strange," Ruth said. "In my dreams, train rides took me to magical places, to caves with underground rivers and mountains with secret trails to the peak.

"Once, we took the train to the countryside. We had packed a picnic lunch and we wandered through the forest until my father found the perfect place for our blanket. The leaves were beginning to fall and there was a cold wind. But we laughed and laughed. My father told his favorite joke about the fat postman who always got in trouble with the German Shepherd watchdog. He never quite outsmarted him. My mother turned our modest meal into a feast, spreading thick slabs of homemade bread with butter and strawberry jam. We blessed the sandwiches with a prayer. Thank you, God, for your bounty, we said. That was the only train ride that I ever took. So how could this one be bad?"

Ruth was not really asking a question. Ruth was not speaking to her. She was lost somewhere, deep within herself. It was hard to imagine her living as a survivor in Jerusalem. Did she suffer from guilt, from remorse? How did Ruth feel when she sat in the auditorium listening to the Eichmann trial testimony? She sat so still. From what Susan could see, there was not a sign of emotion.

The survivor at the next table was leaving now. Susan watched as she reached into her handbag in search of a few *agorot* for a tip. She opened a worn leather coin purse and dumped out the coins. She seemed to be counting them, touching each one to be sure it was real. She placed a few on the table and began to leave. But, after a moment's hesitation, she returned and put one of them back in her purse.

Ruth reached for a handkerchief and blew her nose loudly. It sounded like the shofar on Rosh Hashanah. *Wake up, it said. Wake up, you American Jewish girl who knows nothing of suffering. Face east and daven. Pray to your God, if there is a God.*

They were walking once again, through the narrow winding streets of Jerusalem. It was quiet except for the screeching of the cats who were running everywhere—up trees, down alleyways, fighting with each other as they pulled fish bones and chicken legs out of garbage cans. The stench invaded her nostrils. For a moment, she gagged, overcoming the impulse to throw up. A sour, acidic taste remained in her throat.

Nothing soothed it. A cold drink. Hot tea. A mint lozenge. It would not go away. It was the same sensation that she felt when she saw survivors. Always, her mouth burned when she saw them wandering the streets of Jerusalem, their numbered arms carrying heavy shopping bags as they left the *shuk*. Inevitably, she felt nauseated when she imagined Uncle Yakov trapped in one of the death camps, his torn trousers hanging from his bony frame.

The same acid burned in her throat when she sat in the auditorium, listening to the testimony. There were three witnesses scheduled to testify about the prison guards in Ward 8 in Mauthausen and the first was a woman who had worked in the laundry. When she raised her right hand to take an oath, the ceiling spotlights hit the numbers on her other arm.

Survivor Number 129: blonde woman wearing bright red lipstick. Dressed in a green sheath that is much too tight. Around her neck, a glittery gold necklace.

"Of course, I'll tell the truth about those bastards," she said, even before the lawyer asked her a question. "I washed their shirts and briefs and pressed their uniforms." She was sweating under the lights, fidgeting from side to side as she spoke like a smoker who was missing her fix. Her eyes darted about. She crossed and uncrossed her legs. She held up her hands for the camera. "See these hands?" she said. "They are scarred from lye."

Susan squinted. She could just about see the burn marks on the woman's hands, brown scar tissue, an ugly residue from the liquid lye that the Nazis used in their laundry.

"Tell the court about your family and how you ended up in Mauthausen," the lawyer asked her. That was always the first question, Susan noticed. How? The lawyer asked. How did a normal family get caught in the Nazi net?

The question provoked Susan. No one had dragged her normal family to a camp. They were safe in their three-bedroom home with a dramatic view of the bay and a garden filled with blue hydrangeas. The only train her father traveled on was the suburban line with a dingy smoking car and a red leatherette bar. During high school, Susan often traveled to the city, sitting next to him as he read the *New York Times*. He folded the paper lengthwise, a technique that travelers used to save space. When he was done, he handed her the folded newspaper.

"Check out that Holocaust story on page six," he said. "It's all about the reunion of a Jewish family from Hungary. They ended up in four different DP camps but found one another after the war." Her father had underlined parts of the story with his Waterman fountain pen, its black ink blurring the letters and leaching through the newsprint.

Susan was used to this. Everything he read was underlined or asterisked, accompanied by a cryptic note to himself in the margin. Next to the story of the Budapest family's reunion, her father had written: "How many Hungarians were shipped to Mauthausen?" He read the newspaper, consumed by his obsession with the Holocaust. He wanted her to share his obsession, but when she protested he got angry. "You're a Jew, too," he said. "Don't you care about what happened to your people?"

She had written so many lists about this question:
Yes, I am a Jew.
Yes, I do care about what happened to the Jewish people.
No, I am the next generation.
No, the world has changed and we have to move on.
No, I will not be obsessed with death.
All crossed out.

The woman on the witness stand shivered before she spoke. It was a whole-body shiver that started with her head and rippled down to her legs. "Bastards," she repeated. "They tore our lives inside out. My father was a tailor. He made suits for wealthy businessmen who came to our home in Linz to be fitted. He made *bekishes* for the rebbes, long, black silk coats that were worn on Shabbos. Our house was full of black thread, curling on the cushions of the parlor sofa and stuck in strange swirls to the floral rug in the dining room. I can see him with ten straight pins in his mouth, adjusting the linen pattern on the dummy." She took out a floral handkerchief and mopped her face.

"We were so unimportant," she continued. "Petty little nothings. Why did they have to destroy us?"

The lawyer was waiting for her to answer his question.

"They told us to pack a bag. My father packed a sewing kit with his sharpest scissors and four spools of black thread. Just in case they needed a tailor, he told me. I packed my diary. My mother sorted our clothing into two piles and handed me a thick green sweater. She said that it might be very cold where we were going. When I asked her where that was, she never answered me. One hour later, there was a knock on the door. Two Nazi soldiers had come to escort us to the central depot. One of them took the sweater from my arm. He told me that I wouldn't need it." She stopped speaking and asked for a glass of water.

"Who was at the central depot?" the prosecutor asked.

Susan knew the answer. She had heard him ask the question before to a man who was shipped to Auschwitz.

Susan's earphones buzzed incessantly. At times, the static was unbearable. She listened to the soothing female voice of the English translator although she understood most of the Hebrew. Once a week, after hearing the nightly half-hour Eichmann trial reporting on *ABC* in New York, her father would call her the next day at the pension at a prearranged time.

She would hold the phone and just let him talk. "Eichmann just stands there calmly and smirks. Even when he watches the footage of the camps, with the mountains of bones, he doesn't blink. I watch every night. I can't stop myself from watching. Sometimes, I turn it on and turn it off. But I always turn it on again," her father said.

When she didn't speak, her father asked, "Are you there?"

"Yes," Susan said, keeping her voice low. "This phone is in the pension and I don't want to disturb anyone."

He was reading to her now, from an editorial in the *New York Post*. "We are scandalized by an interview with *New Yorker* Eichmann trial reporter Hannah Arendt. Who is she to say that the Jews were cowards, going to their slaughter like sheep?" Her father's voice cracked. "I've read her writing," he said. "It's cold, analytical, and disappointing. I couldn't finish it."

"Analytical is good, isn't it?" Susan said, sure that her remarks would tick her father off. "You've always told me to be analytical, to think my way carefully through things, to avoid being impulsive."

He was quiet for a minute. "Don't be a wise guy," he said, hanging up the phone.

She'd tried to be respectful but who said he was right? When she cried, he always told her to stop crying. When she overreacted, he always told her to have a stiff upper lip.

He called again after reading the April 14th issue of *Life* magazine with a photo essay on Eichmann in jail by Gjon Mili. Timed to the opening of the trial, the piece included photos of Eichmann mopping the bathroom floor in Djalameh jail near Haifa, where he'd been held, draping shirts and underwear that he'd washed himself over the bars of his cell window, and cutting breakfast margarine for the matzos, which were served to him during Passover, one week before the trial. The author wrote that, "...trapped, he [Eichmann] appeared smaller and yellower than his legend. Stripped of the brutal system he served, he had no strut."

"It's a brilliant analysis," her father said. "No strut. No power. Just a man washing his underwear."

His phone calls were always the same, full of anger and sadness as if Susan could comfort him, as if she could tell a little story that would make him laugh. Most of all he wanted her to agree with him, which she rarely did. After several moments of silence, he would hang up. When she woke the next morning, she wasn't sure if they'd spoken at all.

On Saturday mornings, Susan and her father were up early while the rest of the family slept. They talked while they ate jelly doughnuts filled with strawberry jam. On the kitchen table, a swirl of sugar. Her father drank black coffee in a white mug with the name and address of the local synagogue printed in dark blue letters. It was a modest building of yellow brick with a ragged *mechitzah* dividing the men's section from the women's. The building smelled of mold and the sea since it was fewer than a 1000 feet from the Atlantic Ocean. There was always sand in the wine-colored carpeting.

Her father was a passionate Zionist who'd never visited Israel. In fact, he had never crossed the Atlantic since arriving in America as a boy of 12. "I've been to Europe and it wasn't so great," he said. There was no need to leave. Everything was here. The streets were paved with gold. He despised the protesters in Union Square Park, the rabble-rousers who complained about low wages and hunger. "They're lazy," he told Susan. "In America, anyone who wants to succeed can do so."

There was no reason for her father to leave America. But Susan, ah, that was a different matter. It didn't surprise Susan that while he didn't offer her money for a trip to Europe, he was willing to pay for the entire trip to Israel. She could always see the *Eiffel Tower* or *Big Ben*. She could always snap a photo of the changing of the guards in front of Buckingham Place. But walking the cobblestone streets of the old city of Jerusalem? That was another matter.

At least once a week, he went to his top dresser drawer and took out the smooth stone that was wrapped in one of his white cotton handkerchiefs, hemmed with his initials embroidered in one corner. Yakov had given the stone to him before he left Europe. Scratched in it were the words *Gut Glik Libe Yakov*. Her father ran his fingers over the stone. "Good Luck, Love Yakov; it's all that I have left of him," he said. "When he handed me the stone, I had nothing for him so I reached in my pocket and gave him my lucky silver coin, the one with Russian writing that I found in the marketplace when I was five years old. I watched him drop it into his pants pocket."

Susan had heard the story of the stone and the coin hundreds of times. In each telling, the stone grew larger and heavier and the coin more valuable. It was a coin that belonged to the Tsar, one that was stolen by a royal guard in St. Petersburg. It was dropped accidentally in the streets of their shtetl when the Russian soldiers rode through on horseback during a pogrom. And the stone, ah, the stone, it was from prehistoric times, an ancient relic of civilization.

At the ulpan, the subject for the week was the weather. The Moroccans joked about it during their lunch break. "She's taught us six different words for hot," Ezra said as they interrupted each other with examples. "Who cares?"

He sat across the table from Susan, staring at her. She'd seen him in class but they hadn't talked since he walked her home. Her face became flushed and her forehead sweaty. Ezra was so different from the boys Susan dated at home. They were all college boys who came from good families and drove around town in their fathers' Chevrolet convertibles. There was Sam who drank too much and Bruce who talked too much. They were predictable and boring. Ezra was passionate, artistic, and political. Ezra was exciting. His eyes were darker than the darkest olives in the *shuk*, black with flecks of brown.

"We're in a heat wave," Susan said, jumping into the conversation about the weather. "It's been a week now without a breeze. I keep my shutters closed and I sip water all day long. It's so hot that it's hard to think."

"Think about what?" Maya asked her. "In Israel, you don't think. You just work!" Maya ironed sheets in the laundry of the King David Hotel. They were soft cotton sheets with the hotel's monograms on them. Each sheet was inspected by her supervisor. "If I scorch one," she said, "they will cut my salary in half."

The guests that Susan saw stepping out of taxis and limousines and entering the King David would never tolerate burned sheets. The men were dressed in perfectly tailored pinstripe suits. The women wore designer dresses, a cloud of pastel colors. A few steps behind them, the bellhop followed, their matching tan leather bags loaded onto his luggage cart.

"I worry about burning things," Maya said. "I worry all the time."

"Worrying doesn't help anything," Ezra said. "I believe in acting. You can't change life in Israel unless you are willing to speak up. Being afraid means that you are doomed to a life of servitude, like the slaves who built the pyramids in ancient Egypt."

They knew about those slaves. Every year they read about them in the Passover Haggadah. "That was Egypt," Maya interrupted, "not Israel in 1961. We are free here." She paused, and added, "Almost."

In class, they'd each written a composition on the weather. Maya's began, "In Casablanca, the sun always shines. It is a friendly sun, not like the sun in Israel which is harsh. In my dreams, I am back home, smelling my mother's cooking as I wake up." She read her words to the class, wiping tears out of her eyes.

Susan read after Maya. "In the summer, I spent my days at the beach by the ocean, digging for clams and catching crabs. Our house was not kosher but my father forbade me from bringing them home. It was cruel but I left them to die on the white sand. The sun was hot but there was a strong breeze from the Atlantic. I would sit on the sand and smell the tide coming in. Although my father disapproved, I came home after it was dark."

4

On the scrap of paper, Susan had written the address. It was near the Central Bus Station in Jerusalem. Her teacher had suggested that a man there could help her. Micha spent his days researching the Holocaust. Susan found his building and walked up the four flights to his apartment. They'd finally managed to connect on the telephone and he was expecting her.

Micha's business was tracing lost friends and relatives. He had *contacts*. When he opened the door, Susan was surprised. His hair was gray and he had a beard and long side curls. He wore a black velvet kippah. She was afraid to shake his hand but, surprisingly, he put his hand out to shake hers. His hand was warm and a little moist.

"So good to meet you," he said. "Come in, come in." The room was small and full of furniture. There was a green velvet settee and dining table with six matching chairs covered in green striped damask fabric. Hanging on the windows were ivory lace curtains. Susan thought it very Middle-European in look, like an apartment in Freud's Vienna that she'd seen in a magazine rather than one in 1960s Jerusalem. On the table, Micha had placed a yellow lined pad and a fountain pen, the tools of his trade.

On a massive sideboard across the room were stacks of papers organized into green folders. Susan began to count his folders. She guessed nearly 50. Years ago, when she found herself counting the number of performers who were taking a bow onstage, she was convinced that something terrible would happen if the curtain closed before she finished. The same fear took over when she was walking down the street, jumping over lines in the sidewalk as she counted them. One misstep and the rest of her life would be forever stained. It was irrational. Her counting habit was clearly out of control in Jerusalem.

Micha pointed to the first pile. "That's Auschwitz," he said. "They're in chronological order." The Auschwitz pile was the highest and the folders were fat, with colored tabs sticking out. "I've got my own coding system. Yellow means new material. Orange refers to things that are still in the works. Blue is old material." The tags in the Auschwitz stack were predominantly orange. The folders were worn and Scotch tape was holding them together.

"Do clients come to you?" Susan asked. She hadn't thought of herself as a client until the moment she asked the question. She'd seen clients in her father's waiting room: a carpenter who was crippled when a car struck him as he exited his vehicle on the driver's side without checking for oncoming traffic; a middle-aged man about to file for bankruptcy after his café closed; a young woman in tears, contesting a divorce.

There were clients who tapped their feet nervously and clients who shredded tissues on the dark blue carpeting. After they left, Susan's father would give her the task of getting down on her hands and knees and picking up the fuzzy white pieces. "Such sadness," she said as she dug her nails into the carpet, pulling out the tear-soaked remnants of their pain.

Her father's quest had become her quest, too. She was a niece looking for an uncle she'd never known. She took out the stone, rubbing it gently, before handing it to Micha. "I'm trying to find out what happened to my uncle, Yakov Reich," she said. "He was last seen in Rozwadów, a shtetl 215 kilometers northeast of Krakow."

Micha squinted at the stone. "People have brought me photos of tombstones before, images shot at old Jewish cemeteries where the stone is crumbling. But this is my first actual stone." He was already writing the inscription on a clean page of his pad.

He stood up and took a green loose-leaf binder from a file cabinet in the corner of the room. He opened the book to "R" and began to read. "There are 16 names under Reich," he said. "It's a common name, but there's no Yakov." Then, he took out a thinner binder marked "Krakow and vicinity." There was no Yakov Reich listed there, either.

"These lists are so incomplete," he told her. "Every week, I add a few names or move names from one camp to another. Just yesterday, I found Rachel Slovinsky. Her cousin told me that she'd last seen her in Prague. Rachel liked to paint and draw so we assumed she was sent to Theresienstadt but there was no record of her there. There was no record in a DP camp and there was no death certificate. Two weeks ago, a man came to see me with papers from his aunt. She was frail and could not come herself. His aunt had lived in the Jewish Quarter in Prague and she'd sent her nephew to see if he could find out whether any of her old friends survived. He came with a list she'd given him. It was written in a shaky hand but on it was Rachel Slovinsky, her best friend. Next to it, his aunt had written a note: 'The family was shipped to Mauthausen. Never heard from them again.' Things happen by accident. Bits of recorded memory rub against each other. I can't promise you much," Micha said.

He wrote down the basic facts and Susan gave him a picture of her father, taken the first year he arrived in America. He was standing with a group of boys. The setting was the playground of his public school on the Lower East Side. Her father stood in the back row, the oldest and the tallest student in his third-grade class, his eyes set squarely on the camera. "I'm not here for long," that was the expression on his face, as he stood amidst a group of eight-year-olds. He was wearing a jacket that was much too short and several inches of his arms stuck out from his sleeves.

Micha asked her a few questions about her grandparents. What did she know about their life in Rozwadów? Did they have a business? She closed her eyes and imagined the map of Poland, a universe of stars and planets and comets, shooting back and forth, all revolving around Krakow. The type was very small. The names were foreign. When she squinted, she could just about read the word, Rozwadów.

Once, she'd written a paper on the Daughters of the American Revolution. Her fifth-grade teacher insisted that a drawing or a chart accompany the work. *No problem there with lineage*, she thought, remembering that the DAR women could trace their ancestry back for generations. *Amanda Smith, that was her name, had great-great-great-great-grandparents in Tudor England.*

Susan's own chart was much more modest. "All I know is that my grandparents separated before World War One. My grandfather and his oldest son left for America in 1908. My grandmother remained in Poland until 1920, after the war, surviving by having her children sell bootleg cigarettes and liquor to the soldiers." Susan blushed. "Not much to tell, really," she said to Micha. "Plain folks, not very different from thousands of other immigrants who fled pogroms in Europe. Except, maybe they were a little taller."

She could see that Micha sensed her frustration. His eyes said, you are discouraged and stymied. "Don't despair," Micha said, suggesting that Susan visit two other offices in Jerusalem. He gave her their addresses and phone numbers. "Just keep asking questions," he said. "You might be lucky and find some answers." To comfort her, he added, "If I find anything out, I'll let you know." I'll start with Auschwitz and Mauthausen, He placed two yellow sheets of paper with the name Yakov Reich on them inside the corresponding folders and tagged both with yellow markers.

The sight of those folders filled with names reminded Susan of Arlington National Cemetery, across the Potomac River from Washington, D.C. She had visited there once and been struck by the rows upon rows of tombstones, some dating back to soldiers who fought in the Civil War. Sons, husbands, fathers, and grandfathers. There were just too many lost souls buried there and too many colored tags in Micha's folders.

It was nearly 2 p.m. and she was starving, her grumbling stomach loud enough to be heard by passersby. Across the street, she spied the falafel shop that Rachel had praised. The owner was from Casablanca. He came from the next alley and his family knew hers back home. Whenever she stopped there, Rachel confessed to Susan, he would wink at her, his heavy, dark eyelids closing over his dark eyes. Then, he would put four chickpea balls in her pita instead of three. It was the least he could do to alleviate the suffering of a fellow Moroccan.

The man behind the greasy counter was missing his two front teeth and when he opened his mouth Susan could see a glint of gold. He wore an embroidered kippah with pink and green birds flying across a field of blue. Someone had lovingly made that design for him. Each bird was different in size and color. There were large pink birds swooping down and small pink birds hopping on a branch. The green birds flew in the clouds at the top of the kippah in a single line. Susan noticed that his fingers were long and slender.

The shop was filled with the smell of pita bread just coming out of the oven, puffed and lightly brown. It was an aroma that didn't last long, fading by the time the owner stacked them. He placed one on top of another, making a pita tower that rivaled the Tower of Pisa; it, too, was leaning. "A falafel, please." He didn't seem to hear her, so she said it again, emphasizing the word "please." He nodded, writing nothing down. Then, a stream of questions: did she want sweet pickles, chopped lettuce, diced tomatoes, finely cut parsley and cilantro? Did she want extra tahini sauce poured over the fried chickpea balls? Did she want hot sauce, his homemade *charissa*? And if so, how much? He motioned with his finger, using his thumb and first finger to measure the amount. "More," she said, raising her thumb and index finger in the air, almost an inch apart. The man in front of her was adding more heat, shaking the red sauce vigorously over the pita. "It's never spicy enough," he said, handing the bottle to her.

Ezra told her that falafel was an acquired taste to the Moroccans. At home in Casablanca, they ate couscous and spicy stews with bits of chicken and meat. It was also an acquired taste for Americans like Susan, although her guidebook devoted three pages with colored photographs to the charming falafel shops of Jerusalem. There was even a small map with each shop given a four-star rating. Three red stars meant that their sauce was very hot. Four was a warning to Americans (beware: super-hot!). She noted that this shop, only three stools wide, was not included on their map.

It was always that way with guidebooks. They missed the best restaurants with three tables on a stone terrace, hidden on the eastern edges of the city. They missed the stalls in the *shuk* with the finest olive oil and the plumpest firm green olives. You had to hear about those places from a native. Guidebooks were for tourists who were too lazy to explore on their own.

Micha had given her two addresses to search for Yakov but she was coming to picture that to be a serious sleuth in Jerusalem meant to take risks, to sip Turkish coffee with strangers and sit on park benches, determined to strike up conversations.

Susan took her falafel outside and sat down on a stone wall that ringed a nearby children's playground. The kids were climbing the jungle gym, chattering to one another as they did tricks. A skinny girl swung from one bar to another almost two feet away. The leap was bold and Susan held her breath, hoping that she would succeed. For a moment, the girl on the jungle gym was suspended in the sky, her dark, almost black skin and thick black braids a stark contrast to the sky, her thin body dressed in mismatched clothes. She looked like she was wearing her older sister's pants, rolled up so she would not trip. It was not a leap Susan could have made as a girl. She remembered only being able to cross halfway on the monkey bars, falling to the sand below in embarrassment. Afterwards, there was a large bruise on her left leg, black and blue and then fading to orange and yellow.

Survivor Number 130 past by: a gray-haired man with a scraggly beard, the numbers visible on his arm. He planted his wooden cane loudly on the sidewalk as he walked. He stopped to pick up a discarded newspaper. He was carrying a ragged shopping bag filled with carrots and onions. A man who most probably lived alone, on his way home to cook a pot of vegetable soup.

Susan looked at the addresses Micha had given her. One of the offices was about a half-hour away up Jaffa Street, near the Central Post Office. It was a crowded area that she usually saw from the bus window. Workers were hurrying into the post office to mail letters on their lunch hours. There was often a long line out the door. It was always slow at the post office or the bank or at any city agency. People were just not in a hurry to serve you. If it was time for their tea break, you had to wait.

Pushing forward with the search for Yakov felt daunting. She imagined a road map with hundreds of barely marked streets crisscrossing each other. A turn to the right might lead her back in a circle. A turn to the left might prove a detour. She was fearful of the journey knowing that she did not have a good sense of direction. When she walked in New York City, she found her way by place markers: a building covered with ivy or a brick wall painted with graffiti. She was often confused. Struggling to figure out which way was uptown and which way was downtown. She walked east when she meant to walk west. A real sleuth would never have this trouble.

She couldn't abandon the search, though. She thought of her father pressing the stone into her palm before she left. "I never knew what happened to him," he said to her. "Please do this for me. Knowing something is better than knowing nothing."

Was that always true? Knowing something could be worse. Why would her father want to know that his brother was tortured or gassed? Wasn't it better, she thought, to just fade away, to be lost in the history called the Holocaust, to be an invisible body without numbers.

The building on Jaffa Street was a three-story concrete structure, with a used clothing store on the ground floor. It was not distinguished architecturally from the buildings around it, and was probably built hurriedly in the late 1920s. The stucco was cracked in several places, as if a spider had woven its web on the façade, and two overflowing garbage cans stood like sentries on either side of the front door. Inside the store, rows of open cardboard boxes, their sides peeling, were stacked everywhere instead of shelves. Customers were pulling things out of the boxes and stuffing them in shopping bags. In the center of the room there were shirts, dresses, and pants crumpled on a black plastic table. There was a sign with the words "KOL BEGED BACHANUT AVAR KVISA!" in large black block letters, assuring customers that every garment was clean. A young mother, surrounded by her flock of four, stood there holding the clothing up in the air to check for holes. Her face was red and her eyes darted from side to side. She was hoping, Susan was sure, that her neighbors would not see her.

Susan thought of the thrift shop on Second Avenue where the clothing was piled in a mountain on the floor. She loved to shop there! It was Mt. Everest, a slippery slope of satin lingerie from the 1920s, sequined dinner jackets from the 1930s, and organdy prom dresses from the 1950s. You never knew what you would find. On Tuesdays, the day when the owners replenished the mountain, she always arrived early, ready to duke it out with another customer who was pulling on the sleeves of the same jacket. "I saw it first. No, I touched it first!" Not letting go until the opponent gave up.

It was the ultimate quest. If you had an eye and good taste, you could find something unique, a scarf or blouse that your friends would envy—a designer garment that ended up on the concrete floor of a hole-in-the wall store up the block from the most popular kosher-style deli in New York City. She'd packed one of these treasures in her trunk: an oblong, red and blue rayon scarf with bold stripes and polka dots, fringed with white. Retro 1940s.

The thrift store in Jerusalem, though, was all about survival. Susan watched as the woman held the pants up in the air to gauge its size and then rotated them backward one more time to check for stains. She threw a rejected pair of navy pants back on the heap and moved to the other side of the table.

A woman with a strong German accent answered the buzzer. "Can I help you?" she asked. Susan could hear her asthmatic breathing. That was such a funny word, "help." She hadn't said "who's there" or "hello." She'd gotten right to the point: "Can I help you?" meant who are you and what do you want from me? Susan explained that Micha had suggested that she contact her. "I am searching for my uncle who was lost in the Shoah," she said. The only sound that followed her words was that of the buzzer, letting her enter the building.

She walked up a flight of narrow stairs. Someone was cooking cabbage and the smell was overwhelming. The pungent odor of coriander lingered on every step. When she got to the first landing, the smell seemed to emanate from the open door at the end of the hall. A woman stood there waiting. In her hand was a large wooden spoon. "Come in, come in," she said. "Pardon my appearance." She was wearing a flowered apron that had large orange stains and was very much in need of washing. As she spoke, she picked off a piece of cabbage stuck to one pocket and put it in her mouth.

The apartment was tiny. There was a kitchen with a blue Formica table and two rickety chairs and a parlor with an oversized dining table covered in a lace tablecloth. It was piled high with papers. Down the hall, Susan could see a small bedroom, with a narrow bed big enough for one person. It did not take much detective work to figure out that she lived alone. In America, living arrangements were harder to figure out. Single women often had double beds, but Susan and her friends had found their own way of figuring things out. They counted the toothbrushes in the bathroom.

She directed Susan to the parlor couch, its dark blue fabric covered with white cat hair. "I'm not much of a housekeeper," she said apologetically. She made a valiant effort to lift a hairball from the cushion before Susan sat down. Susan smiled. "I'm not here because of your housekeeping skills. I hear that you might be able to help me find out what happened to my father's brother, Yakov," she said. "We think that he died in the camps but we have no proof. There are no records whatsoever."

Her name was Shoshana and she was a survivor of Auschwitz. She looked about 60 years old with dyed hair the color of a persimmon, gray roots showing. Her face was covered with dark sunspots and wrinkles from too much exposure and the blue veins in her hands were prominent. Despite her small size, she looked tough to Susan. Messing with her would have been dangerous. It was the way she moved her arms and the set of her chin. She seemed to be saying, watch out, I have been a prisoner. Never again!

"You've come to the right place," she said as she took out a clean sheet of paper. Then, out of the blue, she asked, "Have you been listening to the Eichmann trial?" Without waiting for Susan to reply, she answered the question herself. "Of course you have. In this country, everyone is glued to the radio. I went to Beit Ha'am once but I found being there too hard. When I hear it on the radio at home, I can distract myself, mop the floor, water my plants, bang a book on the table. When I sit there on one of the hard benches, all I can think about is my father and my mother and my sisters and brothers, my entire *mishpacha*—all perished. I am the only survivor." She was doodling on the paper. It was the face of a man with a mustache. He resembled Adolf Hitler.

Yakov would have to wait. Shoshana had to tell her story. In seconds, she began recounting why her parents had named her Fruma. As the youngest child of seven, she was to be their pious, obedient daughter, the one who would take care of them in their old age. It did not turn out that way. When she came to Israel, after the Holocaust, she no longer believed in God. There was no one for her to take care of and no one to take care of her, and she had come to hate the name Fruma. "I became Shoshana, a rose," she said, pointing to a miniature white rose bush in a plastic pot on her windowsill. The plant only had one flower. Its leaves were yellow and Susan spied tiny aphids crawling up the stems.

Suddenly, the flashback ended. Shoshana was back in the present, asking Susan what she knew about Uncle Yakov. It was the same difficult question, thrown at her from every direction, one to which she could only give the slightest of answers. There was no photo. He had blue eyes like her father's and he was tall and thin like her father. After that, who was sure? Maybe there was a dimple on the left side of his face when he smiled. Or maybe it was on the right? Her father couldn't remember. He thought that he had a mole by his ear. But maybe it was really by his nose.

Shoshana explained that she used her own catalog system for her research. Instead of colored tags, there were Jewish stars, the same blue as the stars and stripes on the Israeli flag, on her folders: one for new cases; two for persons reported missing for two to five years; three for Jews lost for up to eight years; four for Jews lost for a decade or more; and five for Jews who vanished *before* the Shoah—Jews who went out one day to buy a loaf of bread and never returned.

"That was my grandfather," she said, picking up a five-star folder that was dog-eared in one corner. She read through it every week. Her mother told her that they never knew what happened to him. It was an early Sunday morning in the winter, a day when it was impossible to walk without a scarf wrapped around your face. He put on his heaviest coat and his boots and went out in the snow to buy bread from the bakery three streets away. He was a stubborn man who had his ways and he just would not eat the bread from the bakery around the corner.

"Doesn't sound stubborn—" Susan started to speak but Shoshana interrupted her. She wrung her fingers as she spoke. When he didn't return, her grandmother and her mother went out looking for him. No one in the bakery had seen him. No one in the neighborhood remembered him passing by. "He vanished." Shoshana dabbed her eyes with a handkerchief and stopped talking.

"It's hard looking for someone you have never met," Susan said, trying to be sympathetic while finding a way to return to Yakov's story. "No one in my family really remembers him, except my father. He's obsessed with my finding out what happened to him. His sisters have forgotten what he looked like. Except they all tell the same story of Yakov having the brightest, bluest eyes in the family, the color of a perfect, cloudless sky."

"That's not much of a clue," Shoshana said, jotting down a few words. She reminded Susan that while the Nazis spoke of Aryans with blue eyes and blonde hair there were plenty of Jews who had blue eyes and blonde hair, too. Shoshana had brown eyes, like Susan's. No one in Susan's family had inherited her father's blue eyes.

She went to the corner of the room and picked up a rolled map. "Let's try to trace your uncle's journey," she said, as she smoothed the worn map of Europe, backed with canvas. She knew the names of hundreds of shtetls and, with a pointer, started to name them. "By now I know the map by heart. See that red dot?" she said. "That's Przemysl in Galicia."

Susan looked for Krakow on the map and then dropped her finger on a dot not far from it. "He came from Rozwadów, a little village on the San River," she said. During World War One, the town was filled with thousands of Austrian troops, camped there because of its strategic location. It turned out to be a blessing for poor Jewish families who sold chocolates, cigarettes, and liquor to the soldiers. That, Susan explained, was how her grandmother and family survived during the war years when she was separated from her husband. According to family legend, they earned enough money from selling cigarettes to build a two-story brick house, which might have been true, because there was a brick factory with a large kiln in the village.

It was hard to imagine such a palatial dwelling since the only photograph that Susan had ever seen of the town, in a history book, was blurry. There were a few stone houses on the town square but most of the buildings were of a single story and made of wood.

Susan felt like she was losing steam. She was getting tired of telling the same story. There were moments when she wanted to add in imagined details of her own, to flesh out the story so that it was more dramatic. The life of a narrative, after all, was in the vivid details. They carried the loose cigarettes in a burlap bag that usually held onions or potatoes so the cigarettes often had a strange oniony smell. They hid the money in thick woolen socks that their mother knitted to fight off frostbite. She invented a story about her father being mugged, punched in the eye by some hoodlums who wanted to steal his money. He gave them three coins and they let him go but he never told his mother. Susan wasn't sure if he had ever told her this or whether it was purely a figment of her imagination but her father and Yakov would smoke a few cigarettes before they got home. No one would miss them, they thought. Sharp-eyed, their mother always did. She counted out the coins and the cigarettes and then, discovering that four cigarettes were missing, smacked them hard four times on both cheeks.

The anecdotes were building in Susan's imagination, like lint collecting on the delicate fabric of oral history. It was too late for her to remember what her father actually said or what he didn't say.

It was impossible to unravel what he remembered from what he had forgotten or from what she had invented.

Shoshana was taking notes. Susan could not read what she was writing but Shoshana stopped to underline one word three times. "Blue," perhaps, or "stone"? She was left-handed and she used her right hand to cover her notes.

"Have you spoken to anyone from Rozwadów?" Susan interrupted. "Someone who might remember Yakov?" She had to take the offensive. Being a sleuth meant extracting hidden information.

Her bold words startled Shoshana. "There's a woman from Rozwadów who lives near Bnei Brak," she said. "Four years ago, she came to see me to ask for help in finding her sister." She pulled a torn, yellow sheet from the pile of papers. "Here it is. Her name is Chaya Birnbaum and she lives on Ha Rav Desher Street."

Without a moment's hesitation, Shoshana began to read Chaya's account: "My sister and I were best friends. She was four years older than me. She was a student at the girls' yeshiva on the town square and I was still in the younger grades. One hot July day in 1941, she did not pick me up at school. I stood at the entrance and waited but she did not come. After an hour, I walked home alone. The house was empty when I arrived. My mother, I thought, was probably out shopping at the marketplace. Food was scarce since the Nazis arrived but she usually managed to get a bag full of half-rotten potatoes to make potato soup. My older brothers were not home either. They worked at the brick factory until dark so I didn't think that anything was wrong. But there was.

"Our economic situation had worsened during the 1930s. Trade declined dramatically and antisemitism increased. Jews were beaten up. Shops were broken into. Every day, before we left for school, our mother cautioned us to be careful. Keep your head down, she said. Don't talk to anyone. Don't smile and don't laugh. I could never understand why we should not smile. After 1927, it was harder and harder for Jews to emigrate—either to America or to

Palestine. With the arrival of the Germans, life for the Jews in Rozwadów deteriorated. If your family was smart and lucky, you escaped east, crossing the San River to the side controlled by the Red Army. My brothers did that, leaving work one day at the brick factory and never returning home. They ended up in labor camps in Siberia. One of them, Isaac, survived and he lives near me in Israel. My mother and father vanished. I learned later that they were caught in the Nazi roundup of Rozwadów's four hundred remaining Jews and shipped to one of the extermination camps. Neighbors found me in the apartment and took me east. After the war, I settled in Israel. I found my brother but we never knew what happened to our sister, Bluma. There is no record of her anywhere."

Susan reached out and took the paper. The handwriting was hard to read and the ink was smeared. Maybe Chaya knew Yakov, Susan thought. Maybe the two families bought bread at the same bakery or they both worshipped at the stone Rozwadów Synagogue on the market square. Maybe Yakov and her father had squirmed on the same hard, wooden seats as Chaya's brothers, cold air blowing in through the broken glass windows, their rebbe running his fingers through his gray beard as he davened, his body swaying. Over and over the same prayers turned toward Jerusalem.

Shoshana handed Susan a small black-and-white photo of the two sisters when they were young. They were wearing identical Shabbos dresses, handmade by their mother. The girls were staring at the camera. Neither was smiling. Susan noticed that Chaya was clutching the hand of her older sister. Everything was perfect. Their hair neatly combed and decorated with bows; lace trimming their ankle socks.

"Life was good then," Susan mused aloud. There they were sitting for a portrait, capturing their life before everything fell apart, before their shtetl was consumed by pain and suffering. Behind the girls was a landscape with a mountain and gentle rolling hills and no clouds in the sky. The backdrop was the one that Susan had seen in family portraits, probably taken in the same photographer's studio. A dark, dusty room in the back of the building. Susan imagined herself posing for a portrait: sitting on one of the upholstered chairs, her hair neatly braided, her pinafore pressed. The flash of the camera. There was no hint of rain, no sign that trouble was brewing. There was no pogrom over the horizon, no Nazi storm trooper about to snatch a person off the street and ship him by train to a work camp.

Susan had never been to Bnei Brak, although she had heard about it, of course. Every Jewish child who has ever read the Passover Haggadah knows the story about the haggling back and forth of the rabbis in Bnei Brak on the night of Passover. How Rabbi Elazar, Rabbi Akeevah, and Rabbi Tarphon spoke all night long about the departure from Egypt and how they disputed whether the story of the flight of the Jews from Egypt should be told at night.

Susan remembered arguing with her father over the puzzling interpretation that "the days of your life" referred to the days alone and that "*all* the days of your life" included the nights also. It was, she insisted, rabbinic gobbledygook. Where there was a way to interpret something within the laws, the rabbis would find it. Once, she'd ridden in a Shabbos elevator operated by a non-Jew, a Shabbos goy, hired to stop the elevator at every floor. It was kosher, her friend told her, as long as you were not doing work. Susan thought that the whole design was ridiculous. *Leave it to the Jews to come up with that solution. What a joke!*

Her father defended the rabbis. Their wisdom was beyond strictly rational comprehension. His words were puzzling. Here was a man trained as a lawyer suspending logic. "You can never outthink a rebbe," he insisted. When she protested, he waved his hand in the air, dismissing her words.

Shoshana advised that Susan should call Chaya and go see her. Handing her Chaya's phone number, she added, "And do it soon, I hear that she's not well."

Susan left, clutching the folded paper, tempted to curl it up into a ball and throw it into the nearest garbage basket on the street. She felt like quitting. She was tired of following clues. She wanted to strike out on her own. Live her own life. Forget about this Uncle Yakov assignment. She crumpled the note in her pocket, and placed it on her bed stand when she got home. She lay there staring at it for several hours. It was her life, after all, not her father's. She had to follow her own dreams. Back and forth, thoughts swiveling. *Call Chaya. Don't call Chaya. Stop this nonsense.*

But she couldn't stop. Being a quitter, that was worse than anything. Breaking your promise, that was sinful. She unfolded the note and walked across the street to the pension to use their telephone to call Chaya. The phone rang for a while and Susan was about to hang up when a woman finally answered. Her voice was soft and she spoke in heavily accented Hebrew. The connection was poor and there was static. "Speak louder. Please speak louder. Shoshana, who?" the woman kept saying.

They agreed to meet on Thursday afternoon. Susan would take the Egged bus from the Central Station in Jerusalem and Chaya would meet her at the bus stop on Rabbi Akiva Street near her apartment. She would be wearing a purple hat for identification.

All week, Susan could not stop thinking of the meeting with Chaya. On the street, she passed a beautiful dark-skinned woman in a purple turban. Her face was heavily made-up, especially her eyelids which were thickly coated in lavender shadow. Her lips were a deep wine color. This woman, Susan was certain, had not escaped from the Nazis. She had never walked the streets of Rozwadów.

Later that day, Susan saw another purple hat. This one was on a woman dressed in a dark gray suit who was entering the garden of the pension across the street from Susan's apartment. She was carrying a leather briefcase. Probably one of the reporters at the trial, Susan thought, looking at her neat figure. Her hat was a cloche, shaped to her head, and it had three small, gray feathers that seemed to spring from behind her left ear. A taxi had left her off at the pension and she entered hurriedly.

Testimony at the trial had been especially heated in the last two days. Susan covered her ears as she walked down the streets, trying desperately to muffle the sound. Loud, louder, loudest. The announcers' strident voices echoed, bouncing from cobblestone to cobblestone.

Two German women who had been female guards at Auschwitz and Mauthausen took the stand. One of them, Marla, cried throughout her testimony. "I was so young," she kept saying. "I was afraid they would kill me. They were totally evil but I was a coward and I obeyed," she told the prosecuting attorney. "I saw him once point his finger at two people and order the guards to take them to the crematorium."

She was talking about Eichmann, of course, the man in the glass cage, the trial that all of Israel was glued to, at home, in the office, at school, even at the ulpan on Wednesday, where the Moroccans heard Marla's testimony blasting during their lunch break. Ezra was the first to criticize her. "Phony tears," he said. "I don't believe for one minute that she was sorry." He stared at Susan, waiting for her to speak.

"Maybe Marla was desperate. Who knows what we would have done?" Susan could see the frown on Ezra's face.

"Don't be silly," he said. "We would never have followed orders to kill someone."

Rachel believed that Marla sounded contrite. "There are so many things that we do that we are sorry for doing," she said. Rachel's face was so sad. What had she done, Susan wondered, that she now repented? A lover she'd rejected in Morocco? A promise that she'd failed to keep? When Susan looked at Rachel's face, it was impossible to read. She passed the pita to Susan and lowered her head to say a blessing. "Amen," they said in unison. Then, tearing off a bit of pita, she scooped up a dollop of baba ganoush, and swallowed it in one gulp.

In class, they talked about Marla's testimony. Esther Wolff was convinced that Marla's repentance was phony. "Even without seeing her, even with just hearing her shaky voice over the radio, she sounded like she was lying." She had her point of view and made no effort to be objective. Rachel and Ezra raised their hands. Susan decided not to speak. It was a tactic that she knew well, the same silent response that she fell back on when her father went off on one of his rants about the persecution of Jews all around the world.

Count to ten first.
One: Do not show emotion.
Two: Straighten your spine and your shoulders.
Three: Remember not to grimace.
Four: No fidgeting.
Five: Think hard.
Six: Don't take him head-on.
Seven: Hold your breath.
Eight: Be smart.
Nine: Be smarter.
Ten: Count to ten again.

Ezra was convinced that Marla was a liar. "When I was ten years old," he said, "I knew what was right and what was wrong. It's ridiculous to blame everyone else. *Shakran. Liar,*" he kept saying. Then, turning to Esther, he asked, "That's the right word, isn't it?"

Susan knew that Ezra saw everything in black and white. There were no grays to him. There was the moral path—where Moroccans would be treated like German Jews and other Europeans—and the immoral path, where they were a lower caste, subject to the whims of the ruling majority. To Ezra, they didn't have to bow their heads and obey. There were ways to protest, even against the Nazis. Marla should have done something, anything.

"If my boss tells me to punch one of my fellow workers, do I have to do it?" he asked.

Rachel shook her head. "Not the same thing," she said. "Marla had a gun to her back, a knife to her throat, and gas chambers down the hall. How brave would you have been in her situation?"

They read a summary of the trial in the newspaper prepared for students at the ulpan. It said that Marla, a camp guard, confessed her sins in the testimony. That she admitted that she knew what she was doing and did it willingly. They debated the meaning of the phrase "of her own free will." No one could agree.

Susan had been thinking of Ezra for days, dreaming of him. Her head resting on his muscular shoulder, his dark skin hot and smooth. "*Motek*, sweet one," he kept saying to her. "*Motek*, I love you." His arms wrapped around her. When he spoke in class, Susan couldn't take her eyes off of him. He was so smart, so charming.

This time, he followed her out of class and took her hand boldly, swinging it as they turned the corner. "I'm working late tonight," he said. "Can I come by your place afterwards?" Before she answered, he leaned in and kissed her. Then, they kissed again.

She had almost fallen asleep when she heard a light tapping on her bedroom window and a voice with the slightest hint of a French accent, "*Motek, Motek*, I'm here." She pressed her nose against the glass and he surprised her by kissing it. "*Motek*," such an endearing word. No one had ever called her that in any language. She tiptoed to the front door, unlatched it and let him in, careful not to wake her roommates. There were four of them in the suite, sharing four small bedrooms, a kitchen, and a bath. With the exception of the light in the bathroom, the apartment was dark.

Susan held Ezra's hand, guiding him into her room. Within seconds, their clothes were heaped on a worn wicker chair by the bed, his concrete-crusted T-shirt flung on top of the pile. Susan reached into the nightstand drawer and took out one of the condoms that her friend Barbara had given her as a present before she left. They had argued about whether she would need them. Barbara was sure that some Army soldier would sweep her off her feet. "You're looking for adventure," she told Susan, squeezing the package into her hand.

In her head, she heard her father answering Barbara. "Not my daughter. She's dutiful. She listens to me. I know what's best for her." And Susan began fighting with him. "Not always! I'm 18. I'm my own person. I'm not like my friends. They're ordinary. Why can't you trust me? I'm smart like you." But she got not a word back in reply. Just his blue, censoring eyes.

Did it really matter? She wasn't a virgin. Sometimes, though, she still believed that she was. Her back seat sex with Bob didn't count. How could it? There was no passion. Nothing memorable. A little groping, three lukewarm kisses, a few seconds of discomfort, and it was over with. She was left staring out the window with Bob asleep behind the driver's wheel.

With Ezra in her bed in Jerusalem, surely it would be different. Just looking at him excited her. His dark eyes a deeper shade of brown than she'd ever seen. His beautiful hands and long, tapered fingers. No amount of construction work could alter their exquisite shape.

Her friends at home were busy preparing for graduation now. The senior prom, end-of-year parties, final exams. Susan had escaped. It was her father's idea that she travel to Israel, but maybe he was right after all. Maybe she could be her own person here.

Although it was April, it was cold inside her bedroom with its stone walls and stone floor. They were lying in each other's arms under her floral quilt. His skin was so smooth. She touched his shoulders, then pulled her hand back. He took her hand and moved it back to his shoulder. "Don't be afraid," he said. "Don't be afraid, *Motek*." She put her arms around him and hugged him tightly. "*Motek*," Susan said as Ezra pulled her panties down. She didn't resist. Susan kicked them off her toes. Then he entered her, shivering when he came.

When she woke in the morning, Ezra was gone, off early to his construction site. Susan looked at the clock and realized that she had an hour to get to the Central Bus Station. She put on a white long-sleeve blouse that buttoned at the neck and a long navy skirt. *Now I look like one of those Yeshiva girls*, she thought as she combed her hair in the mirror.

She made it to the bus to Bnei Brak with one minute to spare. As it turned out, she was the only woman on the bus whose hair was not covered. There were two empty seats. One was next to a Hasidic man who was davening. He didn't look up when she approached. But his body language said, do not sit next to me. The other was next to a woman in her sixties. Her hair was covered by a shiny black wig that was obviously artificial. She had two shopping bags stuffed with vegetables and spices at her feet and Susan had to scoot around them to squeeze into the seat next to her.

She was reading a Yiddish newspaper. On the front page, Susan saw a picture of a woman testifying at the trial. *It must be Marla*, she thought. The trip was about an hour and a half and Susan began to write down questions for Chaya. Once, in high school, Susan heard a local journalist talking about the craft of reporting. "Don't just come in and make up the questions as you go along," the journalist advised them. "Make up a list and put the questions in order. Be prepared to bring the person back to your subject when he or she wanders off in the wrong direction. Everyone takes a detour." Susan's lists were a way of ordering and reordering her life. Moving priorities up and down. Just upgrading or downgrading an item felt like she was actively shaping her life.

Susan's list for Chaya was basic:
What years did Chaya live in Rozwadów?
Did she ever meet Yakov Reich?
Did she know any members of the Reich family?

She did not want yes-or-no answers. She wanted to know details. How poor were they? How religious were they? Did the children go to school? What did the inside of their house look like? She had begun to write down a fourth question when her neighbor leaned over to her and asked, "Do you have family in Bnei Brak?"

Susan shook her head no and was about to speak when the woman asked another question. "Are you spending Shabbos there?"

The directness of her questions surprised Susan. Here was somebody she'd never met before grilling her on her weekend plans. Israel was a small country, true, but who said that every Jew had to know all of your business? The clerk in the drugstore had to know exactly why you needed aspirin and whether you were listening to the trial. The crossing guard had to know what neighborhood you were from in New York City. Jews should not have secrets from one another. They were a *mishpacha*, one family, except for the Moroccans, who were the black sheep.

Susan explained that she was meeting a woman who grew up in Rozwadów. "I'm trying to find out if she ever knew my Uncle Yakov," she said. There was an immediate "Aha! You're meeting Chaya," the woman said, for the first time looking Susan directly in the face. "I'm Tzipora Goldman and Chaya's my neighbor. I've known her for years. I met her when she first arrived in Israel at the Office for New Immigrants where I worked. She's been ill recently, one bad chest infection after another."

Tzipora was tapping her foot nervously. That was a sure sign, Susan knew by now, that her life story would come pouring out of her. The foot tapping was like a metronome, beating out the struggle for survival. "I come from Krakow," she said, "but I never was in a camp. I hid out for two years on a farm. I'm one of the lucky ones—no numbers."

Suddenly, Tzipora was in no mood for chatting. She reached into her bag, took out her well-worn Book of Psalms and began to pray. Susan wanted to ask her where she hid out and what life in Krakow was like, but their conversation was cut short. It was that way in Israel. Questions, followed by more questions, followed by silence.

A little over an hour later, they arrived in Bnei Brak. "You'll get off when I do," Tzipora said to her while she gathered her packages. She'd covered her wig with a dark beret, to make herself more religious, Susan thought. There was no room for a stray hair or a bit of elbow showing in this city.

The street was crowded with shoppers. Although it was Thursday, many were already beginning their Shabbos errands. The women wore flowered house dresses which reminded Susan of the shifts that women used to wear to clean their houses in the States. Their legs were covered in thick beige cotton stockings with dark seams. No one was wearing makeup and no one was wearing jewelry, except, of course, gold wedding bands and cheap metal watches. Within a few seconds, she spotted Chaya.

There was her purple hat, of course, distinctive, looking handmade. It was shaped like a turban, with alternating strands of purple and black curving upward, angled to one side. Her hat was so French, like the chapeaux that Susan saw in French magazines where the elegantly attired models strolled the streets of Paris. She was dressed in a dark gray tunic, its tweed fabric gathered with a black satin sash, and decorated with pearls. The influence of Milan or Vienna. She didn't belong here, on this dirty, crowded street in Hasidic Bnei Brak.

Susan nodded as she walked over to greet her. Chaya took Susan's hand and held it for a moment, then, surprised, turned to her friend Tzipora. "We met on the bus," Tzipora said. The two women were such a stark contrast. Tzipora with her bad wig and Chaya with her French chapeau. Although they were both born in Poland, their lives had diverged dramatically. It baffled Susan.

They walked down the street and turned left at the corner. The sidewalks were littered with wrappers from popsicles and shells from sunflower seeds. Susan had seen young Israelis spit them out carelessly. At times, she had to jump sideways to avoid the shells mixed with saliva landing on her skirt. Everywhere, their remains left a sticky residue on the concrete.

The neighborhood was shabby. Old concrete buildings lined the block. They seemed to lean on each other, dominos which would fall if someone gave the first one a little shove. Beggars kept approaching her. They held out their hands and blessed her. It is a special mitzvah to give tzedakah in the Holy Land, they said. God wants you to help me, a woman kept chanting in garbled Hebrew. God wants you to help feed my five children! She smiled, revealing four missing front teeth. Susan dropped ten *agorot* into her cupped hand. Her fingers were filthy and her nails ragged.

Chaya stopped in front of a four-story building with a large pot of red geraniums on one of the top steps. She bent down to deadhead a dried flower and then reached into her bag for her key. "I've lived here for ten years, almost as long as Tzipora," she said. The heavy wooden door creaked as it opened. The lobby was dark and smelled of stale cooking oil. Susan thought she detected the strong smell of urine, too. It reminded her of many of the lobbies in the tenement buildings on the Lower East Side of New York. No matter how much bleach you poured on the wood, you could not purge it of the smell of piss.

Tzipora lived on the second floor and she left them on the landing. She shook Susan's hand and opened her door. There were no words wishing Susan good luck in her search. Just a firm nod goodbye.

Chaya lived one floor above, in a dark apartment at the back of the building. A blue and gold Star of David hung on her door. Next to it was a small framed picture of sunlight on the hills of Jerusalem. It looked like it had been cut out of a travel magazine. The hills were tinted pink and the sky was blue. A golden light suffused the top of the sky. True believers would say that it was the light of the Torah, God's light.

They entered a narrow hallway with wooden hooks on the wall for coats. To the right, Susan could see a small kitchen. On the counter, Chaya had already lined up cups and saucers to serve tea. There was a plate of cookies. This was clearly the ritual: a proper tea with starched, white cloth napkins. Susan wondered where Chaya had learned this. Certainly not in Rozwadów, where the few pieces of pottery were most probably cracked.

Chaya took a plump lemon out of her shopping bag, held it to her nose, and smelled its perfume. Then, she sliced it into thin wedges. "There are no better lemons than the ones from the Promised Land," she said, emphasizing the word "Promised." She stared at Susan when she spoke, as if she was checking to see whether Susan shared her Zionism.

Zionism was a tricky business. Susan definitely did not agree with that traditional longing that the words "next year in Jerusalem," which ended the Haggadah and the Seder, implied. She loved New York City too much. Zionism, that was her father's shtick. She was a Jewish girl born in America. A New Yorker who never experienced life in a shtetl or a beating in a pogrom. She'd read about these events but they were distant, someone else's history. Try as she could, they were not hers.

Still, especially in this year of the Eichmann trial, 1961, she felt guilty that she was not more strongly drawn to Israel. The ethos of Herzl and the pioneers didn't move her. Growing up in an Irish Catholic neighborhood, she did wonder what it was like to live in a land where Jews were the majority. And the search for Yakov was her excuse to find out. She never admitted this to her father but she was tired of dusting Christmas cards with glitter.

"Rozwadów is clear in my mind," Chaya said as they sat down at the table. "I forget what's on my shopping list but I remember every little detail about the town." She described it as a simple place where most of the people were poor. Her family, she said, was lucky, at least before the Nazis arrived. Her father was a produce wholesaler which meant that they were upper class. They had matching white china dishes with gold embossed rims and heavy silver cutlery with leaves carved on the handles and their Shabbos dresses were made of silk with lace trim, made by the local tailor. She poured tea as she spoke, caressing the delicate floral, bone-china cup with her slender fingers.

Chaya's mother had a beautiful soprano voice and she sang to herself all day long. When she closed her eyes and sat very still,

Chaya said, sighing, she could still hear her mother leading the rounds of *Dayainu* at the Seder table. They had an upright piano with real ivory keys, which was rare in Rozwadów. Her father traded it for several truckloads of vegetables. It was his gift to her mother Alisheva on her 30th birthday. When Chaya was six, her mother taught her to read music. They often played duets together. "Chopin's Etudes. Oh, how my mother loved them. Chopin was born in Poland, too," she said.

By the time she was ten years old, her father's business was closed, the piano confiscated, and the china and silver sold. It was too dangerous to wear her Shabbos dress on the street. They were afraid to light candles, even with the shades drawn. Without his own business, her father eked out a living sorting merchandise in the back room of a store. On the street, he didn't dare wear a kippah. She poured tea for Susan, her hand shaking slightly as she lifted the cup.

The pace of the narrative was too slow for Susan, who took advantage of the pause in Chaya's story to ask a question. "Did you ever know a man named Yakov Reich? He was my uncle. He stayed in Rozwadów when my father left for America in 1920." The questions tumbled out of her. "From what we know, he worked in a dry goods store. He would have been in his thirties when you were there."

Chaya took out a sheet of paper and drew a square. "That was the town square as I remember it," she said. She pointed to the first store on the corner. It was the bakery where she bought challah and honey cake. The woman there always gave her a chocolate cookie. Next to it was the produce store. The owner had a black beard and he was constantly polishing his apples. "Occasionally, one would fall and he would give it to us kids," she said.

She paused for a moment at the next store. "This was the girls' yeshiva." She drew a box but, then, suddenly erased it. "No, no, it was the synagogue. The boys' yeshiva was next to the shul and after that was the girls' yeshiva." She was moving around the square identifying buildings.

"A dry goods store? There was a store where we bought socks. It was on the other side of the square. The owners were a man and his wife. They had a daughter who was handicapped. She sat on a chair in the corner behind the cash register making strange, guttural noises." Chaya said that she was afraid of her and that, no matter how she tried, she couldn't stop staring at her. They had a large selection of hair ribbons and she always wanted a new one. She didn't remember a young man helping them. Perhaps he was there but he didn't make any impression on her.

For a few seconds, Susan's heart raced. This woman actually remembered Rozwadów. She'd been close to Yakov. Perhaps their arms had touched as they passed each other on the cobblestone street. Perhaps he'd sold her the hairband with three rose buds in a row, the one Susan had seen in the photo of Chaya and her sister.

"Think hard," Susan said. Her voice was a bit harsh, almost a command.

"I just remembered something," Chaya said, responding to Susan's question. "One time, there was a fellow helping out in the store. It was getting dark and he told me to go straight home. The Germans were already in town then and he seemed worried about me shopping alone." She remembered telling him that she was a very fast runner and that no one could ever catch her.

Chaya sighed. She hadn't been caught and transported to a camp but she had suffered, hidden away, eating leftovers, and praying that no one would discover her hiding place. Her face was drawn and she closed her eyes for a moment, unable to talk.

Susan was sweating now. There was more to Chaya's story, more to be unearthed. "Do you remember his eyes?" she asked her. "What color were his eyes?"

"I don't remember," she said. "But I do remember him giving me one coin too many when I paid. I tried to return it to him but he refused. He said that it was a little present for me, money that I could spend the next time I came in. His face was sad. He didn't think that there would not be a next time. It was as if we were saying goodbye forever. "Walk straight home," he told me as I was leaving. "Don't talk to any strangers. Don't talk to any Germans." He walked me to the door and watched me make my way down the street."

The scene had changed. One minute they were sitting in Chaya's tiny parlor in Bnei Brak sipping tea from china cups, and the next, they were standing in a little store in Rozwadów, crammed with shirts and pants and socks, clothing stacked neatly on wooden shelves. A young man, perhaps Yakov, was behind the counter, waiting on Chaya, a ten-year-old-girl whose life would never be the same. It was as if Susan was standing next to her, eavesdropping on their conversation.

It was only a short time later that the Germans began their roundups and the Jews of Rozwadów, who could still get away, fled east. One day, when Chaya returned home from visiting her friend in the next building, her parents were gone. A pot of water was still boiling on the stove and the book that her father was reading lay open on the dining room table. His eyeglasses lay beside it. Only after the war did Chaya find out from her brother Isaac, who lived in Tel Aviv now, how her brothers escaped across the San River. Moshe, the eldest, died a year later of consumption. They never knew what happened to their sister. "We keep looking for her. Like your Uncle Yakov, she's vanished."

Chaya stood up and walked over to a tall dresser. She opened the top drawer and took out a package. "Here are my treasured memories," she said, taking six small black-and-white photographs out of a worn yellow envelope, bits of paper falling to the floor as she did so. She lined them up on the table in two neat rows. There was a photo of the town square with modest one- and two-story buildings standing side by side around it. In the middle there was a statue and a fountain. Two girls were playing in the water. They were wearing print dresses and they were barefoot, their shoes flung on the grass nearby. A man was standing on the porch of one of the stores looking at the children. The photo was faded and slightly out of focus. It was hard to see his features. His face was thin and his nose straight and strong. It reminded Susan of her father's nose with its high bridge. It was much too fuzzy to be able to tell whether this was Yakov. Chaya turned the photo over and read the date: October 3, 1939—one month after Germany invaded Poland.

Chaya fingered the second photo lovingly. It was, she told Susan, a family portrait, taken in a photographer's studio in Krakow. In the background were clouds and a mountain range. Everyone was dressed up. Clearly it was an important occasion. The photo was taken at the time of her eldest brother's Bar Mitzvah and they had traveled to Krakow by train to go to the studio. "The photographer was not happy with my behavior," she recalled. "He kept telling me to look at him instead of out the window."

Susan stared at the portrait as Chaya talked. "That's me, standing next to my mother," Chaya said. "I'm clutching my mother's hand. That's my father, next to her, dressed in his new black suit. Those are my brothers," she said, touching each one's face. "And that's my sister—see how my mother tied ribbons in her curly hair? My brothers look so serious," Chaya said, "like stone statues. Only my father is smiling." Then, she remembered something that made her laugh. "He told us to be still and stop squirming because the photograph had cost him one week's salary."

Afterwards, they'd walked along the streets of Krakow, stopping in a candy store to buy chocolate and then in a small shop off a side street to buy her brothers new white shirts. The owner had grown up near Rozwadów in Nisko. "For you, my friend, I have something special, he said to my dad, both hands clasped around my father's hands. When he returned from his storeroom, he was carrying white shirts with embroidered collars. Beautiful Shabbos shirts."

The other photos were taken in town. There was one of the

synagogue and another of the marketplace. There was a picture of a group of girls standing in front of the entrance to her school. Chaya couldn't remember when it was taken since there was no date on the back of the photo. "I was probably ten years old," she said.

Susan picked it up and held it close, studying the girls. They were dressed in plain white blouses and long dark skirts. Their hair was braided neatly and their faces were pale. Food was already scarce and their bodies were thin.

"That's all I have," Chaya said. "You can make copies of them if you like. Perhaps my brother Isaac will remember more. He is coming over here to meet you at 2 p.m." She looked at the clock on the wall. It was ten minutes to two.

When she said Isaac's name, Susan noticed that she bit her lip—a nervous tic. "I should tell you a bit about Isaac," she said. "He suffered when he fled east. He worked in the labor camps there and lost a foot to frostbite. He is often forgetful and always depressed. Eight months after he married, his wife died. He never had children. He lives on a small disability pension now, awarded to survivors, but he rarely leaves his apartment. I have never had much luck getting him to talk about our childhood. Today was different, though. I told him that you were looking for an uncle from Rozwadów and he perked up.

"We were fortunate," Chaya said. "We had a house near the marketplace, where wealthier Jewish merchants lived. The rest of the poor folk, the tailors, and the Torah teachers lived in wooden buildings on the crowded side streets."

Chaya's mention of the brick factory and the stone houses on the square reminded Susan of her father's stories. They had been poor, especially in the years before World War One, but the family legend was that they'd lived in a solid brick house.

There was a loud knock on the door and Isaac entered without asking. His hair and beard were gray and his cheeks sunken. Susan saw a man exhausted by life. He limped as he walked, planting his cane firmly on the floor before he moved forward. He was dressed in a tan jacket and shiny black pants that looked like he had worn them for years. In one hand, he was carrying a leather briefcase, its handle cracked in several places. It was the same type of briefcase that the Egged bus drivers carried when they were changing shifts, brown leather with bulging pockets fastened with buckles.

Isaac nodded at Susan and murmured, "Shalom." His voice was low and Susan had to pay careful attention to hear him. He placed the briefcase on an empty chair and sat down beside them at the table. "I hear you are looking for an uncle from Rozwadów," he said. "Not many of us left from there now."

He emptied his briefcase on the table: a map, folded and taped; a schoolbook with a green cover and gilt lettering; a stack of photographs; three newspaper clippings; and copies of carefully folded documents. "My life," he said. "Not much! It's all here. I spread these out on my kitchen table and study them every night. The answer to the puzzle always eludes me. What went wrong? What happened?" He stopped to wipe his eyes.

Isaac had written a detailed history of the town. Written on a yellow legal pad that reminded Susan of her father's office notebooks, he said that it was still a work in progress. There were black lines crossing out words and lots of notes scribbled in the margins.

They looked like Susan's lists. Written. Crossed Out. Written again.

Before Susan could speak, he began reading, enunciating each word now. His Hebrew was clear and, despite his accent, Susan understood everything he said.

Rozwadów, his beloved Rozwadów. He had spent years researching the shtetl, sitting on the hard wooden chair in the reading room of the public library, flecks of crumpling paper stuck to his trousers accompanying him home.

"Most people think that shtetls have no history," he said, "but they're ignorant. The Jewish shtetl of Rozwadów officially dates back to the 1830s. Before that time, the town had grown out of the adjacent village of Charzewice. The town was built on land that was originally owned by a family of nobles by the name of Rozewski. By the 16th and 17th centuries, the land passed into the possession of the princes Lubormirski and Tarnowskis who built a palace there. There was also a small ancient church." Isaac had found a local document which recorded that some 30 Jewish families lived in Rozwadów in 1727.

Susan was surprised. "Jews in Rozwadów over 200 years ago? Where did they come from?"

Isaac shook his head. "Where? I've spent months trying to find out the answer to that question with no luck." He said that he discovered that the Jews took one of the 30 Jewish homes and turned it into a synagogue. Over time, the shtetl became a center for Jewish life, especially when the townspeople were given market privileges to hold fairs two days a week, on Sundays and Thursdays, attracting Jewish merchants and craftsmen.

But life was not always peaceful and there was a wave of persecution against the Jews of Galicia after 1764. Six years later, Galicia was severed from Poland and Rozwadów became border territory between Galicia and the declining kingdom of Poland. Anti-Jewish policies during the late 18th century barred Jews from the liquor trade and from farming. Edicts restricted the marriage of Jews.

By the last third of the 19th century, Rozwadów had slightly over 2000 inhabitants, some 1600 of them Jews. Following the construction of a railroad line, economic conditions improved and stone houses replaced wood huts on the town square. At about the same time, they built a brick kiln in the village.

For a moment, he seemed to gasp. The history was pouring out of him. He paused to catch his breath and then opened the map. Inside, folded on a separate sheet of graph paper, was a map that he'd drawn of Rozwadów, with its town square and its side streets. All of the streets had names and there were numbers next to many of the buildings. On a separate sheet of paper, there was a key with information for each number. Number One was the marketplace, where peddlers sold their produce and wares.

Isaac touched each number as he spoke. "I bought apples from Mr. Fried," he said, "and I went to school with his sons. They were the best students in my class. One of them, David, wanted to be a lawyer. He was going to leave the shtetl to study at the University of Krakow. He never did. The other son, Meir, helped his father with the produce. He always gave me the sweetest, most perfect fruit. He would charge me for six apples and give me seven or eight."

Isaac kept stroking Number One as if to bring back the applecart and his friends. "Three," he said. "That was my yeshiva. Rebbe Mordechai taught the older boys. He had a reddish beard and green eyes. So handsome! He loved us and he always brought us treats. Honey candies made by his wife and mandelbrot cookies stuffed with whole almonds for the holidays."

There was no interrupting Isaac, Susan saw. Lost in his reverie, he could not return to the present moment. He lived in the past, rehearsing over and over the incidents of his former life. Chaya touched his arm, trying her best to shake him out of it.

Susan waited, watching him shift his body back and forth, davening. Isaac on the wooden chairs in his Rozwadów yeshiva, his eyes closed, his hand over his face, his boy's voice repeating the *Shema. Shema Yisrael. Adonai Eloheinu, Adonai Echad.* Isaac in the synagogue on the town square.

Susan remembered peeking through the lace *mechitza* in her shul at home, peering into the men's section where all she could see were gray heads bobbing up and down. Gray heads floating above white satin taleisim. As a young girl, she sat in the women's section, intoxicated by the heavy smell of floral perfume.

Finally, getting up her courage, Susan spoke. "Did you ever know anyone named Yakov Reich?" she asked. "He worked in one of the dry goods stores on the square. He was tall and thin with blue eyes." Her questions poured out, like water flowing from a pitcher.

Isaac didn't respond. Again, she asked, this time her voice insistent and louder, "Yakov Reich, do you recall ever meeting him?"

Isaac looked down at his map. "Dry goods? There were two clothing stores in town," he said, rousing himself. He pointed to numbers Four and Seven on his map. "One was owned by Moshe Schwartz and his wife. Maybe they had a helper. I remember that every morning after Moshe unlocked the rusty iron gate, someone swept the sidewalk in front of the shop and hung out the sign, a pair of pants made out of wood and painted blue. They always took it in at night to prevent it from who-knows-what, harsh weather or pranksters who loved to throw rocks at it when no one was looking. It hung from a chain and creaked loudly as it swung in the breeze.

"The other clothing shop had better merchandise, garments from Vienna. It was for the rich folks in town. The owner lived in a big house on the town square. I can't remember his name. We never shopped there."

He was mumbling to himself now. Something about having to make soup for dinner and needing to pick up bones at the butcher's to make the broth. His mind had turned. A pot of water was boiling over on his stove. "Be careful," he said aloud. "You'll burn yourself." He was pointing at the table as he spoke. Chaya put her finger to her lips.

"Do you recall anything about the fellow who put up and took down the sign?" Susan asked, desperate to draw him back to Yakov.

"I fled across the San, away from the Germans," Isaac said, not answering her question. "I lived and the others died. All except you, Chaya." He reached out and patted her hand. "No more parents. No more brother. Nothing left but hard work. Thin soup for supper and stale bread. But I lived." Then, he turned to Susan and asked: "Do you call this living?

"All morning I've been listening to the Eichmann trial," he said.

"I cry and I scream at the radio. So what if I survived? They destroyed me, too. I cannot concentrate and I cannot work. I live on my pension from the Israeli government. What do I do now? I boil water for soup."

The dark cloud lifted and he returned to her question. "Maybe I do remember the man with the sign. He always waved to me as I walked past. Once, he showed me a silver coin that he kept in his front pocket. It was wrapped in a crumpled handkerchief and he spit on it to make it shine. He let me hold it for a minute. That was the only time I ever saw him smile."

Susan gasped, and then, as if she had entered a meat freezer wearing only a flimsy T-shirt, she shivered. Just like that, in one tiny stream of memory, Yakov had appeared. The silver coin, the treasure picked up on the muddy streets of Rozwadów, the gift of one brother to another.

She hadn't told him about the coin. He had told her. The truth has a way of appearing, out of nowhere. Nothing, and then—poof—something. An empty cartoon cloud and then, a cloud filled with exclamation points.

She inhaled deeply, sucking in as much air as she could. Then she exhaled slowly, trying to hold on to the moment. Trying not to let it pass. "That was my uncle!" Susan said. She felt like screaming. "My Uncle Yakov! My father gave him that coin before he left for America. Unbelievable. You met him! You touched his hand." She reached out and touched Isaac's hand, the hand that had touched Yakov, the hand that had held the coin.

"Do you know what happened to him?"

"I don't know," Isaac said. "I remember that the Germans closed down the store. One day, they took over the place and they turned it into a military supply warehouse. The swinging sign was gone. A couple of weeks later, I fled, never to return to Rozwadów again. Your uncle was probably murdered soon afterwards with all of the remaining four hundred Jews of Rozwadów who were rounded up in July 1942. They were either killed or shipped to a nearby labor camp."

Susan picked up the stack of photos on the table and flipped through them. Then she looked at one of the old newspaper clippings. It was in Yiddish. "What does it say?" she asked Isaac. She could only read one word, *toyt*, death.

"It says that Rozwadów died. That it no longer exists," he said. "That all of its inhabitants were exterminated or relocated. It is a story about Shlomo Katz, one of the old rebbes who managed to escape. He wrote a book on the town. There's a copy in the library of Hebrew University in Jerusalem. I went there once and read it. After the war, he settled in Jerusalem and, when he died, he left his papers to the university. Maybe you can find something about your uncle there." For a moment, he almost seemed to smile. "I can still see that coin," he said, "the sun reflecting off of its surface, the way he rolled it in his hand, the warmth when I held it, the way he kissed it before wrapping it back in his handkerchief and dropping it into his pants pocket."

He didn't say goodbye. Instead, Isaac packed up his papers, kissed his sister Chaya, and left. It was as if Susan had not been there, as if their conversation had never taken place.

But it had. On the bus trip back to Jerusalem, Susan thought about this brother and sister, separated by the Germans, who lived so near each other now but who were worlds apart: Isaac, lost in the cloud of his past, moving in and out of reality, and Chaya, fighting to live in the present, clinging to memories of good times before bad things happened. Juggling good and bad, that was a difficult act. Good news was so much easier to catch. An A+ on a school paper. First prize in a science fair competition. She reached out both hands to catch the good news but there was only air. Within seconds, she fell asleep, waking only when the driver called out Central Station, Jerusalem.

Susan hurried home to do her assignment for class. She was to give a report on a trip that she had taken outside of Jerusalem. She decided to talk about Isaac and Chaya and her search for her uncle, and she took out her dictionary to make sure that she had the correct Hebrew words for "survivor" and "escape." She made a list of words that she might need for her talk, a sort of crib sheet that she could refer to as needed.

Which word was better for a survivor, *shareed* or *nitzol*? It was impossible to figure out the difference from her little Hebrew-English Dictionary, the one that she had used for years. The binding was already falling apart and three pages of words were missing from the letter "B." The verb "escape" was even trickier. There were three choices. She settled on *barach*, listing her second choice, *nas*, in parentheses, just in case.

The next morning, when she arrived to the classroom 15 minutes early, Ezra was the only one there. He was sitting at one of the desks folding flyers and inserting them into envelopes. "It's time for us to meet and share our gripes," he said, without looking up. The Hebrew on the flyer was easy to translate. In big bold letters, it said: "Equal Treatment and Equal Pay." On the line below: "Come and Join Us to Protest the Living Conditions of New Immigrants. All Jews are Equal Under the Law. We Must Eliminate Prejudice and Job Discrimination. Improve Education and Provide Better Housing for the Poor and the Underprivileged."

Equal treatment and equal pay—those were definitely Ezra's favorite words. He was always talking about equality, or rather inequality: prejudice against his beloved Moroccans; substandard housing, walls crumbling with black mold; neighborhoods where there was no garbage pickup; kitchens where rusty water dripped from broken faucets.

"Come to the meeting," he said, reaching for her hand. "It's the only way we will ever change things here. Everything is focused on the survivors and the Germans and the death camps. That was an enormous tragedy, incomparable, there's no way to describe what happened to those Jews. But what about the other issues, the hardships of just getting by in this country? We've all suffered. We didn't have easy lives in Tunisia and Morocco. We fled persecution for a new life in a Jewish state. They closed down my ceramics studio one day. I arrived early in the morning to glaze three new pots and found a padlock on the front gate. A paper was taped to the door: I was to appear at the Judicial Office the following week to plead my case. I had no idea what they were talking about."

"What was the charge against you?" Susan asked.

"Don't laugh," Ezra said. "I hadn't paid enough taxes to the city. The bill was for thousands of Moroccan francs. There was no way I could raise that sum. There was no lawyer who was willing to defend me." His face was flushed and sweat began to drip from his forehead. He moved closer to Susan and was about to hug her when they heard steps in the hallway.

It was Esther, carrying a pile of papers, followed by their classmates. As Esther entered, Ezra placed a flyer on each desk without asking for Esther's permission. "Please join us," he said as he handed one to Esther. Her face reddened as she read the text but she didn't comment. Instead, she crumpled it into a ball and dropped it in the wastebasket, and greeted the class.

Their custom was to begin with the news of the day and Esther always launched the discussion. "How many of you listened to the Eichmann trial testimony yesterday?" she asked. Only Susan raised her hand. Instead of calling on her, Esther began to speak from her notes. Two guards had testified about the way they had stripped the women of their clothing and marched them into the showers to be cleansed. By the squeaky sound of her voice, Susan could tell that Esther was agitated. "Those were not showers," she said. "Poison gas, not water, came out of those showerheads." She looked up, over her reading glasses, to scrutinize the faces of her students.

The showers, always the showers, Susan thought. She could see the silver showerheads swiveling on the concrete ceiling. Susan looked around her. No one was reacting. Not a tear. Not a sigh. Nothing. *The Moroccans cared,* Susan thought. But they were numb. Their life was too hard. They could not bear to think about such suffering.

Susan had read about their suffering, the hardships back home in Morocco. Anti-Jewish riots, looting of Jewish homes and stores, even fires set at a few Jewish schools operated by Alliance Israelite Universelle. The government, whether Spanish or French, provided almost no financial support. Jewish community councils earned their income from taxes on the sale of bread, wine, and meat by Jewish merchants and by contributions from wealthy members of the Jewish Community. Susan looked into their dark eyes. They'd come to Israel for a better, easier life, but it eluded them. Their faces were sad and they were clearly disillusioned.

It was Susan's turn to report on her excursion to Bnei Brak. *Bad timing*, Susan thought. The last thing they want to hear about now is two survivors' tales of woes. More of the same drama that was being played out in Beit Ha'am. More of the number counting.

But there was no way out. "My father sent me on a journey," she began, hoping to gain their attention. Rachel yawned, already showing signs of disinterest. She put her hands over her mouth. It looked like she was trying to suppress a second yawn. Ezra was running his finger along a line in his flyer, proofreading the words. He didn't stop what he was doing to look up. When Susan first told him about the search for Yakov, he'd argued with her. "You're wasting your time," he said.

It was right after they made love for the first time, when they were lying side by side, Ezra slowly stroking her fingers. "Don't misunderstand me," he said. "I'm not callous. I care about the survivors and the Holocaust. I care about the fate of your Uncle Yakov. But I am consumed by the present." Then, rolling on his side and curling his body into hers, he said, "You should be, too."

Despite the cold reception, Susan continued telling her story. "He wanted me to find out what happened to his elder brother who remained in Poland when my father and the rest of his family came to America," she said. "The year was 1920. When they parted, they exchanged gifts. My uncle gave my father a stone that he had marked with loving words and my father gave my uncle a silver coin that he had found on the streets of Rozwadów, their village. Yesterday, I spent the afternoon with a sister and a brother who grew up there. They were separated by the war but found one another again in Israel."

Someone coughed and Susan looked up to see Rachel's hand in the air. "Excuse me," she said. "We've just heard Esther's report on the Eichmann trial, do we have to listen to more memories of survivors? What about the sweet smell of bougainvillea climbing on the rock walls in Casablanca? Why can't we talk about our memories and our losses? The mothers and aunts we no longer see. The floors I scrub till my fingers ache."

"You can speak when it's your turn," Esther interrupted. But Susan didn't have the heart to continue. "Let her speak first," she said, boldly returning to her chair. She folded her crib sheet and slipped it into her pocket.

They worked on grammar for an hour and then broke for lunch. Susan sat next to Ezra at the end of the table, several empty seats between them and the rest of the group. "Don't take it personally," he said, lowering his voice. "They like you but they're fed up. They're so depressed about their lives here and everything, especially now, seems to revolve about the Holocaust. They're sick of hearing the name Adolf Eichmann."

Susan was sick of it, too. Not all the time, but sometimes when she just wanted to stop counting numbers and think about the plump olives growing on the ancient trees on the slopes of the hills. Once, she even tried to count the olives as she popped them into her mouth. Four became five, six became three; she kept forgetting where she was as she chewed each morsel, the tangy brine coating her tongue.

Eating olives was comforting. Why would she ever want to get involved in a protest march with Ezra and the Moroccans? They would laugh at her, a spoiled American girl coming along for the ride. "They will think that I'm phony," she told Ezra.

"Not phony," he said, pulling her toward him and kissing her. "Just swept away by my charm." His charm worked, of course. The smell of his sweaty skin was intoxicating. She leaned against his chest, trying to make her breathing match his. She would join them.

"You can forget Adolf Eichmann, but I can't," Susan said. "I promised my father. It's personal. I've made an appointment with a professor of Yiddish at Hebrew University to have him help me translate the diaries of a rebbe from Rozwadów. Maybe my uncle was one of his students. Maybe there's a clue in his journal."

Ezra kissed her again. "Enough about your uncle," he said. "Sometimes we have to flee the past and forge ahead into the future." When he kissed her, Yakov Reich vanished from her mind. They were harvesting olives in the hills of Judea, stuffing them playfully into each other's mouth, the juice dripping down their chins.

On Friday morning, Susan had an early meeting with Professor Abraham Vishovsky, the head of the Yiddish studies department. He'd agreed to talk to her and when she arrived, he ushered her into his conference room where the rebbe's diary lay on a table. Without a word, he slipped on white cotton gloves, carefully turning the pages as he translated.

"I've been a rebbe in Rozwadów since 1908," the journal began. "I was born in Krakow but came to Rozwadów after I finished my studies to lead the congregation in the main synagogue on the square. At first, I was the assistant rabbi and Hebrew school teacher. I taught all of the young boys Torah. Many of them were poor children, the sons of peddlers, but I gave others private lessons because their fathers were merchants. In the yeshiva, the boys loved me because I was kind and I didn't beat them when they didn't know the right answer.

"There were so many wonderful children. I taught all five of the Shapiro brothers, may their memories be for a blessing. All of them, I suppose, perished now. I taught the Schwartz family, preparing Moshe, Shmuel, David, and Gershom for their Bar Mitzvahs. I taught the Reich brothers, too. Yehudah, who went to America, and Yakov who stayed behind in Rozwadów to work in the store. He came to my shul every Saturday and he sat in the back row. I remember those two boys with their bright blue eyes."

"Oh my God," Susan gasped. "That's my father and uncle!" She could hardly catch her breath.

"One left for America and the other," he continued translating, "I'm not sure. On the night of the last roundup of the Jews, when I managed to escape East, I saw Yakov in town by the fountain. I told him to run for his life because the Nazis would kill him. But he told me not to worry. 'I have a friend who will protect me,' he said. 'Nothing will happen to me.' When I next passed the clothing store it was shuttered closed and the sign had been removed."

Professor Vishovsky paused. "Did you get that all down?" he asked Susan, who had been taking notes furiously. "Amazing. Incredible! He actually knew your uncle. Now, all you have to do is find out who this mysterious friend was. It's hard to imagine your uncle saying that he felt safe at that moment in history. The next day there were no Jews left in the town."

He closed the diary carefully and placed it back in its protective sleeve. "There are not many of these diaries," he said. "Most of the rebbes left treatises on the Torah. Few of them left accounts of their life in the shtetl.

"Is there a list of the members of the Rozwadów shul in the library?" Susan asked. "Maybe I can find a survivor who remembers my uncle."

"We really don't know who survived," Vishovky said. "You will have to search the records at Yad Vashem. Every day new names are added. Once in a while, someone is found alive, and a name is erased." The thought was too much for him. There was pain on his face. Pain in his eyes. Pain in the creases of his skin.

Susan watched him tap his fingers on the desk in a sad,

rhythmic beat. He seemed to be tapping out the names of lost family members: his mother and father, perhaps, a sister, a brother, beloved cousins with whom he, like Susan, had ransacked his house for the hidden piece of matzo, the *afikoman*.

"I arrived in 1945," he said, as if he were reading Susan's mind, "with my aunt and uncle. They found me in a DP camp. We had all been sent to Auschwitz but only I survived." Then, he stood up and reached out to shake her hand. "Find out what happened to your uncle," he said. "It's a mitzvah."

No one had used that word before and it troubled Susan. Why was it a mitzvah? What was so good about digging into the dark, troubled past? Yakov was dead, Susan was sure of that, and the only ending here would be sadness. Why not just let him rest, a vanished soul? She debated with herself endlessly on this. The sleuthing, the questioning, was taking its toll on her. She resented her father's phone calls. He was always pressuring her for good news.

"Don't assume that the ending will be sad," he said, over and over again, the words echoing in her head. "Think positive thoughts and good things will follow. Too much deep thinking on your part." Always, the push-pull about her being smart. It was good to be smart. Maybe it was even great to be smart. But not too smart, ah, that could get you in trouble. That could leave you buried in a pile of negativity.

The Eichmann trial continued to dominate the news. Endless testimony by guards and survivors. Their stories were laced with gory details that were hard to hear. One day, it was the story of the child who was clubbed to death because he stepped out of line, killed because he was crying for his mother. The child screamed all night in Susan's dreams. Another day, it was the woman who refused to undress for the showers. They shot her to warn the others not to follow her example. Susan left the house without showering the next morning.

What good news did her father expect when the entire nation

of Israel was consumed by the trial? Ezra would correct her, she was sure. He would say not the *entire* nation of Israel.

By the time Susan left Professor Vishovsky's office, people were already going home for Shabbos. Most offices closed around 1 p.m. on Friday. Machane Yehuda was crowded with shoppers when Susan arrived to buy challah and grape juice, her share of the apartment's communal Shabbos meal. One of her roommates, Naomi, was doing the cooking. No one in the group kept the Sabbath but they did observe Friday night, lighting candles and blessing the wine and the bread.

On the street, she could hear radios blasting Eichmann trial news. The morning session had been a heated one with the prosecutor interrogating a guard from Auschwitz. He testified that he was only a minor officer, reporting to four other higher-ups. "I never made any decision on my own," he said. The announcer read his statement and added the comment, "That's what they all say."

The guard who testified, the announcer said, was very nervous, with a strange facial tic, and the interrogation was intense. "What exactly was your job there?" the prosecutor asked him. He answered that he was a guard in one of the men's barracks and that his job was to make sure that everyone, no matter how frail, would line up for the work crew. "I used to make the rounds of the cots," he said, "getting the lazy ones out of bed. Then I would line them up and march them to their work. I didn't have the authority to give them a sick day or let them lie there."

The announcer's voice was agitated now. "How can this be?" the announcer asked. "How can they all lack the authority to make a moral decision?" Susan choked when he said those words. When she first arrived in the country, it was easier not to hear them. Europe, the Holocaust, that was the past. That was her father's world. Now, it was getting harder. She could barely swallow when the announcer spoke. Once, she'd seen a fellow student cheating on a chemistry exam. He'd written the formulas on the inside of his palm. She watched him as he jotted down the answers. The moral decision would have been to turn him in. But she hadn't done so. Instead, she looked out the window of the classroom, watching the tugboats pull an oil tanker in the bay.

Her purchases swinging in her mesh bag, Susan walked home to Rehavia, thinking about the Rozwadów rebbe's diary. How could she give up now that someone knew Yakov and had actually seen his silver coin?

By the time Susan made the turn into Rehavia, the radios were silent and Shabbos was beginning to descend on the neighborhood. Across the street, in the pension, Susan could see the cook in his white apron. The dining room table was set. She opened the gate to her alleyway and it creaked, the sound frightening the cats who ran off in every direction. The little orange one who always mewed outside her bedroom window remained. He was waiting for her to feed him.

Inside, Susan could smell coriander and garlic and cumin, the herbs that Naomi used in every dish. It was her version of Moroccan food, not quite as spicy as authentic cuisine but definitely not European-style Jewish cooking.

During dinner, Susan told them about Ezra's march and she invited them to join the group on Sunday. No one was interested. "That's not very patriotic," said Naomi. Her nostrils flared in disgust as she spoke. "Israel saved them. Imagine what their life would have been like in Morocco? They should be grateful for their freedom. Life in a democracy is precious." She accidentally dropped her fork after she finished speaking, the thud a kind of exclamation point.

There was no point arguing with her. That was the Zionist point of view. Settling in Israel meant life in the land of milk and honey. No matter how hard it was, no matter how drafty the apartment, how meager the food, how miserable the work, you were blessed to live in the holy land. *They were only visitors*, Susan thought. They could always return home to their middle- and upper-class lives. The cold shower would inevitably be replaced by a hot one.

After dessert, Susan brought up the Eichmann trial. "It's on everyone's mind," she said. Charlotte frowned, changing the subject. "It's such a downer," she said, the others nodding in agreement. "We're here to imbibe the pioneering spirit of Israel, the 'I can do anything if I want to,' attitude of the Israelis. You don't have to dwell in the past. You can tell your father that you don't want to do this, that you are ending the search," Charlotte said, her southern drawl lingering on the words "ending the search."

When Charlotte spoke those words, Susan blinked. She'd thought of saying them to her father, but had never dared to do so. He would have slapped her. Hung up the phone without a goodbye. Click. The receiver dangling, a loud, buzzing sound instead of his voice.

"Look for Yakov yourself."

"What did you say?"

"He's your brother. You look for him."

All day Saturday Susan thought about the protest meeting. She was worried that the Moroccans would resent her presence. After all, what had she ever suffered? Her hardship list consisted of zero items. When she fell asleep, she dreamed that the Moroccans held a noisy protest outside of President Yitzhak Ben-Zvi's apartment on Ibn Gavirol Street in Rehavia, just a few streets away from her apartment. Afterwards, the group marched down to Beit Ha'am to air their gripes outside the Eichmann trial building. There was a ring of soldiers stationed there and all of them had Uzis slung over their shoulders.

When she woke Sunday morning, Susan remembered a piece of her dream. She was shouting at a soldier who had grabbed her wrist hard. He'd immobilized her and she awoke to find herself thrashing about in her twisted sheets. She touched her forehead and realized that it was completely wet. So was her pillowcase.

There were soldiers everywhere—in the supermarkets, by the

shuk, and by the Wailing Wall. They were tall and thin and handsome in their khaki uniforms. With their guns, they looked mean and menacing. Once, outside the supermarket, she'd seen one of them pin a Moroccan worker against a wall as he searched for a knife. "Don't move or I'll shoot you," she heard him scream. The soldier emptied the man's shopping bag. Inside were packages of cheese stolen from the market. The man kept screaming, "God help me, my family is hungry." The soldier kept shoving him into the concrete wall as if to remind him who was in power. Then, the soldier confiscated the cheese and let the fellow go. He limped down the street, a downcast figure. After the incident, the soldier put the cheese in his knapsack and walked away.

By the time she reached the community center, some 40 people were already there. Ezra was flitting about, greeting everyone with a hug and a "Thank you for coming." The room was set up with a motley assortment of wooden folding chairs. Along one wall there was a long table where people left homemade gifts of food. There was a large platter of fried eggplant with a bowl of red hot sauce and several plates of honey cookies rolled in sesame seeds.

She could see that Ezra had done his homework. His remarks were written out on a yellow legal pad, the kind her father used in his law office. "We are all Jews," he began, coughing to clear his throat. "But some of us are living as second-class citizens. We need to make our voices heard. We need good jobs and good apartments. We need good schools for our children. We cannot be left out because we are poor or because we never lived in Europe or because our skin is a darker shade. We haven't been in the Nazi death camps but we have all suffered."

There was loud clapping from the audience. Amen, one man called out. *B'ezras Hashem. B'ezras Hashem.* "With God's help," two women said. They murmured the words softly, in unison. A third woman kissed her Book of Psalms, closing her eyes.

"We don't want to become the enemy," Ezra continued. "Does anyone remember the story of Goliath?" A few people nodded but no one spoke. Susan hesitated but finally raised her hand. "When I was 12, we put on a play about David and Goliath for all of the parents. Our teacher divided us into two groups. I wasn't very happy because I was a Philistine. The biggest boy in the class was Goliath, his armor made out of cardboard painted orange to look like bronze." Susan stopped and swiveled her head to see how those behind her were reacting to her words. Two women had puzzled looks on their faces.

"Why did you have to be a Philistine?" a woman called out. "Why didn't you just refuse to be in the play?" Two women started arguing with one another. "You can't always say no," one said. "Yes, you can!" the other answered.

"I was a Philistine and we had to fight the Israelites," Susan continued. "My best friend was David, the shepherd's son, a young man without armor. Slender David who shot one smooth stone from his slingshot that struck Goliath in the forehead and killed him instantly."

"That's what happens to enemies," Ezra said, interrupting Susan's story. "One rock to the forehead and we're dead. We don't want to be enemies. We want to be friends who help our neighbors see the light." He was trying to smile as he said the word "light" but Susan thought he looked insincere.

A skinny fellow in the third row broke out in laughter. "What a joke! Are we friends?" he asked. "Do they invite us into their homes for Shabbos dinner? Of course not! We should resist. We need slingshots. We need stones."

Stones. Smooth stones. Just like the one that Yakov had given her father when they parted. Stones found on the ground in cemeteries and left on the top of grave markers, signs that someone had visited. Stones, skipping across rivers.

Ezra straightened his shoulders, a sure sign that he was taking control of the crowd. "Don't worry, I have a plan," he said. "But first, let me begin with what we have to do if we ever get in trouble," he said. "Not that we will."

"What sort of trouble?" asked Jacob, who worked in one of the vegetable stalls in the shuk. "Trouble with whom? I don't want trouble!"

"*Nachon, Nachon*," said the woman next to him. "We already have trouble. We don't need more."

Ezra began to write the basic rules on the blackboard.

1. *If a guard approaches you, do not be confrontational. Do not raise your hand. Do not say anything. If he tells you to move, do so; or, if you can't, just lie down on the ground and be silent.*

One of the women seemed very uncomfortable with his advice. She shook her finger at him menacingly. "If he tells me to move, isn't it better to move right away?" she asked. "I'm afraid that he will hit me with his stick." The crowd around her nodded in agreement.

"No. No. This is passive resistance. Haven't you heard of Gandhi?" Ezra said. "He did this in India. If we have to, we can do the same thing here. The secret to protest is lying down and being still."

A photographer was standing at the back of the room. He wore a cap with the logo of *Haaretz* newspaper on the brim and, without saying a word, he began snapping pictures. Several of the people in the room covered their faces. "No pictures! No pictures," they shouted. Ezra ran to the back of the room and huddled with the photographer. The photographer raised his voice: "How do you expect to attract attention without photos?" he asked. After a couple seconds, he put his camera back in its black case and left.

Ezra returned to the front of the room. His face was flushed and he was clearly excited by what was going on. He was a man consumed by a cause. No matter what would happen, Susan thought, he would not give in. When she closed her eyes, she imagined him kicking and resisting as a policeman tried to arrest him. A blow to the chin, a punch to the nose, deep scratches in the cop's arms.

When she opened her eyes, he was back at the blackboard, writing the second rule:

2. *To be effective, make a list of your goals and arrange them in priority order.*

The second item seemed much more neutral. Why hadn't he started with it? Within seconds, though, a squabble erupted. "I vote that we should put a decent apartment at the top of the list," a very pregnant mother called out. "Where am I going to put this child?" she asked, pointing to her belly that was just about ready to explode. "Four of us are already sleeping in one bed."

A man wearing a torn blue shirt disagreed. "I just want a good job," he said. "That means work that I can count on every day. Not waiting in line every morning to see if someone needs me. I don't call working three days a week a job, do you?" He raised three fingers in the air to make his point.

"Three, you're lucky. I work two," his neighbor cried out. "Sometimes only one."

Ezra didn't seem surprised by their disagreement. He didn't grimace and there was no sign of discomfort. Instead, he began to pass out a sheet of paper that he'd prepared in advance. "Number your choices," he said, "from one to ten. One will be our first priority."

Susan was not sure how she would behave if she were involved in a protest. Just thinking about protesting made her hands tremble and her heartbeat speed up. She'd seen protestors in New York City in Union Square, giving out flyers and admonishing passersby about the evils of the rich. Once, she'd taken a pamphlet from a New York City Communist Party club and read it through on the train home. The enemy, it said, was capitalism in all its forms. Only the people could rise up and demand their God-given rights. There must be income equality and food for all. Susan remembered the last line: "Beware the fat cats! They are all around you."

When she came home, she asked her father who the fat cats were and he laughed.

"Just gibberish," he said as leafed through the pamphlet and threw it in the garbage.

He would definitely not approve of her joining a protest with Ezra. And he would be furious if he saw his daughter's face on the evening news. That would occasion a crisis call. He would grill her. She would cry. She would promise not to participate in any protest again, especially not one critical of his beloved Israel.

Once, on the TV news in the States, Susan had watched protests against segregation in the south. A line of college students, black and white, stood their ground, arms linked. A line of cops with their hands on their billy clubs, swinging from their leather holsters, stood yards away, opposing them. There were close-ups of men chewing gum and spitting on the sidewalk. There was calm followed by violence: people being handcuffed, people being dragged into police vans. Sirens were blaring. A young woman in a Cornell University sweatshirt was wailing as blood dripped down her face from a wound on her forehead. Two medics rushed by with a stretcher, on it a young man, his arms flailing in the air.

In Israel, Susan witnessed tempers flaring in the heat. Zionists stood on street corners accusing critics of being unpatriotic. Sabras would pounce on new immigrants. "We were devoured by mosquitos and we always had dysentery. There was almost no clean water," they would say. "*Kasheh me'od.*" Life was hard, very hard. Unafraid, the new immigrants would yell back: "Life is not much better today. We need jobs and we need homes." Angry voices screaming at one another. "You should be ashamed of yourselves," a man in a uniform shouted at the immigrants. "We've given you everything and you don't appreciate it."

Susan drifted off. She sat in a trance, her eyes closed. A movie was playing in her mind. Loud, unsettling, dramatic. She was standing in front of a public building somewhere in Jerusalem. A guard walked over to Ezra and asked him to leave. Ezra lay down on the ground and refused to budge. She imagined herself standing beside Ezra. Behind them was a crowd of marchers who lay down.

Susan couldn't see their faces. Suddenly, the guard was on his walkie-talkie calling for reinforcements. Within a few minutes, two police cars arrived. Four officers jumped out and began to move among the marchers. One had a megaphone. "Get up and leave before it's too late," he called out. "Do you all want to be arrested?"

A photographer was busy snapping pictures. Ezra was holding his ground. Suddenly, he clapped his hands and everyone stood up. They formed two straight lines and began to leave. The policemen got back into their cars and followed them.

The dream was so detailed, so vivid. They walked on a familiar route: down Ivn Gavirol to Keren Kayemeth, right on Ussishkin, left on Betzalel, on their way to the Beit Ha'am building. A survivor with numbers on his arm walked past and spit at them. A female photographer from the *New York Press* took their picture. It was too late for Susan to duck and she was caught smack in the middle of the crowd. Susan could hear Ezra fielding the reporter's questions. "Why were they here? What was their gripe? Did they realize that it was insensitive of them to make their protest at the Eichmann trial?"

A row of soldiers began to approach them. They'd been given their orders. They were about a hundred feet away. Susan began to run. As she did, she noticed that everyone around her was running, too. She'd lost track of Ezra but Rachel was a couple feet away, holding her side as she ran. They ran without looking back, not realizing that the police had stopped chasing them.

Click. Click. The credits were already running. Ezra played by Ezra. Susan by Susan. Rachel by Rachel. The documentary was over. A scary daydream, one that haunted you for days. Like being swept away by the fierce undertow of the Atlantic Ocean. Or trapped in a wooden frame house as fire raged. In seconds, the wind from the Atlantic whipped the flames into the sky and the house was consumed.

Susan left the meeting, walking rapidly to the café on Ben Yehuda. She arrived there out of breath and sat down at a corner table. Ruth brought her a coffee and a pastry and sat down next to her. The radio was on in the café and the patrons were listening to the trial news. Spliced into the announcer's summary were interviews the reporter on the scene had with bystanders on the crowded streets near Beit Ha'am. "I spoke to several immigrants who were standing on the corner smoking cigarettes," the reporter said, "and I asked them if they'd gone to hear the trial. Only one of them answered, a mechanic dressed in greasy clothes. He said that he worked at a repair shop nearby. He wasn't very friendly. 'No time,' the man said. 'And no interest. I'm too busy trying to earn enough money to feed my six children.'" In the café, the survivor at the next table grimaced when he heard the man's remark. "What a pity," he said.

Susan was worried about Ezra. The movie in her mind had ended. But it was all too real. She had woken from her daydream but she wished it had lasted a little longer. She wanted to know what had happened to Ezra. Had he run away? Or was he locked in a cell in solitary confinement, with thick ankle chains so he could not escape, an army cot, a metal sink, and a wooden chair bolted to the floor. She wanted a romantic ending, where she wrapped her arms around him and comforted him. Words were flying in her head. Crazy! *Meshugah!* Foolish! *Tipshi!* Dangerous! *Mesukan!* Stupid! *Metumtam.* She walked home, took a cold shower, and lay down on her bed.

Outside, the cats were screeching. One story was that the British had brought them to Jerusalem to rid the city of the rats. Who knows if it was true? But they definitely had been fruitful and multiplied. There were cats and kittens everywhere. They sounded like babies—screaming to be fed, screaming for attention. Angry, lonely babies running from alley to alley amidst the stone buildings of Jerusalem.

All she could think of was Ezra. His beautiful thin wrists and delicate fingers restrained by handcuffs. A bad daydream. Nothing more. She tried to go back to sleep but thrashed about in her bed.

The soldiers were yelling at her. The police were waving their sticks. The survivors were screaming at her. Even her father, in America, was yelling: "How stupid of you, Susan, to get involved in all of this nonsense," he screamed. "Stop this immediately!"

Between the cats and the voices, she was up all night, never quite managing to close her eyes. In the early morning, she fell asleep for a couple of hours. When she woke up, she remembered her dream. She was resting on the east bank of the San River, having just fled the Germans in Rozwadów. Her dream was impossible. In high school, Susan always floundered halfway across the swimming pool. She always swallowed too much water and had to turn over on her back, floating to catch her breath. There was no way she could have swum across a rough, cold river. But that's the way dreams are, filled with that strange mixture of real and unreal, probable and improbable. Somehow, like Chaya's brothers, Susan had escaped.

In the morning, she left for school, arriving at the ulpan at the very moment that Rachel was entering the building. "The meeting disturbed me," Rachel said, whispering in her ear. "It took me hours to fall asleep." They walked up the stairs and into the classroom. Esther was already there, writing vocabulary words on the blackboard. Within a few minutes, the bell rang and she began her talk. "The news of the day is not good," Esther said, speaking to them slowly in carefully enunciated Hebrew. "We must be united. Not divided!" She was working herself up to her angry face, her usually sunken cheeks puffed and red. "I heard a reporter interviewing some immigrants outside of Beit Ha'am yesterday. It was really disgraceful." She paused, waiting for a reaction from the class, but there was none. Just stares.

Susan could hardly believe her ears. Esther knew that her students were immigrants but that did not stop her from provoking them. Just before she continued her rant, Ezra entered the classroom. His hair was ruffled and he looked like he'd slept in his clothing.

"Imagine such behavior," she continued without hesitating, "at the very site of the trial of one of the most evil men of all time." Her eyes bulged and her nostrils flared. She stamped her foot twice and then, to stop herself, dropped her hand to her thigh. "That is not a Jewish thing to do," she said. "We cannot afford to be divided. The enemy is all around us. We must stick together no matter what."

A hand went up in the back of the room but there was to be no discussion. Ezra didn't try to speak. He sat there with his head in his hands, swaying back and forth in his seat. From behind, he looked like one of the old men in the synagogue davening, only he was not wearing a kippah and he didn't have peyos.

After class, he walked her home. "You took over my brain," Susan said. "A frightening scene. Somehow, somewhere, we were protesting and the police charged us. I ran and I lost you. When it was over, I was terrified."

Ezra started to speak, then stopped abruptly. "I need to talk to you," he said as he leaned over and kissed her, just before her gate. "I'll see you later tonight."

5

The secretary in the Yad Vashem office was very helpful. She directed Susan to a bookcase filled with loose-leaf books arranged alphabetically. Susan had managed to locate a list of Rebbe Katz's pupils and she wanted to see if she could find anyone who was still alive. She spent an hour writing down all of the pupils who listed Rozwadów—most were deceased, although there were some survivors.

There were eight Shapiros listed from Rozwadów. Only two had survived and one of them lived in Jerusalem. Susan wrote down his address. There were eight members of the Schwartz family. Moshe and Gershom had survived and they, too, lived in the city. Gershom had appended a little paragraph to his family entry. "I cannot begin to count the number of Schwartzes who were killed by the Nazis," he wrote. "Not only in Rozwadów but in Krakow, too. Lawyers and doctors and merchants and housewives. At least three Torah scholars and one building engineer. Ours was an educated family that the Nazis extinguished."

The librarian suggested that Susan look in the Rozwadów Memorial books, explaining that they were created by *landsmanshaften*, or fraternal and memorial associations, based in Israel, New York, and Belgium. Perhaps there were members still alive who knew Yakov. Susan checked the names of active members, noting that one lived in Haifa and one in New York. There were addresses but few listed phone numbers.

Susan called one of the Shapiros that afternoon. His name was Avner and he lived only a short walk from her apartment in Rehavia. He had supplied Yad Vashem with the names of lost family members, all of whom were listed as having lived in Rozwadów. He answered the phone with a rather gruff hello, seemingly annoyed by the call interrupting his life. She stumbled at first, but quickly regained confidence. He interrupted her after a few minutes. "You can speak to me in English," he said.

At first, he seemed reluctant to see her. "I don't want to talk about the Holocaust," he said. "It's enough that I lived through it. This country is obsessed with the camps, the marches, the gas chambers."

"Please, please, see me," she said, explaining that her father was desperate to find out what happened to his lost brother.

"What was his name?" Avner asked. When she answered Yakov Reich, Avner let out a cry, a long exhale accompanied by a moaning sound that seemed to unnerve him. Another gasp, the sound of someone sucking in air, a second long exhale. Susan could hear him struggling to catch his breath. "Yakov. Yakov, of course, I knew him. We studied with the same rebbe and we were very good friends. You must come over today," he said, giving her his address. "I have something to show you."

Susan gasped. "You knew Yakov! You knew Yakov!" She kept saying the words aloud. She'd spun the dreidel and it had landed on the letter Nun. Nun for the Hebrew word *Nes*—a miracle. The Chanukah oil lasting for eight days.

Nes Gadol! A Big Miracle. Avner not only knew Yakov, he had something to show her. For a moment, she flashed back to her childhood, sitting in a circle on the school rug. A dozen nine-year-olds at show-and-tell with photos of their immigrant grandfathers and grandmothers. Her Rozwadów *bubbe* in her somber dress. Three sentences that she'd written and memorized: her name was Tovah Reich and she was six inches taller than any other woman in her village. Her hair was thin and she twisted it up on top of her head in a tight knot. She only spoke Yiddish.

What did Avner have to show her? Would it be a clue? Was it possible that Yakov was not dead?

Susan hadn't really wanted to come to Israel. But the idea of being a heroine, of being recognized as the resourceful young woman who reunited two brothers appealed to her. What a story! Susan, the shrewd, aggressive American girl who unraveled a mystery. Front page in the *New York Times*: a picture of her father and his brother, arms linked with the headline "Two Brothers Together After 41 Years." The story would trace their journeys since 1920, when one remained in Poland and the other emigrated to America. Her father would speak about the miracle of finding his brother. "I thought he died in the camps," he would tell the reporter. "Imagine my joy in finding him alive in Israel." She would recount how she'd found him. False leads. False starts. Clues dropped here and there. It was a fantasy that often consumed her as she traveled back and forth to the ulpan. It was on her mind now as she walked to meet him.

Avner Shapiro lived over a candy store on Jaffa Street, not far from the main post office where he worked as a clerk. It took her almost an hour to get there and, on the way, she stopped to buy him flowers. She rang the bell and he buzzed her in. He was waiting on the second-floor landing.

She looked up and was completely surprised. Avner was definitely not the man she expected. He was not wearing a kippah and he had no peyos. His hair was combed in a slick pompadour that reminded her of the publicity photos of Elvis Presley and he was wearing a bold, striped shirt and tight jeans. All he needed was a guitar. She guessed that he was in his mid-fifties but he looked, at most, like he was in his mid-thirties.

His apartment was small but carefully furnished with modern blonde wood and chrome pieces, not the dark mahogany cabinets that were ubiquitous in Israel. His table was a glass oval on a wrought-iron base that looked like an atom with matching iron chairs. On the walls there were black-and-white lithographs, striking images of men working in factories. Each bore the initials "AS" in the corner. Clearly, it was his own work. On a small table in the corner of the room, there were two art books on Picasso and Klee. One was open to a full-page spread of Picasso's *Guernica*.

"Please sit down," Avner said. "Forgive me if I was rude to you on the telephone. I just can't stand all of this Holocaust reporting in the news. Since the Eichmann trial began, that's all we hear. Yad Vashem is always calling to invite me to be on a panel or to speak but I never go. I survived, so what? I don't want to be on a stage. I don't want to be reminded of it all the time. But, when you mentioned your Uncle Yakov, I had to see you." He cleared his throat as if choking on something.

Avner was anxious to tell his story. "We sat next to each other in the boys' yeshiva from the time we were seven or eight. For years, we davened together." He touched his kippah-less head. "You can see that I'm not religious now," he said. "But in those days in Rozwadów, every boy was educated by the rebbe. My father was a merchant. He traded goods back and forth from Krakow to Rozwadów. We were better off than most of the other Jews. If I recall correctly, Yakov's father left for America in 1908 and could not return because of the outbreak of the war. He was fortunate, though, because his mother was resourceful and the family survived selling bootleg cigarettes and whiskey to the soldiers stationed near the San River. When they left for America in 1920, he remained."

There was no time for Susan to take notes. The story was pouring out of Avner now, like the raging waters of the River San in the spring. Tumbling over small boulders as it cascaded past the village. "It was a difficult decision for him," Avner said. "He asked my opinion and I told him to go. I said that if I had the chance I would have gone. But he agonized about leaving the village. He was afraid of New York. He was afraid to live in a big city. No matter what I said to convince him, he wouldn't leave. He had a job and friends and that was all he needed. I felt as if he wanted to tell me something more but that was all he said at the time.

"Yakov worked for one of the dry goods stores and he earned a modest living. The owner trusted him and treated him like a son. He would often eat with their family and, after his family left for America, he slept for a while in a windowless room in the back of their house. We would have dinner together almost every week and we occasionally traveled to Krakow, which was our big city.

"Eight years after his family left, I became engaged and Yakov was my best man, standing just behind me at the chuppah. 'You'll be next,' I told Yakov then, but he never married. The matchmaker tried to make a *shidduch* for him, but none of them ever worked out. He'd saved money and he rented two rooms in a small, stone house just off the square in 1937. He once invited me over for breakfast there in his kitchen, the sunlight creating patterns on the stone floor.

"I would always ask him if he was lonely living by himself, without children and a family. He said that he wasn't. That his life was good and that there was nothing that he would change. He didn't seem to miss his family. On top of a cabinet, there was a family portrait, taken just before they left for America. 'I was working that day,' Yakov told me, 'and I arrived too late for the picture.' Next to it were three small photos that he'd received from America. There was one of his father and mother standing proudly behind his two brothers and two sisters. That photo was dated 1936.

"Then, in 1939 our world exploded. The Germans arrived in Poland. It wasn't long before the Nazis came to Rozwadów.

Everyone was afraid. Jews were forced to shut down their businesses and—poof—the clothing store was gone.

"A week before the store closed, Yakov met me on the street. 'Come with me,' he said. 'I have someone I want you to meet.' We walked to the end of town and followed a narrow dirt path into the woods. Avner knew this trail. We'd often take long walks there, especially in the summer to escape the dust and heat of Rozwadów. The woods were cool and green and deserted.

"After walking for ten minutes, we paused in a little clearing. A man was waiting for Yakov there. He was dressed in a German soldier's uniform and the minute I saw him I felt afraid. Yakov leaned over to me and squeezed my hand. 'Don't worry,' he said, 'Karl Bregner is my friend.'

"Bregner extended his hand and I shook it. It was a strong shake and I remember that his hand was smooth and warm. He was clearly someone who hadn't done hard labor in his life. By that time, I had already decided to flee across the San River the next night and Yakov knew about it. I could not imagine why Yakov had arranged this meeting.

"'Karl has a plan that will keep me safe,' Yakov said. 'I'm going to work for him in the German army supply depot as his assistant. With my fair skin and blue eyes, no one will know that I'm a Jew. I told him that you were my best friend and he has offered to help you, too.'

"When I first heard Yakov's words, I thought what a fool he was, how stupid of him to be taken in by some German soldier, perhaps four years older than Yakov. This was a trick, a ploy. Bregner would protect him until it was no longer safe to do so. There was no such thing as a German being loyal to a Jew. I'd heard of Jewish women who in desperation became mistresses to German military men. They were safe until they were arrested and herded into cattle cars with the rest of the Jews. Yakov was so naïve, I thought.

"His blue eyes were wide open and he was almost smiling. He

stood shoulder to shoulder with Bregner, their hands almost touching. I looked at the two of them and I was afraid."

Susan was leaning forward on her chair now, not to miss a word. She could feel that something important was coming. Entering a confessional booth, where Jews were not allowed. Avner on one side of the glass, Susan on the other.

"I have a little secret to tell you," Avner whispered. "Sometimes, I would eavesdrop on my mother's conversation with her sister, whose neighbor was the subject of considerable gossip. He was a bookseller who went from town to town hawking old and new books. My aunt whispered that men would visit him late at night. She would peek through her curtains and see young men slipping out his back door early in the morning. A *shandah,* my mother said. A shame. 'He is such a good-looking man. What a waste. What's wrong with him?'

"They would go on and on, giggling uncontrollably, with my aunt making bad jokes about what went on when two men were in bed. Somehow, when Yakov and Bregner stood in front of me, all I could think of was my aunt's neighbor, the man who loved men. Maybe that was Yakov's secret. I felt sad and ashamed and afraid all at once."

Susan gasped. She felt the blood rushing to her ears. Then, for a moment, things turned gray, as if she were going to faint. The room was a blur, in and out of focus. Objects were spinning in a circle; she felt that she was about to experience a major attack of vertigo, like riding on The Whip at Coney Island. That she was about to throw up. She was fighting to keep her balance. Her work as a sleuth was not supposed to take her in this direction. Her father would go crazy if Avner's story was true. She could see him wringing his fingers together, the blue glass stone on his law school ring moving in and out of view. Her father, shaking his head back and forth. *No, this is not true. This is not true.*

Avner sighed. "It was not exactly what I expected," he said. "The Torah tells us about procreation, about sex between a man and a woman. Men can be friends. But love, sex? Impossible." Even as he spoke, Avner was sweating. It was 20 years later but clearly he hadn't made peace with Yakov and Bregner as a couple even though he was a progressive man.

Susan turned her head away. She was listening to his words but she could hardly look at his face. Yakov and Bregner, lovers? Like Susan and Ezra? Their legs entwined in the bedsheets. In the history books on Eastern Europe, she had seen photos of engaged couples, Yeshiva *bochurim* in tall black hats, white shirts and long, black coats, with their betrothed in flowing dresses that swept the ground. They walked several feet apart and only met in public places. No touching. The engagement was short, ensuring that there would be no sex and babies before marriage.

Gay lovers in Rozwadów? Susan could imagine a Jew who'd fallen in love with a Polish farmer's daughter and gotten her pregnant. The family gave money to the farmer's family and shipped the boy off to a distant shtetl. Every day, his parents davened that no one in town would find out about their scandal. But Yakov and Karl? How was that possible?

Susan remembered the red-haired man in her synagogue. Once she heard one of the sisterhood women refer to him as a "fairy." He was pale-skinned and he sat on his front porch with his friend, a dark muscular fellow, probably Italian, his shirt open to reveal chest hair. They would wave to her as she walked past but they never invited her to join them. In shul, he davened in the men's section, his slender body swaying up and down. Susan fancied that one day she would see him open his wings and take flight.

"They were lovers, I could feel it," Avner continued, "and I was stunned. We boys often gossiped about the rebbe from the neighboring shtetl who liked boys too much. He offered to tutor us privately for half price but our parents always said no. We were warned to stay away from him. He was, our mothers said, a dangerous, evil man. On the surface, Karl was the enemy, but I could tell that he wasn't a sexual predator. The way they looked at each other. Don't be shocked at what I'm saying," he said. From the expression on Avner's face, Susan could see that he was trying to measure her response. She had no words for him and he began speaking again. "This fellow Bregner, he was a man who, although I could barely understand it, loved Yakov. And Yakov...how had my best friend, this Yeshiva *bocher*, turned out this way? How could he love a man?"

For hours after meeting Bregner, Avner sat in his bedroom, curtains drawn. "I was trying to understand what I'd just seen and I couldn't. I felt guilty for not feeling angry at Yakov or ashamed. But we'd spent our childhood together. Rejecting him felt cruel." Avner said that he only saw Yakov one more time. They met on the street the next morning in front of the store and they walked around back to the storeroom to talk.

Susan thought of taking notes but somehow she felt paralyzed and couldn't reach into her handbag for a pencil and paper. Better to sit and listen.

"Yakov took my hand and squeezed it. 'I trust you,' he said to me. 'I wanted you to know the truth. I wanted you to meet Karl.' He stopped speaking for a moment and sighed, his shoulders moving up and down as he did so. It was a big effort. I remember every word he said."

We first met nearly nine years ago, in 1930, in a club in Berlin. When I was in Krakow, I saw an ad in a newspaper for the Eldorado. It was well known, even in Krakow, as a place where men could socialize. I saved my money and bought train tickets from Krakow to Warsaw and Warsaw to Berlin. On my first night in town, I met Karl Bregner. We were both waiting in line to enter the Eldorado. He was dressed in a military cadet's uniform and I thought he was very handsome. He offered me a cigarette. I didn't smoke but I took it.

After that I spent the week with Karl. He was leaving town for an assignment elsewhere and I was returning to Rozwadów.

"It was hard, Yakov told me, for him to keep such a big secret."

I knew the truth about myself years earlier when my family left for America. That was one of the reasons I stayed. My mother would never have stopped crying. My father would have thrown me out of the house. A young man who loved men was a shandah, a big sin. My whole family would have been damaged, stained. Maybe I would have had more of a future in America, but at what price?

Then Avner said Yakov gave him a stone with an inscription on it. Avner stopped talking now and reached into his pants pocket. "I carry it with me every day," he said. "A treasure from my childhood." Avner took the stone out of his pocket and rubbed it gently before placing it on the table.

Without a word, Susan reached into her pocketbook, took out her father's stone and placed it next to his. Fraternal twins, with the same inscription. One stone was smooth and dark gray, its surface almost polished. The other was smooth and light tan, with veins of white running through it. But the words were identical.

She was sitting in front of a man who had been Yakov's good friend, almost like a brother. She could hear her father's questions pouring out, one after another, as if he were in court, interrogating a reluctant witness. *What happened to Yakov? Did he survive? What else did Avner know?* A torrent of questions.

"Do you know what happened to Yakov?" Susan asked. "Did you ever hear from him again?

"I never did," Avner answered, "although I tried to find him after I came to Israel. There is no trace of him," he said. "I hope that you have better luck."

Luck was such a funny word. It implied that things just happened. That you didn't need to be clever to decipher a puzzle or to unravel clues. Susan knew that wasn't true.

"I will need more than luck," Susan said, as she put her father's stone back in her bag.

After she left, she debated whether she should tell her father what she'd learned about Yakov. He prided himself on his old-fashioned values. The thought of his accepting a brother who was a homosexual—that would be difficult. Men behaved in certain ways according to her father's traditional social code. They opened doors for women; they helped them with their coats. They supported their wives and raised their children right. In his mind, right did not include a man having a male lover and right most assuredly did not include his brother Yakov having a Nazi soldier for a lover.

Susan herself was shocked by this revelation. For her father it would be unimaginable and deeply painful. He was a Democrat politically but he had his fears: television that would ultimately stop children from reading, makeup that would make his daughter look like a whore, fancy clothing that was elitist and wasteful. He liked simple foods and an occasional cigarette. He didn't drink. He spoke about the evils of segregation and the plight of black people although he never uttered one word about homosexuality. Sexuality was never discussed. Certain subjects were just taboo. Once, when she asked him where babies came from, he walked out of the room.

According to her father, Yakov would have been either a victim or a hero. Those were the only two alternatives—killed by the Nazis who brutally murdered the Jews or rescued by his own wits and good fortune. In love with a Nazi soldier, that was invented fantasy. A myth to besmirch his good name. He would be very angry. "How do you know that Avner didn't make up that story?" he would ask her. Ever the lawyer, he would say that there was no proof. Facts had to be proven like theorems in geometry.

Ezra showed up just before 9 p.m. He knocked on her window and she opened the dead bolt on the door and let him in. The apartment was quiet since her roommates were up north touring Safed and Tiberias.

He was exhausted. "I didn't sleep all night," he told her as he collapsed on her mattress, his weight making a crater in the center. "I had my own nightmares. I was handing out flyers on a street corner when a policeman approached me. He grabbed the stack of flyers from my hand and told me that I was under arrest. He shoved me into a police car and took me down to the station where they interrogated me endlessly. Who was I? Where did my family live? Where did I work? First, a skinny fellow asked questions and then they sent in a husky, intimidating man to ask the same questions again. The room was hot and I asked for something to drink but they didn't give it to me. I asked if they could provide me with a lawyer and they said that I was not entitled to one."

"What are you afraid of?" Susan asked. "Your dream doesn't make sense to me. After all, Israel is a democracy."

Ezra laughed. "Yes and no," he said. His voice turned serious. Now, he was transformed into the commanding presence in front of the meeting room, his lips pursed. "I despair," he said. "I love this country. I'm proud that I'm a Jew. But there are times when I'm angry, when I see Israel as a police state with all the police being Ashkenazim. If you are dark-skinned like me, you are considered dangerous and you have questionable rights. In my dream, they threw me in a cell with two cots and a sink and locked the door. An hour later, the guard showed up with another prisoner, a Moroccan worker who, under the influence of alcohol, had swung at his boss. 'He cursed me out as a filthy black scumbag,' the fellow said to me as he flung himself on the other cot. His name was Henri and he had four children, all under the age of six. 'I should have known better,' he told me. 'Now I'll lose my job.'

"A few minutes later my cellmate asked me why I was in jail." Ezra sighed. "What a nightmare. But at least my dream had a happy ending. Thank God, my family rescued me. A couple hours later, my family arrived at the station. They were told that they had to pay a fine to have me released and that I would have my day in court. I was to go before the judge the following week. What a joke. Me standing before the judge without a lawyer."

It wasn't a joke even in a dream. Susan knew that. Standing before a judge without a lawyer meant serious trouble. Her father had taught her that. "Never," he said, "try to represent yourself. You will trip yourself up that way. You will always self-destruct without a lawyer." He was a true believer, convinced that lawyers were the good guys who saved people from themselves.

"I've something to tell you," Susan said, as she reached forward to stroke his forehead. "I learned something about Yakov, something *disturbing*." Ezra was staring at her now, seemingly relieved to change the subject away from his frightful nightmares. Susan had surprised herself by saying the word "disturbing." She wanted to tell him slowly, not to blurt it out. Slow and steady, that was the best way to deliver bad news, her father told her. He would demonstrate how she should clear her voice, straighten her posture, and tip her chin up. But she couldn't follow his instructions now. She was trembling. "I met with Avner Shapiro today, a refugee from Rozwadów. He and Yakov were good friends."

She was starting to feel panicky. There was a lump in her throat that she always felt when she ran out of words or when, no matter how she tried, she couldn't remember the right answer on an exam. *Just pick your first choice when you panic*, her father always told her.

The correct answer is A. No, A crossed out. B. No, C is closer to the truth. No, safer to stay with A. Don't panic.

"Yakov didn't go to America for a reason," Susan said. She coughed. Then, she coughed for a second time. Ezra's eyes widened and his irises turned from dark brown to black. Somehow, liberated, rebellious Susan felt nervous, almost ashamed to tell him what she'd learned. "There was something wrong with Yakov," she said. She was struggling to find the right word. Was there a right word?

"Just say it," Ezra said, reaching for her hands to steady her. "Just tell me." She bit her lip so hard that she tore skin and tasted blood. Sour and salty. "Yakov was homosexual and he didn't want to shame his family." Susan exhaled, a stream of air long enough to float a falling balloon.

Ezra was sitting up straight now, shaking his head back and forth. "What? I don't believe you." His face was flushed. "People will make up all sorts of things," he said. "On my construction site, there's a fellow that we all think is homosexual. He tries to hide it but we can tell. I feel sorry for him. He seems so uncomfortable. He avoids eye contact. When we tease a beautiful girl who walks by, he looks the other way. He works side by side with us but we don't invite him to eat with us and we never invite him into our homes. I am ashamed of myself."

Ezra seemed to be struggling. "That's how I was brought up. Men who liked men were outcasts." He was sweating profusely and Susan could see that his hands were trembling. She started to speak but stopped herself. What was the point? She felt her face flush. She felt conflicted, too. It was hard to imagine Uncle Yakov that way.

Ezra was staring at her now. "Too much stress," he said. "It's not *our* problem. Enough about Uncle Yakov." He pulled her toward him. "Thanks for coming to the meeting. I turned around to see you but you were gone."

He was massaging her neck now and the muscles of her shoulders, his strong hands loosening the tension. She was unbuttoning her blouse and slipping off her pants. Just being near him excited her. He reached down to fondle her breast, the nipple suddenly taut. She could feel him hard against her, pressing against her thigh, then her bare belly, then entering her with a sigh.

For some strange reason, the cats had stopped screeching and the radio was not blasting news of the Eichmann trial. For one moment, it was just the two of them, lost in each other, wrapped under the covers on a chilly Jerusalem night.

Early the next morning, Ezra left for work and Susan took the bus to Hebrew University where she asked the research librarian for help tracing a German soldier: Karl Bregner. She knew little about him except that he was stationed in Rozwadów in 1939. The librarian disappeared for 15 minutes and returned with a reel of microfilm. It was a complete listing of the German soldiers in the Krakow area with basic information on their commissions and activities. "The Germans kept good records," she said.

Susan put the reel in the machine and spun it until she reached the letter B. Then, she turned it slowly. There were many Bregners. The reel spun so fast that she missed the Ks. There was a Manfred Bregner and Manfred Bregner, Jr. from Krakow and a Richard Bregner from Berlin. When she got back to the Ks, she saw the name Karl Bregner: he was assigned to the Krakow area in 1939, age 35. His entry said: single, 1.88 meters tall, blue eyes, religion Protestant, originally from Munich. Studied at the Military Academy in Munich. Responsible for supplies in Rozwadów and Chief of Supplies at the Mauthausen Camp, 1940 to 1945. Deceased: 1945. It didn't say how he died. After the entry there was an asterisk with a note: see photo appendix p. B3.

Susan asked for a copy of the entry and then for the photo reel. When she reached p. B3, she saw, for the first time, Karl Bregner's face. Although the image was grainy, and slightly out of focus, Bregner was definitely a handsome young man, with a high nose and arched eyebrows. His hair was light and parted severely to one side and his eyes were light, too. His skin was very pale. She could see why Yakov was attracted to him. *Oh my God*, she thought, *that's what Bregner looked like. I can't believe I found this.*

She stared at the photo all the way home, running her index finger up and down his face, trying to reconstruct his life story. He and Yakov had fallen in love at a time when Germans were not supposed to mix with Jews and at a time when homosexuals were imprisoned. It seemed impossible to Susan that Bregner could have saved Yakov. She was certain that they were both dead.

She carried her copy of the entry and photo to the café. The place was full and Ruth was busy waiting on tables. As usual, the latest news from the Eichmann trial was blasting from the radio. Eichmann's lawyer had objected to some testimony and the lawyers had squabbled for nearly an hour. Two people in the audience had fainted and the trial had been interrupted for half an hour while an ambulance took them away.

A nurse from the Auschwitz infirmary testified on medical

experiments performed on women prisoners. The Nazis introduced new techniques of sterilization and a group of young women in their twenties were selected for the procedure. "They wept," she said, "and some of them became hysterical. The doctors had to anesthetize them." After she spoke, two women who had been sterilized gave their accounts. Their voices were so soft that they could barely be heard.

At a corner table, an old woman began to cry. Ruth stared into space. Susan tried not to listen to the testimony but it was impossible to keep their words out of her brain. Barbaric surgical tongs holding their vaginas in position. Pain. Blood. Tying their tubes. Experimental drugs. Injections of carbon dioxide. They were about her age at the time, maybe a year or two older. Guinea pigs in the Nazi labs.

Ruth sat down next to her. "How is the search for Yakov coming along?" she asked. It had been several days since they'd spoken.

"I don't know whether he is alive or dead but I have learned some shocking things about his life after 1920—things I never would have expected." Susan told Ruth about Avner's friendship with Yakov and about their last meeting in the woods outside the shtetl. "That's when Avner met Karl Bregner," Susan said.

Ruth gasped. "Karl Bregner? Her face became pale, and sweat suddenly beaded on her forehead. Her right hand began to tremble. "Karl Bregner," she said again, in complete disbelief. "I never thought I would hear that name again. He ran the supply room at Mauthausen. I remember him." She was shaking now, unable to control herself. "I saw him once driving in a car with a blonde woman, probably his girlfriend."

"Well, she wasn't," Susan said. "She definitely wasn't." Ruth's eyes were staring at Susan now. It almost seemed like she had stopped breathing. "Despite what you saw, Bregner didn't have any girlfriends. But he did have a boyfriend." Susan paused and swallowed. "My Uncle Yakov was his boyfriend and I wonder if somehow, Bregner managed to hide him from the Nazis during the war. Did Bregner have any helpers or special workers that you recall?"

"I remember Bregner because he was so handsome," Ruth said. "I hated myself for thinking that, but he was." Susan took out the photograph and showed it to her.

"That's him, definitely, that's him." Ruth's voice was agitated. "His eyes were almost violet. In my two years there, I only went to the supply room two or three times. It was a big room with barred windows. At least ten prisoners were there folding garments under the supervision of several soldiers. But I only remember Bregner. He was the boss."

She sat there stunned. Something big had happened. Some profound chunk of painful memory had come loose in her brain. Ruth was lost in another world.

Susan was determined to be aggressive, to bring her back. "Do you think that Bregner might have done something to save Yakov?"

Ruth shook her head. She was shivering now, uncontrollably. "There were eyes everywhere," she said. "Eyes when we were sleeping. Eyes when we were eating. Eyes when we were working. There was never a moment when I felt that I was not being looked at."

She hadn't answered Susan. Maybe she hadn't even heard her question.

"I dreamt once that Bregner took me to a dance," Ruth said. "I was wearing a pink satin gown and a diamond tiara and he picked me up in a black limousine and we drank champagne and danced and danced. When I woke up, I was soaking wet on my cot, shivering under the thin, dirty sheet they gave us for a blanket."

"He must have had a powerful personality," Susan said, all the while reflecting on Ruth's remark that she had only seen him in the warehouse on a couple of occasions. How vivid her memory of Bregner? Who knows what Susan would have felt had she been in Ruth's situation. "According to the German records,"

Susan said, "he died in 1945. That's the last mention of him that I can find."

Ruth didn't respond to the news of Bregner's death. She sat shell-shocked in silence. Susan couldn't help thinking that Ruth knew something that she was not telling.

Meanwhile, there were other leads for Susan to track down. There were several survivors from Rozwadów who lived in Israel. She hoped that one of them, perhaps the man who lived in Haifa, could confirm or add to Avner's story. She was planning a trip up north and she invited Ruth to join her.

"We can visit my father's first cousin on the kibbutz," Susan said. "He's a farmer. I'm sure that he will put us both up."

At first, Ruth didn't want to go. "Digging into the past is always painful," she said, wincing. "Nothing good comes of it." The next day, though, when Susan saw Ruth in the café, she'd changed her mind. "You can't go alone," she said. "It's too hard for you." She bent over and kissed Susan on the cheek. The kiss was a complete surprise. It was the first time that Ruth had ever shown Susan any affection.

They would leave Friday morning and take off three days of school and work, returning to Jerusalem late Sunday night. Susan called Nahum Steinberg in Haifa and arranged to speak to him on Sunday. Then, she called her cousin Herschel. They'd never met and he was happy that she was coming. He knew little about her and to be safe he kept reminding her that the kibbutz was definitely *not* religious.

Susan laughed. "Not a problem," she said. She read that it was founded as a Marxist kibbutz. According to her father, this cousin had arrived in Israel when it was still Palestine, leaving Rozwadów in the early 1930s. He was a passionate Zionist and a passionate Marxist. It was a hard life, and her father had learned from another cousin who had visited the kibbutz that the children slept in separate buildings, only joining their parents for the noontime meal. His cousin had married Alisheva, a survivor whom he met in

Israel, a woman who had been the subject of medical experiments for two years in the camps. They had three children. After the birth of the last child, she took to her room and never came out again.

Susan and Ruth met at the Central Bus Station where they boarded the Egged bus for the four-hour ride to Haifa. Her cousin had arranged for someone to pick them up and bring them to the kibbutz. Susan slept for much of the ride, dreaming about marching with Ezra. This time they were protesting in front of the Knesset. Instead of 30 stragglers, there were 300 of them, carrying banners that read: Do Not Discriminate. All Jews Should Have Equal Rights! Susan was carrying an Israeli flag. The police formed a line and pushed them back. The protestors did not lie down. No one was arrested.

When she woke up, the bus was just arriving at the Haifa terminal. It was very crowded. People were hurrying home for Shabbos, hands gripping shopping bags. Outside the station, Susan saw a battered green truck with the name of the kibbutz on it.

The driver called her name as he opened the door so that they could climb in. It was a bumpy 15-minute ride to the kibbutz, which was located slightly north of the city, surrounded by Arab villages and farms. They passed a shed for cows. Three chickens and a black rooster were pecking the dry ground near the shed, looking for stray feed. A large black dog barked. He did not look friendly. By the time they arrived, the farm workers were no longer in the fields.

They stopped at a modest stucco house with a tin roof. A man was waiting for them there and Susan had an eerie feeling when she looked at him. He strongly resembled her father—the same build, the same broad forehead, the same ears and the same blue eyes. He shook her hand over and over again. "Welcome, welcome, welcome," he said. *Nayim Me'od, Nayim, Me'od, Nayim Me'od.*

He carried their bags inside to a small bedroom with two narrow beds that had clearly been made up with the only decent sheets they had. Everything else in the house was frayed and stained. There was a white lamp that had been glued together in three places and a couch pillow with stuffing leaking out in every direction. The flowered plastic tablecloth was faded. She couldn't resist the urge to touch it as she passed by. It was very greasy.

On the wall were several framed certificates from the kibbutz. There was one for farmer of the year and another for best kitchen worker. Evidently, Cousin Hershel was not a slouch.

How their lives had diverged. Hershel was a farmer who wore coveralls and milked cows. Her dad was a lawyer who wore white shirts and ties and carried a leather briefcase. The children of two brothers who most probably had beards and wore peyos, raised in Rozwadów, students at the local yeshiva. Hershel now bronzed from his life in the sun. Her father was fair. Yet they shared the same blue eyes.

Shabbos dinner, Hershel announced, was always served buffet-style in the social hall with everyone helping out. There was no need to dress up. Then, trying to be a host, he added that there was a little hot water. "If you want to take a shower, you better do so soon," he said. "It usually runs out."

Susan ran into the shower. It was warm for about a minute and then, with no warning, was freezing cold. That's how it was in Israel. Things were black and white, left and right, at extremes. There just didn't seem to be a middle. She jumped out, put on a clean blouse and pants and, seeing no one in the house, found Ruth and Hershel sitting outside on lawn chairs.

"My wife does not come to meals," Hershel said as Susan sat down to join them. "I bring food back to her. She is not well." He didn't explain what was wrong with her. Susan had already heard the story. Some of her friends were sterilized but her treatment at the hands of the Nazis was to take experimental drugs. Mind drugs. She'd never been the same. When Hershel married her, she was quiet about her past but some time after she gave birth to three children, she fell apart. The nightmares started coming. Every night she screamed out loud for help. The psychiatrists prescribed tranquilizers, which left her in a drugged-out state. Hershel prepared food for her and when the kids visited for lunch, she rarely talked to them.

Ruth and Susan followed Hershel on the gravel path as he led them to the wooden dining hall that the kibbutzniks had built themselves. "It was my design," Hershel explained, pointing to the graceful, vaulted ceiling.

When they entered the hall, Susan could hardly believe what she saw. In the front of the cavernous space, on a white wall, there was an enormous portrait of Karl Marx. It was an image that Susan had seen before in a school textbook and in *Life* magazine. Marx, with a full head of hair, mustache, and bushy gray beard, his penetrating eyes watching them under heavy brows. He was dressed in a black jacket and white shirt, with a black ribbon crossed at his neck as his tie. In his black-and-white garb, he resembled the rabbis Susan saw on the streets of Jerusalem. He was the god of the kibbutzniks, the man who inspired them from the first day when they arrived in this desolate spot to till the rocky soil and do battle with the mosquitos. Forget the Torah that they'd learned in the shtetl. *Das Kapital* was their new bible.

And here was Karl Marx presiding over Shabbos dinner at her cousin's kibbutz. It was uncanny how this man whose writing challenged philosophers like Hegel, Voltaire, Rousseau, and Aristotle now looked over these rugged Jewish farmers.

The children had been fed earlier and they were already sleeping in their dormitories. It was only the grown-ups who lined up for baked chicken, soggy green beans, and sliced potatoes. They were a straggly lot. The man behind Susan in line wore jeans and sandals, his T-shirt revealing formidable biceps. Susan had never seen an Israeli who looked like this before. On reflection, though, she realized she'd seen him in travel posters and magazines. He was the man featured in the Jewish National Fund ads, the ones that urged Americans to make *aliyah*. *Come to Israel*, the posters said, *and look like him*. In the poster, he stood in a field, hoe in hand.

The sky was cloudless and his face was tilted up under his straw hat. He was the quintessential pioneer. The campaign was designed for young people like herself. It was a reminder that Israel was populated with pioneers, not just survivors.

The dining hall was set with long tables. On each, there was challah and grape juice. There were Shabbos candles by a stage in the front of the room. Susan wondered if anyone was going to say a prayer.

She moved slowly along the buffet, helping herself to chicken, rice, and a vegetable stew of chickpeas and beans that Hershel wanted her to taste. Then, she sat down next to him and waited.

A woman stood up and walked to the candles. She said the blessing out loud and lit them. Then she spoke again. "Let us be thankful," she said, "for the bounty of our land. We can be proud of our hard work, our spirit. This would not have happened without all of us. Remember, comrades," she said, "we are a collective, a family of workers. None of us is more important than another." *Nachon,* a man called out. Correct. *Nachon.*

Another woman stood up to speak. This was their Friday night custom. Instead of prayers, there were testimonies, commentaries, and criticism. "We have to repair the children's playground," she said. It had been two weeks since she'd spoken about the problem and nothing yet had been done to fix the broken swings. Ruth leaned over and whispered that this was the oddest Shabbos dinner that she'd ever attended.

The food needed salt and seasoning. "We raise our own chickens and grow the vegetables on the kibbutz," Hershel explained. The kibbutz was founded in 1933 when no one else had settled in the area. The land was very swampy and many people came down with malaria. They were up to the challenge, he explained, because they were all young Zionists, pioneers in the State of Israel. Proud Marxists and dedicated workers. Nothing was too much for them.

For a second, Susan thought he looked sad. She'd come to

recognize that face as a sign that a personal story was coming. There was no joy without sorrow. He'd first come to Palestine in 1929 by himself. Although he tried to convince his family to come with him, they would not leave Rozwadów. This was about ten years after Susan's father's family left. When things started to get bad in the early 1930s, he went back to Rozwadów, hitchhiking for many miles, because he wanted to convince his family to leave before it was too late. They were stubborn. They refused to believe that their world would collapse. None of them survived.

"Why didn't they come?" Susan asked Hershel. Their refusal was just like Yakov's. "What held them there?"

The shtetl was so poor and there were few jobs. The Germans were at their door. There were letters from America and from Palestine speaking of streets paved with gold and redeeming the holy land. It was impossible to understand why they clung to their humble, poverty-stricken existence.

Yakov was another story. If it was true that Yakov loved Karl, she could understand. It added a romantic element to the tale. It made it more than someone who had just taken the wrong turn in the road and gotten lost. That was not Yakov. No, he was a man who would not part from his lover. No matter what.

After dinner, they returned to Hershel's house, choosing to sit outside under the stars instead of in the small living room. Ruth was interested in Hershel's work on the farm and she asked him about his daily chores. He got up at 4 a.m. every day except Saturday, when he slept till eight. First, he cleaned and checked the chicken coop, collecting eggs. Then, he joined a comrade to milk the cows. After he finished his animal chores, he went out to the fields and weeded and hoed. Hershel read the workers' newspaper put out by the collective of Socialist kibbutzim but he did not read books. In fact, Susan only saw one book in his house. It was a book on the proper care of farm animals. There just was no time for reading novels or history and definitely no time for studying Torah.

Hershel remembered Yakov. He was a quiet fellow, he said.

While the other boys made jokes, Yakov didn't speak. He always stood in the second row, preferring the shadows to the sunlight. When the rebbe called on him, he blushed and, occasionally, he stuttered when he was answering.

"I wanted to say the words for him, but I couldn't." Hershel said that they saw one another frequently after Yakov's family left in 1920. He was living with the owner of the shop and he seemed lonely. When Hershel became involved in the Zionist movement, he couldn't convince Yakov to join him. That was the only time Hershel remembered Yakov expressing a strong opinion. Yakov didn't think that all Jews belonged in the Promised Land.

Oh, how disappointed her father would be to learn that his beloved brother was not a Zionist.

No, Yakov said that it was better for Jews to stay in Poland where they had been for centuries. By 1930 in Galicia there was already an active group of secular Socialist-Zionists, *Hashomer Hatzair*. Yakov would not attend meetings. He thought that they were all a bunch of troublemakers who would make life harder for Jews.

Once, Hershel succeeded in convincing Yakov to sit in on a meeting. The subject was making aliyah and the speaker was a young man from Krakow who brought flyers to distribute. He'd just returned from Palestine and he told them about the efforts being made to reclaim the land. This was our chance, he said, to transform our lives. In Palestine they would no longer be peddlers or petty merchants.

Yakov left the meeting before it was over. He told Hershel later that he was sorry that he'd attended. He accepted his family's emigration to America even though he'd chosen not to go with them. That was about moving up in the world, about making money. He didn't agree with making aliyah, though. He didn't want to become a farmer.

"He came to say goodbye to me when I left for Palestine," Hershel said. "We shook hands and we hugged each other." That was the last time Hershel saw him. When Hershel returned to try to convince his family to join him, Yakov was away. Hershel stopped by the store but he wasn't there. "I left him a note," Hershel told Susan. "I told him I was sorry I missed him and I wished him good luck."

Hershel didn't have any photos of Yakov but he did remember that his front tooth was chipped and that he had a mole on his left cheek, near his ear. He had funny toes, too, Hershel told her. The second toe on both feet was longer than his big toe. Hershel had noticed the odd shape when they were boys swimming in the San River.

The pieces were coming together. She was getting closer to the truth. Now was the time to ask tough questions. Did Hershel know anyone else from Rozwadów? Was there someone else who might have interacted with Yakov?

Herschel was quiet for a moment. Then, he said that there was a fellow from Rozwadów who worked in a hardware store in Haifa. Hershel had bought some fencing there for the kibbutz. They'd instantly recognized each other. Since that time, he'd visited several times. He lived in a small apartment near the port. As it turned out, he was the person Susan had called. She was to see him on Sunday morning.

It was almost midnight and Susan and Ruth retired to the room they were sharing. There were two narrow beds with mattresses so hard that it was difficult to fall asleep. Susan usually slept on her right side but she could not get comfortable. She tried the left but that was worse. Finally, she gave up and lay on her back looking at the ceiling. The moon was out and slivers of its light made a pattern on the wall. Ruth had fallen asleep right away and she was snoring lightly.

Instead of counting sheep, Susan found herself counting the pieces of the puzzle that made up Yakov's life. She knew more about him now than his height and his eye color. He was quiet. He was not a Torah scholar. He was not a Zionist. He was not interested in making money. She knew where his mole was and she knew about his peculiarly shaped toes. She didn't know, however, what had happened to him.

In the middle of the night Alisheva screamed. It was a wail, really, that pierced the night air. "Help me, help me!" she called out. "I'm being strangled." Susan heard Hershel comforting her. "It's all right," he kept saying to her. "No one is here but me, darling. You're safe."

Again, her screams, "I can't breathe, stop strangling me." And again, his soft words, "Shhhhh, we have company. Shhh, you're safe in Israel. There are no Nazis here."

Hershel apologized to them in the morning. They were peeling hard-boiled eggs in the dining hall when he spoke. "I hope that Alisheva didn't wake you last night," he said. Ruth hadn't heard her and Susan said that she hadn't heard her either, even though it was a lie. Better a lie than the truth, she thought.

He spoke about her nightmares. In the beginning, they were only occasional, he said. Then, they became frequent and more violent. The children were frightened. He took her for daily therapy. She was in a group with other survivors.

Hershel didn't think that the group sessions helped. When she came home, she was always more agitated. They told him that she was silent there, rarely saying a word. After a couple of months, they decided that it would be better if she did not attend. Her nightmares continued to get worse. She was always being killed. Sometimes, they were attacking her with a knife. Sometimes, they were strangling her. Sometimes, they were forcing her to swallow poison. The drugs prescribed by the doctor put her to sleep but inevitably she would wake up in terror.

During the day, Susan and Ruth walked around the kibbutz, stopping to chat with neighbors as Hershel gave them a tour of the farm. They looked up to him, almost saluting when he arrived. He was a founding father of the kibbutz and a hero, a *gibor*. He had battled the mosquitoes and put down roots in this swamp. Many of them thought that he'd turned it into paradise. Some of their children disagreed, having begun to leave for the cities. Still, he swaggered as he walked, pointing out each and every accomplishment: the long pipeline that brought fresh water, and the row of trees that he planted as saplings, now more than 20 feet tall.

In the kibbutz barn, the smell of freshly cut hay was overpowering. There was a new calf, only a few weeks old. Hershel knelt down to inspect it, softly caressing its thin legs. It was suckling on its mother. Mother and calf didn't move; they knew his smell and touch. Outside in the fields they were planting tomatoes. The seedlings, raised in greenhouses, were now five inches tall. Hershel took two trowels and handed them to Ruth and Susan. Then, he placed two plants in their hands. He showed them the right way to plant, digging a hole, filling it halfway with water, placing the plant gently inside and then filling it up with soil. Susan noticed that he was careful to anchor the plant in the ground. "Don't touch it too much," he said. "It's like pie crust. Too much handling and it's ruined."

Susan's aunt had given her the same advice when they baked an apple pie together. "Keep your fingers off the dough," she advised, adding that she raised her daughters the same way. "When you have children, don't fuss over them too much," she said. "Let them breathe."

Hershel laughed when he looked at Susan's tomato plant. It was leaning sideways, almost touching the soil. Without saying a word, he bent down and replanted it, heaping soil around its stem as protection.

"I'm not much of a farmer," Susan said, watching him correct her work.

At dinner, Hershel recalled a few more things about Yakov. He loved music and he had a beautiful voice. That didn't surprise Susan, whose father also loved to sing. Hershel remembered that Yakov always hummed or whistled to himself. The rebbe often asked him to be quiet. "He was not quite aware that he was doing it," Hershel said. "I envied him because I couldn't sing," he explained. Once, Yakov told Hershel that he thought that anyone could be taught to sing. It was just a matter of careful listening. "He tried to teach me a melody, 'Raisins and Almonds,' a Yiddish lullaby, but I couldn't master it. He would sing a note and wait for me to copy it, which I couldn't do. Finally, he laughed and said, 'Well, maybe I'm wrong. Maybe there are some people who can't sing.'"

Susan knew that song. Her father sang it to her as a child and although she didn't have much of a voice, she could sing that tune. It was ingrained in her DNA. Ruth knew the song too. "My mother sang it to me. Every Jewish child in Eastern Europe knew that melody."

Susan noticed that no one at the kibbutz brought up the subject of the Eichmann trial, and as they walked, she asked Hershel why they didn't. Surely there are survivors at the kibbutz who were glued to the radio, she said. She told him that radio news all over Jerusalem was blasting the latest trial testimony. There was absolutely no escaping it.

There were survivors at the kibbutz, Hershel said, but they were not in the majority. At the time of the mass immigration of Holocaust survivors, many of the kibbutzim suffered from labor shortages since many of their members were in the military. The kibbutzim desperately wanted to attract survivors but it was not an easy process. Young survivors wanted time off for education, which was often not possible given the rigors of life on the kibbutz. Some survivors were not in good health and the work was just too hard for them. For many, the organization of the kibbutz reminded them of the camps and they preferred living in cities. Those who ended up at the kibbutzim were usually family members of settlers who arrived from DP camps.

By the time they came here, Herschel said, the kibbutz was eight years old. All they wanted to do was fit in. We were busy planning how to cultivate new land and how to build a larger barn. None of us had time to think about Hitler and the Holocaust. "Why should we?" he asked Susan. "Why think about bad times when you can think about good ones?"

She had no real answer to his question. Hershel's recipe for living was simple. All you needed to do was to dig a hole, plant a seed, and watch it grow. His upbeat philosophy reminded her of her father's rosy view of American history. There was no arguing that the Founding Fathers had ever done anything wrong. "Be positive," her father always said. "Don't allow even one negative thought to enter your brain."

On Sunday morning, Susan and Ruth left the kibbutz in the car of Hershel's neighbor Shulamit, heading for Haifa. She promised to drop them off at the café on Nathanson Street where they were to meet Nahum Steinberg during his lunch break. Shulamit was a fast driver and her heavy foot landed on the brake as she whizzed around curves. Susan was thrilled that the drive was short. Breakfast backed up in her throat, leaving a sour taste. Twice she gagged. It reminded her of riding on the Tilt-a-Whirl in Coney Island. That ride definitely made her throw up.

Ruth sat in the back, seemingly oblivious to the driving. She'd been quiet for most of the weekend and Susan wondered what was on her mind. Something was clearly troubling her. But there was no time to talk. They exited the car and walked down the steep hill to the café. There was only one man seated in the sunlight. He wore dark sunglasses and a navy baseball cap. He stood up as they arrived, bowing to them and then pulling out chairs for them to sit. He lit up a cigarette, obviously his third because the ashtray held two butts. His complexion was quite pale and he looked like he didn't spend much time out in the sun.

He motioned to the waitress and they all ordered coffee. Susan noticed that he had a slight tremor in his right hand, which became obvious when he lifted the cup to his mouth. Before she could say a word, he spoke. "I *knew* Yakov. We were good friends."

Good friends? What clues would Nahum Steinberg add to the puzzle?

Nahum seemed to be picking up in the middle of a story. "Our favorite pastime was skipping stones across the river," he said. Yakov was very good at it. In fact, he was the village champion. He taught Nahum how to find the perfect stone, the one with a flat surface. Only flat stones had the magical power to bounce across the water. Once, Yakov's stone skipped halfway across the San, rising and falling and touching the water six times before it sank. "We boys clapped and whistled. Yakov did not welcome the attention, though. He was a shy fellow, definitely not interested in our gossip, especially not our tales about the pretty young women in the girls' yeshiva.

"Boys and girls were kept apart in those days and married off young by the time they were 20. The rebbes did not want any hanky-panky. That, however, did not stop the 13-year-old yeshiva boys from looking at the budding yeshiva girls. There were jokes and, occasionally, pranks. Yakov never joined in our antics."

Susan thought about their world. Boys and girls with a wall between them. No touching. No feeling. Still, the boys did look at the girls and did notice, when the rebbe or their parents were not looking, which ones had developed breasts. How did a boy who was attracted to other boys fit into this shtetl world? She thought of him, lying in bed alone. *Was he sad? Was he angry? Was he ashamed?*

Nahum unzipped a small portfolio and he placed a stone on the table. "He gave me this one as a present on my birthday in June of 1940. The Germans had already arrived and we were all very nervous. A few days afterward," he said, "I saw Yakov getting into a car driven by a German soldier. I thought he was being arrested and I was very sad." The stone bore the same inscription as her father's.

One week later, Nahum and his family were rounded up and shipped to a nearby work camp. After that, they were transported to Mauthausen where they stayed for six months. Then, it was on to Auschwitz. He was the only survivor.

Nahum lit another cigarette, his fourth. "One more thing," he said. "When I was in Mauthausen, I once saw the German soldier who had Yakov in his car. I'm sure it was him."

Ruth jumped in. "Where did you see the soldier?" she asked. Before she finished her first question, she asked a second: "Did you ever talk to him?"

Susan thought she seemed anxious, maybe even frightened.

"In the supply warehouse," Nahum said, "I think he was the commander there." Nahum washed the floors in his ward and once he was sent to pick up soap and other cleaning supplies. "I saw him standing outside the building but I never spoke to him."

Ruth was perspiring heavily now, sweat visible on her forehead. She was tapping her foot incessantly, unaware that she was doing so. She kept reaching into her pocketbook to pull out her pack of cigarettes although she'd just lit one up. She was almost in a trance, sitting there, waiting upon Nahum's every word.

It was strange, Susan thought, that Ruth never told Nahum that she'd been a prisoner in Mauthausen, too. There was no apparent reason to keep this a secret. Susan decided that she would not bring it up if Ruth chose not to do so. Survivors were touchy about what they were willing to remember. It was selective, like hearing.

Once, Susan helped out at an old-age home where most of the residents wore hearing aids. They told her to speak loudly and slowly to them and to enunciate the words carefully. Often, she had to repeat things two and three times. Once, though, when she was particularly frustrated that the woman she was helping had not heard her, Susan joked about it with a co-worker. "It looks like I will have to repeat the instructions for the fourth time," she told her friend. Within seconds, the older woman leaned forward and spoke to Susan, "You do not have to repeat it for the fourth time," she said angrily. "I heard you."

That memory came back to Susan whenever she spoke to

survivors. Even the ones without hearing aids were selective, picking and choosing what they were willing to hear or not hear, reveal or not reveal.

Ruth asked about Bregner's assistants. It was such an odd question. She couldn't figure out why Ruth wanted to know who worked for him. What difference did that make? Clearly, it mattered to Ruth.

Nahum thought for a few moments and ordered another cup of coffee. He boasted that it was his fourth cup of the day. "There were two Germans who worked in the back room," Nahum said. "They never came out while I was there. I heard them laughing and making noisy toasts. I heard the clink of their beer mugs." Nahum signed. "We barely had water to drink."

"Why are you talking so much about Bregner when you're looking for your Uncle Yakov? Bregner is probably dead," Nahum said. "All those Germans, they carried cyanide pills. They didn't want to rot in prison. That was OK for Jews but not for Germans who were taught never to surrender."

Nahum changed the subject. He asked if they were listening to the Eichmann trial, confessing that he couldn't turn it off. It was an addiction, like drinking coffee or smoking. It didn't matter who was testifying or how gruesome the subject was, he had to listen.

"Some folks here say that the Israelis are making too much of the trial," Susan said. "That they're mired in the past, weeping and wailing and judging. *Not everyone has a number on his arm,* my friend Ezra says. He's a Moroccan and he's angry about the way his people are treated here. It's a world dominated by Ashkenazim."

Nahum nodded. That was true, he said, but really it was the German Jews, the *yekkes*, who had the most power. Polish Jews, they were a lower class, not quite as low as the Sephardim, but poor and illiterate. "We have the right skin color," he said, "but we are not from Berlin or Vienna."

It was 1:30 p.m. and Nahum had to return to the hardware store. He shook Susan's hands and reached out to shake Ruth's hand, too, but she did not extend hers. Her face was somber, her lips tightly pursed.

The bus back to Jerusalem left about 15 minutes late. Two suitcases, tied together with rope, had fallen apart and the passengers were busy picking up the mess and trying to find rope to tie the bags together. The driver was angry, yelling at them that they only had five more minutes and that he would leave without them. Egged drivers were gruff, Susan knew this already. They had to be if they were ever going to close their doors. "On time" in Israel meant almost being on time, ten minutes late. There was none of that German precision—the famous European trains that Susan had read about that left at 10:00 a.m. and not 10:01. That was OK for civilized, cultured folks but not here in the Middle East where engines often overheated and tempers did, too.

Susan watched through the window as one of the passengers came running with a frayed piece of rope. He struggled to stuff his belongings back into his bag and then wrestled with the rope, tugging and tugging till he could join the pieces together and tie a knot. People on the bus clapped when he did so, relieved that they would finally be leaving the terminal. When he came aboard, he passed out candies to everyone. A *matanah*, he said, for your patience.

Ruth said nothing. She seemed disinterested in the drama, choosing instead to read the latest edition of *Haaretz*. The headline read: *Eichmann Trial Testimony Heats Up*. Underneath it, there was a large photo of a crowd outside the Beit Ha'am building. Next to it was a smaller photo of the meeting that Susan had attended, under it a caption: *A group of Moroccan immigrants gathered to vent their complaints about their treatment in Israel*. Evidently, the photographer had managed to shoot a couple of photos before he was asked to leave the meeting. Ezra was standing next to the blackboard, holding a stack of flyers.

Ezra loved protesting. Susan knew that. It was his mission in life. He couldn't just sit still and vent, like most other Israelis who gathered in the cafés to complain about having no money or working too hard or suffering from the weather, the *hamsin* that lasted over a week and caused everyone to take refuge indoors from the suffocating heat.

Ruth handed her the newspaper and closed her eyes. There was a second story on the trial, an interview with Hannah Arendt, a *New Yorker* reporter. She was a celebrity, the author of *The Origins of Totalitarianism*, published ten years earlier in Britain as *The Burden of Our Time*. Susan had tried to read it twice, never quite getting more than halfway through the book. Arendt described the rise of antisemitism and what she called the New Imperialism which she believed led to World War I. The heart of her book was an analysis of Nazism and Stalinism. Her prose was dense and the argument often too theoretical for Susan.

Now, here Arendt was in Jerusalem covering the Eichmann trial and living across the street from Susan in the pension. Susan had recognized her, having seen her photo in the New York papers. She had dark, wavy hair cut short and a long straight nose. She was dressed in a gray jacket that resembled a man's suit and she wore laced-up black shoes. She carried a briefcase that was fat with papers. Susan thought of trying to talk to her the next time she saw her, but she didn't have the courage.

In the interview, Arendt answered the reporter's question. What surprised Arendt so far about the testimony? "The pettiness, the bureaucracy of it all," Arendt replied. "Eichmann," she insisted, "was not a real intellectual. He was a petty player in the Nazi scheme of things, taking orders. He was doing his job."

Her comment struck Susan as radical. The trial was supposed to put evil on display. Eichmann was the personification of evil, crafty, cunning, and vindictive. The testimony was to reveal to the world that there had never been such evil before. Calling him petty reduced the evil, made him a pawn in the process.

Susan's father was not happy with Arendt's interpretation. He called after he read the story. "Why let him off the hook? There's no such thing as a pawn in the face of evil. Arendt's got it all wrong. I know that you don't agree with her."

He didn't give her a chance to say a word. Maybe Eichmann really was a minor player. Maybe, despite all the debate among Holocaust scholars, Hitler was the master puppeteer pulling all of the strings?

Susan wanted to ask Ruth why she was so interested in Bregner but Ruth had fallen asleep, her hands clasped together as if she were praying, a strange pose for a woman who was not religious. She looked older when she slept, signs of gray hair apparent in her hairline. For some reason, the trip had worn her out.

When they arrived at the Central Bus Station in Jerusalem, Ruth hurried off, her goodbye slender and forced. "See you," was all she could say. She didn't thank Susan for the weekend at the kibbutz. She took a few steps and then came back, touched Susan's shoulder, her lips parting as if to speak. A moment of hesitation, then a flustered "See you" for the second time as she left the station.

When Susan returned to her apartment, she found a note from Ezra in her mailbox: *Where are you?* He'd written in blue ink. Beneath it was a second sentence in pencil: *Still not home? I miss you. Protesting has worn me out. Call me if you can.* Below was a phone number. Susan walked across the street to the pension. She knocked on the door and waited. A woman with a German accent answered. "Can I help you?" she asked. Behind the woman, there was a telephone on a small table.

As she usually did, Susan asked politely if it was possible to use their telephone. She would pay for it of course. The woman hesitated. "Is the call local?" she asked, obviously recognizing that Susan was American. "Yes."

"OK," the woman said as Susan handed her the fee.

At first, the number was busy and Susan had to wait. She sat in the parlor observing the European-style furniture, the velvet curtains and the lace doilies. There was a silver coffee set, rimmed with ornate flowers and vines on a rosewood sideboard and dainty floral demitasse cups and saucers lined up on glass shelves in the china breakfront. In the hall, Susan saw a grid of cabinets, which served as the mailboxes for the guests. One of the cubbies had the name *Hannah Arendt* written in Hebrew letters.

In the background, Susan could hear the radio broadcasting a summary of the day's testimony. The second time she dialed, a man answered. He asked her to hold on while he got Ezra. Seconds later, she heard Ezra's voice.

"I saw you in the newspaper," Susan said. He laughed. "I didn't know that I was famous," he said. Ezra gave her a quick report on the latest protest work, explaining that the police had begun to shadow him and his followers. One of the officers, when no one was looking, even came over to shake his hand. "You're doing an important job," he said, adding that his mother was from Tunisia. "The police are trained to keep us in check," Ezra explained. "They expect that we won't give up and that we'll keep doing what we're doing. That's the game we're playing." He asked her about the trip to Haifa. "Any major discoveries?"

"Too much to tell you now," Susan said. "I'll tell you later."

Ezra invited Susan to join the protesters for dinner at 8 p.m. They were meeting in a small Sephardi synagogue, tucked into a ground-floor apartment of a building housing Moroccans. It was a working meeting to make posters and stuff envelopes. Susan wasn't sure that she should come.

"I'm an outsider," she said. "Folks resent me." He didn't agree. "They want you there," he said. "You're with me."

She hung up the phone. Just as she did so, the front door of the pension opened and Hannah Arendt entered. Susan stared at her. Arendt looked past her, as if she weren't there. She checked her mail and disappeared up the stairs to her bedroom on the second floor. If she had only walked a bit slower, Susan would have tried to talk to her, to ask if Eichmann was really just an ordinary man who followed extraordinary orders. But Arendt had no time for her. As

Susan exited the pension, she heard the sound of typing from the floor above. It was Arendt recording her notes from the trial. Susan could still hear the tapping as she crossed the street to her apartment.

Dinner was informal, a potluck with a stack of fresh pita bread, bowls of hummus, baba ganoush and olives. Someone brought a chopped Israeli salad of cucumbers and tomatoes. They ate quickly. Ezra wiped the table clean as he sorted the rally handouts into piles so they could collate them easily.

"We've changed our venue," he said, announcing that "the next rally will be outside the offices of The Jewish Agency on King George Street. They're the ones who are responsible for the lives of immigrants. We have to pressure them to make changes." The new flyers were filled with statistics that called attention to the vast discrepancy between the quality of life for the Sephardim and the Ashkenazim. At the bottom of the economic scale, Sephardim often earned salaries that were less than one third that of the Ashkenazim. One of the flyers had photos of dark-skinned children with bare feet.

A mother stuffing the envelopes didn't like the photos. "We are proud, Ezra," she said. "We shouldn't print photos of our children that make them look neglected." She tore one of the flyers in half. Her anger stirred the group. Another woman sided with her, adding that poverty didn't mean neglect. "We're better parents," she said. "Or, at the least, as good as the Ashkenazim we work for. We clean their kitchens and their bathrooms and we keep our own houses clean, too. We're nannies for their children. They trust us. Doesn't that mean that we are responsible? Who here would let your child out on the street with no shoes?" Ezra solved the dispute by removing the old flyer from the table. He substituted another one with the photo of a pair of Moroccan boys, dressed in their finest clothing and wearing colorful kippahs, strolling down one of the narrow streets of the Old City.

The photo reminded Susan of a book she once found on her

local library shelf. They were black-and-white images taken by James Van Der Zee, a Harlem-based studio photographer. The people in his book looked perfect—hair coiffed, their clothing elegant, the studio setting regal. The introduction to the book said that Van Der Zee wanted to show black people as beautiful. He had no space for poverty or bare feet. Susan reflected, *how does any group want to be seen by the outside world?*

Ezra walked her home but he didn't come in. The meeting had exhausted him and he had to go to work early. She could feel him moving away even as they kissed.

When she went inside, Susan found a fat envelope in her mailbox. It was an answer to a query that she'd sent in to the research librarian at Mauthausen. Someone at Yad Vashem had suggested that Susan write them to see if they had any records of the Germans who served there. There were two letters, one in German and the second, a translation, in bad English. They did have records of the Germans who worked at Mauthausen, the clerk wrote, although she didn't think the records were complete. They'd sent some lists to the Eichmann prosecutors but she was attaching the list for the Mauthausen supply facility. Six Germans were assigned to that building, Number D3, as it was known at the time.

Susan let out a scream. At the top of the list was the name Karl Bregner. Below it were five other names, none of them names that Susan had ever seen before. Susan copied down the list on a separate sheet of paper. She would show it to Ruth to see if she recognized any of them. If one of them were alive, perhaps he would know more about Yakov. Maybe Karl Bregner's secret was not so secret.

She had also asked the clerk whether any of the Germans on the list had survived. There was an asterisk next to the names of the three men whose death certificate she'd found. The others were a mystery.

The next day, at the ulpan, Esther announced that she had a surprise for the Moroccans. Through a friend who was politically connected, Esther had gotten them tickets to attend the Eichmann trial. It was a rare opportunity for immigrants and she waved the tickets in the air proudly. There was a sound in the back of the room, just like a loud boo at a baseball game when the team you're not rooting for scores a run. Susan looked back to see where it came from but the booing had stopped.

Esther repeated her announcement, hoping for a more enthusiastic response. "Israelis are clamoring for tickets," she said. "Even sabras haven't been able to get into the trial." She paused, waiting for applause. The room was silent, except for the squeak of a chair leg on the stone floor.

"We'll be going on Thursday," Esther said, "during class time, so you won't have to miss any work. There's a translation in case you prefer listening in French." Susan was sitting two rows behind Ezra. She could see that his ears were red. Rachel was sitting next to her, opening and closing her fingers into a fist. She was not happy about the *tiyool*, this field trip planned for the class.

Esther had prepared a handout on the Holocaust for the day's translation exercise. On the top of the page was a list of new vocabulary words: death camp, gas poisoning, ration card, prisoner, sterilization, and experiment. Below the list was a little map with dots locating many of the concentration camps: Majdanek, Bergen Belsen, Mauthausen, Auschwitz, and Dachau.

The passage to be translated came from the testimony of an Auschwitz prison guard. Esther had simplified the Hebrew slightly for the group and she called upon Ezra to read and translate the first sentence. Annoyed, he asked if she could call on someone else. But she held her ground. "I'm the teacher here," she said, smiling as she delivered her dictum. "It's not too difficult for you. Translate!"

Ezra resisted. It was not the difficulty of the passage that bothered him, he said. It was the politics. "I can't stand this obsession with the Holocaust." He leered at Esther.

She stood her ground and shook her finger at him. "You immigrants are so ignorant about what it took for Israel to be established. We suffered. We died. We were gassed to death. We've built this state on the bones of those who died in the Holocaust. The least we can do is purge this evil from the face of the earth." Esther was almost shouting now, her face bright red and her hands twitching.

Susan could hardly believe what was happening. It was a revolution in the classroom. Several other students turned their handouts face-down in protest. No one was willing to read.

Esther was staring at her now. Susan imagined what was going through her mind. That nice American girl, she will rescue me from this hostile situation. She will calm everyone down and translate the passage. What a trap. If Susan agreed, Ezra would be furious. If she disagreed, all hell would break loose.

The moment passed. Esther backed down. "We do not have to translate this today," she said, regaining her composure. "But remember, we will all be meeting at Beit Ha'am on Thursday morning. Please be sure to bring your identity card or they will not let you in." Then, she dismissed class early.

6

To get into the morning session at Beit Ha'am, Susan had to arrive early, before 8 a.m., in order to be processed by security. She handed the guard her ID and they took her picture and searched her for weapons. They emptied Susan's handbag and opened her lipstick case and compact, too. They took all of the cards out of her wallet. After that, they escorted her into a holding pen until it was time to let the spectators enter the courtroom. There was to be no talking and no note-taking and cameras were strictly forbidden.

There were ten Moroccans from her class, looking scared and overwhelmed. There were two survivors looking gray and full of despair. There was a student from Hebrew University who was writing her dissertation on the Holocaust. Susan recognized a bus driver on the Number 6 line and the man at the stamp window in the Central Post Office. The reporters were in a separate holding area, behind a glass divider. Hannah Arendt sat in the front row, a notebook in hand.

Esther wore a black dress and black stockings for the occasion, as if she was in mourning. She avoided looking at Ezra although she greeted Susan. "We have seats just behind the reporters' section," she said, a clear sign that her friend, who'd made the arrangements, had clout.

A bell rang and they were shown into the courtroom. The guard ordered them to walk slowly, one behind the other. "No talking," he said. "Absolutely no talking." The famous glass booth was empty. Eichmann had yet to arrive. Two workers were cleaning the glass door and a third man was testing the microphone in the booth. In front of each seat there was a pair of headphones for translation. Susan turned the dial on hers to English. Ezra and the Moroccans turned theirs to French. The man on Susan's left set his headphones to German.

At 9 a.m., a door opened and the judges entered. Everyone was asked to stand. Five minutes later, two guards escorted Eichmann into his glass cage. A man behind Susan screamed out, "Haman!"

Every Jewish child knew the story of Purim. How Mordechai, the Jew, saved the Jews of Shushan from wicked Haman's plan to exterminate all of the Jews in the kingdom. Dressed in a blue and purple gown with a gold crown on her head, Susan had once played Queen Esther, Mordechai's cousin, in a Hebrew school production. The audience clapped loudly and shook their noisy groggers when Haman was hung on the cardboard gallows that they'd taped together, gallows that were originally intended for Mordechai, the Jew.

Susan was thinking about Eichmann's fate. Of course he would be judged guilty, but how would they kill him? If they gassed him, the way he'd gassed millions of Jews, where would they bury him? There would always be some fanatic who wanted to dig up the grave, a loyal follower who wanted to lay fresh roses on his stone.

She could see the headlines: *Brawl erupts at Eichmann grave; two men injured, three arrested. Paint splashed on Eichmann tombstone: You should have died in an oven.*

They would have to cremate him and, in the middle of the night, dump his ashes in the Mediterranean Sea. His final solution. He would be washed away, as if he never existed.

Eichmann looked smaller and thinner on the stand. His face was pale and his eyelids seemed heavy, like a man who needed sleep. He looked more like the clerk in the post office, who kept putting his glasses on and taking them off, and whose lips were tightly pinched together as he worked. Eichmann's hairline was receding and he wore thick eyeglasses.

In the newspapers, he seemed more frightening but here in Beit Ha'am he looked like a man who could be pushed over with a light shove. A tap on the shoulder and he would fall down.

Israeli newspapers referred to him as "the caged monster." They painted quite a different picture of the man. There were cartoons of him screaming orders at nearly naked Jews. He towered above them, his angry face distorted.

The prosecutor announced the next witness, a woman who'd been in three different camps: Auschwitz, Majdanek, and Mauthausen. She limped to the witness stand and took the oath, barely able to hold up her deformed right hand. "Of course, I will tell the truth," she said, baffled by the question.

She was a trained nurse, a profession that made her valuable to the Nazis. The Germans were afraid of catching diseases from the Jews. Their eyes oozed contagion. Their skin was covered with pustules. Her job was to clean them up so that they could work. Those who did not heal were gassed.

She started to cry. "Why was I given this burden?" she said, turning to look at Eichmann. The prosecutor asked the witness to enter the names of three people she treated into the court record. One was a 14-year-old girl who had been raped by a German officer. "She tried to kill herself," the nurse said, "with a rusty metal fork. When they brought her to me, she already had sepsis." Susan grasped her shoulders to try to prevent herself from shuddering.

It was horror after horror being reported over and over to the world. The Jews in the camps, the prosecutor said, had suffered extraordinary pain. No other people had ever experienced such torture. Rachel leaned over and whispered something to Ezra. Ezra leaned over and whispered something to Dina. Something was about to happen.

There had been a big debate at their last meeting. "We must not do anything," the shoemaker insisted. "Protest is treason," he said. "People who are convicted of treason are hanged!" He made a gesture showing a noose tightening on his neck. Rachel disagreed violently. "I clean toilets," she said, "but I hate my work. I used to work in a flower shop arranging bouquets. I think that we should all stand up and shout. Disturb the trial. Make a lot of noise! Who cares if we are arrested? What are we, cowards?"

The woman who took in laundry stood squarely in the middle. "I'm used to getting rid of stains and dirt," she said. "You have to do it slowly and carefully. If you do it too harshly, the spot becomes a hole!"

"Mild protests never work," Rachel said. Back and forth, one side, the other, and the middle. Finally, in desperation, they'd come up with a plan. They would stand up in unison. They would chant aloud in unison, telling the world about their suffering. They'd rehearsed it at the meeting. Ezra would start to stand first and they would follow his lead.

Now, here they were in Beit Ha'am. The moment had come. Ezra was perspiring heavily. Susan watched the beads of sweat dripping down his forehead. She reached for his hand, discovering that his fingers were cold and trembling. Bold, brave Ezra. How could that be? They'd talked so often about this moment—when all eyes would be focused on him and the Moroccans, when the plight of the Moroccans would become known to the world. Ezra squeezed her hand so hard that she felt a sharp pain. Not a word out of his mouth but fear in his eyes. It was hard for Susan to imagine Ezra afraid. He leaned on her when he started to stand up, and she could feel his knees buckling. Several of the Moroccans began to stand, watching him for their cues. Suddenly, though, Ezra shook his head, and fell back down on the wooden seat. Susan and the Moroccans followed his lead.

The chant that they'd rehearsed was never spoken. The chant that Ezra had crafted was never heard: "We are suffering, too. We live in *Eretz Yisrael* yet we are in pain. Moroccans are second-class citizens. We are living through our own Holocaust." Instead, they sat silent, mute, chanting the words to themselves, in increasing decibels. Louder silence, still louder silence.

The reporters were busy scribbling in their notepads and the news cameras were busy capturing the trial on tape. The guards were all on alert, the Moroccans' attempt to stand up seen as a warning of trouble to come. Three guards stood nearby. Then, three more joined them. Esther was afraid. She feared that her students would stage a full-scale rebellion. She clenched her teeth and waited.

But Ezra's head was hanging down, almost between his knees. Sunken, defeated, a balloon without air. The session was over and the audience was escorted out of the courtroom. Ezra, Rachel, and Susan walked out together, linking their arms. One of the guards touched Ezra's elbows. "I saw you start to stand up," he said. "You made the right decision. We would have handcuffed you and thrown you in jail for disturbing the peace."

"I was a coward," Ezra said to Susan. A tear was rolling down his cheek. "I thought that I had the courage but I didn't." Susan squeezed his hand. "Sometimes, sitting down is the right thing to do," she said.

After she spoke, she was angry with herself. She sounded like her father. He told her not to be a coward but at least once a week he warned her about being too brave.

Lecture Number 199: Being Brave Does Not Mean Making a Fool of Yourself.

Would you argue with your teacher over raising your grade?
Would you ride your bicycle with your eyes closed?
Would you walk on thin ice if a friend dared you to do so?

Susan recognized the photographer who had been at their meeting. "We meet again," he said, snapping a photo of her linked arm in arm with Ezra and Rachel. Then, turning to Ezra, with his tape recorder in hand, he asked, "There's a rumor that you were going to stage a protest at Beit Ha'am. Is that true?" Ezra didn't answer. Rachel, too, was silent.

But Susan could not keep quiet. Words poured out of her. "Who are you to question us?" she said. "We don't have to tell you what our plans were or weren't. Why don't you ask us about our grievances, about the quality of our life in Israel? Why don't you write about our unfulfilled dreams?"

Before she knew it, she was on dangerous ground.

"*Your* grievances," said a man nearby, who overheard her words. The words made him angry. "You're an American girl, a spoiled American girl. You ought to be ashamed of yourself," he said. Seconds later, an overripe tomato landed on her face, liquid dripping down her cheeks, seeds leaving her face speckled. The photographer raised his camera and caught Susan in shock, her eyes bulging, her teeth clenched. This was definitely not good. Her father watched the trial news diligently and she was sure that he would see this photo of his daughter being pelted by a tomato. He'd be furious.

How could a daughter of his be so disrespectful? What had he done wrong when he raised her? She could hear him debating with himself angrily. Pacing back and forth, brewing cup after cup of black coffee. Then, without a moment's hesitation, he would call Josh, his old law school buddy, who now lived in Tel Aviv. Josh would call Susan and read her the riot act. The message from her father: behave, or else NO MONEY.

When she looked to her right, Susan realized that Hannah Arendt was only a couple of feet away. "Miss America," Arendt called out, clearly speaking to her. "What are you doing here?" There was no time to answer as the police were now pushing to disperse the crowd that had gathered. Standing by the curb with its motor running was a waiting police van. Inside, Susan saw a homeless man she recognized. She often gave him a few *agorot*, careful to drop the coins into his hand without touching his filthy fingers.

He was screaming for water. *Mayim, Mayim*, he said. "It's too hot in here." The guard walked past him, pretending not to hear. The man cried again. "*Mayim Bevakasha*. Water, please. Have pity on me. I'm homeless. In Casablanca, I had a home and a family. It was small but it had a roof and a purple flowering bougainvillea vine that climbed over the roof of a side terrace. I would sit out there every morning and smoke my pipe. What has happened to me? Why am I living on the streets?" She imagined him in an embroidered blue and green tunic, patting the head of his favorite dog. Before him was a silver tray with tea and sweets.

They walked for about ten minutes without saying a word. Ezra was silent and it was impossible to read his feelings. Rachel kept wringing her fingers. She seemed sorry that she'd ever attended the meeting and her eyes were teary.

Susan didn't dare call her father, so she called Ruth. "I can't explain now," she said, "but we came close to getting in trouble at the Eichmann trial. Nothing bad happened, but it almost did. Close call. I left there so quickly that I forgot my pocketbook. The guard said that to get it back I have to go to the police station at the Russian Compound off of Jaffa Road. I need you to do that for me! Please! Can you meet me around the corner from the station? Bring along a paper and pencil so I can write a note authorizing you to pick up my handbag. I'm afraid to get it myself, just in case that New York photographer catches me on camera again. All I need is another photo of me in a New York newspaper and my father will explode."

Ruth came by taxi after having stopped at the bank to withdraw cash. Ruth's face was red and Susan could see that she was furious. "You shouldn't get involved in this stuff," she said. "It's bad, very bad business. There's no place for protest in this country. Haven't we suffered enough?" Sweat was dripping down her forehead. "What were you thinking?" she asked Susan. "I don't know why I came to rescue you. They should have arrested you and thrown you in jail."

The officer at the front door directed Ruth to a window where she handed in Susan's note and filled out a form for lost property. As she pushed it through the slot, the woman behind the glass partition let out a cry. "Ruth," she said. "It's Ruth. I recognized you immediately." She came running out, slamming the door shut as she entered the room. "I can't believe it. It's Ruth. Remember me? We had bunks across from each other at Mauthausen."

Ruth was trembling violently. Her hands shaking up and down. She was not able to speak. "Ruth," she said. "Do you remember me? I'm Bracha."

Still, not a word from Ruth. She stood frozen, paralyzed. She was avoiding eye contact and her head was tilted downward. "Ruth, Ruth, it doesn't matter anymore," Bracha said. "It isn't how we survived," Bracha said. "It's that we survived. Each day a test. I was fortunate because they needed me to repair their uniforms. You had no choice. You made the only decision you could. When I watched you sneak out at night, I felt sorry for you. Maybe you loved him. He was so handsome. Maybe you didn't and he just was a way to stay alive."

Ruth had covered her ears with her hands and she was shaking her head violently. She clutched Susan's pocketbook and ran out of the office and onto the street. Susan saw her and ran after her. She was running so fast that Susan could barely keep pace. She ran across the street against the light. A green truck almost hit her. The driver was screaming at her, "Crazy lady! Watch where you're going!"

She ran down another street, almost tripping on a crack in the sidewalk but just managing to right herself. She banged into a woman carrying a bag of apples and they scattered in every direction. She was desperate, frantic to get away.

Finally, exhausted, she ran into a small park and collapsed on a wooden bench. Susan found her there crying. "Go away," Ruth said as Susan approached. "You can't help me now."

A picture window shattered by a small stone. Cracks radiating outward until the glass collapsed. No words came out. Susan sat next to Ruth, finally deciding to put her arm around her shoulder. "You can trust me," she said.

"It's a horrible story," Ruth began. "I wanted to tell you earlier but I was afraid." She was so pale now, as if sunlight had never touched her skin.

"Mauthausen was brutal," Ruth said. "Every day, someone we knew disappeared. I had no real skills. I failed at my work in the sewing factory and the cook threw me out of the kitchen because I kept burning food. Pots boiled over on my watch. After a while, no one wanted to give me work. That was dangerous. If you were not valuable, you were gassed. Twice I was on the list but, at the last minute, my name was erased. I didn't know why.

"One evening, a German soldier came into the barracks and called my name. I recognized him from the supply warehouse. His name was Walter Kruck. He ordered me to go with him. His car was outside. He told me to sit in the back seat. He drove to the camp gate, he presented his ID, and then drove several miles until we came to a house in the countryside.

"As I learned later, it was not his house. No one was home and we sat in the parlor, in the dim light. He told me that he was married and that he had two young daughters, Elsie, age six, and Renate, age eight. He smiled when he mentioned his daughters' names. Then, he opened his wallet and held their pictures up in the air for me to see. "Beautiful, sweet girls," he said. Originally from Munich, the family had moved to his parents' country house near Karlsfeld during the 1930s. He saw them now once a month for a long weekend.

"My knees were hitting each other, making a clicking noise. I didn't know why he had taken me there and I was afraid. The Nazis had their laws prohibiting sexual relations between Jews and

Aryans but we girls knew better. There was a brothel at Mauthausen, where non-Jewish women worked but that didn't stop camp officers from sexually abusing Jews. We girls in the barracks, we were prey for the soldiers. My friend Faigel told me how one of them raped her in the laundry room. She showed up at lunch with a black eye and a cheek that was beginning to swell. None of us said a word. We sat there slurping our watery soup as the soldiers looked on.

"Two weeks later, she woke in the middle of the night. She was reliving the brutal rape. She told us how he had shoved her into a closet, unbuttoned her dress and dropped his pants. He threw her against the wall and put his hand over her mouth. He told her not to cry out or he would slit her throat. Within seconds, his erect penis was inside. She felt pain as if her insides were tearing apart. Then, he motioned for her to get dressed and return to work. We heard these stories often. Each one was slightly different but our fear was palpable. I was thinking of Faigel's brutal attack when Kruck started to speak.

"His voice was calm and soothing. 'You want to live,' he said. 'Don't you? I can make that happen. Without my protection, it will only be a matter of time before you're beaten, or raped, or killed. I am Karl Bregner's very good friend. We trained together and I can count on his loyalty. If I ask a favor, he will do it.'

"He got up from his chair and joined me on the couch. He put his arm around me and began to stroke the back of my neck with his fingers. 'We can make a little arrangement, can't we?' he said. He pulled me toward him and kissed me hard."

Ruth started to cry. "I was a virgin. I knew nothing. Husbands and wives made babies. Lovers held hands. 'I don't want to force you, Ruth,' he said, as he led me to the bedroom. 'You have free will. You can say no.'"

But could she? Free will, to Ruth those were false words. Once, there were visitors scheduled from the Red Cross. They were marched through the lunchroom where the prisoners were dining on chicken stew and lentil soup, a large roll with butter on every plate. It had been months, years, since they'd seen such food. Before their arrival, the guards warned them: don't gobble the food down. Act like it's normal. Acting, that was what she was being asked to do. Acting as if she had free will and could actually turn him down, tell him no, I will not be your mistress, not now and not ever.

Ruth's hands were trembling and she was looking off into the distance away from Susan. She could not tell this story looking directly into Susan's eyes.

"Then, he raped me. He would not, of course, call it rape. We'd discussed the matter. We had an agreement. My silence translated as yes, as permission. Yes, I will do anything you want me to do to stay alive. I closed my eyes and my body felt like it belonged to someone else. This was not my body he was entering, banging against me ferociously. An earthquake that lasted too long, minutes rather than seconds. His sweat dripping on my chest. I was too numb to sweat, too frozen.

"There was no fire in me and definitely no feeling. When it was over, he asked me if it felt good. I lied and nodded yes. That made him happy. He slapped me on the back, the sort of great-news-old-chap slap that men seem to give one another, told me to get dressed, and drove me back to my barracks.

"'No talking about this, remember,' he said during the drive. 'If you say one word, the arrangement is over.'

"Bregner had arranged every detail. Usually, you were grilled entering and leaving the barracks. The guards would enjoy running their fingers over the women's breasts to make sure that they were not carrying weapons. But no one touched me this time. No one asked where I had been and why. The guard outside the door let me in without one word. I tiptoed down the aisle in the dark, felt for my bunk bed and collapsed.

"After that, I saw him on Monday and Thursday nights, sometimes on weekends, too. When three women near me disappeared late one afternoon, never to return, the girls thought we were all doomed. The next day, three more vanished. But my name was never called. They all said that I was lucky."

She said the word "lucky" with such sorrow in her voice. Susan wanted to comfort her. But she didn't really know how. Once, when a boyfriend jilted her best friend, Susan tried to lessen the pain. She told her friend that the fellow hadn't deserved her, that she was better off without him. Her comfort was a disaster. Her friend despised it. "He did deserve me," she insisted. "We deserved each other. How do you know? You have no right to comment on my life!"

She remembered that moment now. Maybe it was best not to try to console Ruth since consolation often backfired. Still, despite herself, words came out of her mouth: "You did what you had to do to live," she told Ruth. "You wanted to live!"

Ruth wasn't listening. She hadn't finished telling her story, the deep secret that she'd buried for nearly 20 years. Now, with the Eichmann trial blasting on the radio, she'd begun to dream about him again, she said.

"In my dreams, everything is different. Walter is a passionate lover, a man whose touch thrills me. Just being near him excites me. I am not the unwilling mistress of a German officer. Rather, I'm a young woman in love with a handsome soldier in a perfect uniform, his body muscular and his skin soft. I can't wait for him to arrive. I count the days. I count the hours.

"Where do these happy dreams come from? Why am I dreaming them?" Ruth spoke softly now. "I know the truth, but it's too much to bear. I know what would have happened if I'd resisted but I want it to be a fairy tale. Perhaps I read too many children's books when I was a girl. The heroine was a princess with golden curls, dressed in a pink ball gown. In her hair, a diamond tiara; on her feet, sparkling silver slippers. She was dancing a waltz with her handsome prince. When I was little, I remember asking my mother to read the story to me over and over again. 'You're our little princess,' my mother would say. 'I promise you that we will dance at your wedding.'"

As she said the word "wedding," Ruth's fingers curled into a fist and she pounded her chest. It reminded Susan of asking for forgiveness during the Yom Kippur service. Over and over again, for each sin, a pound on the chest, a rhythmic plea to God. In a trance, Ruth pounding her chest, her eyes closed.

"Of course, there was no wedding," she said. "No mother. No father. No picture books. No adoring prince. Nothing left from my childhood. Just Walter in his German soldier's uniform and me in my flimsy cotton dress and torn green sweater, a present from Walter so that I would not shiver in the cold. On my feet, worn leather shoes that Walter had managed to steal to replace the shoes, two sizes too small, that I'd been given when I entered the camp." She was shaking her head back and forth. "He was a Nazi. I was a Jew. But he gave me shoes."

Ruth began to sob. "There," she said, "I've confessed." She looked up at Susan, startled by her own words. "I'm guilty. Somehow, I must have loved him," she said. "I feared him. I hated him. I needed him to survive. But, in my dreams, he is not a rapist. He is not a man I fear. In my dreams, he is my lover and I am his love, a young woman wrapped in his warm arms." She reached into her pocketbook and took out her wallet. Then, she carefully took out an old photograph. There were four men in the photo, three of them dressed in German uniforms. She put her fingers on the faces, identifying each one. "That's Bregner," she said. "He had the highest rank. He was the leader. They were always hanging out together. That's Walter Kruck," she said, her finger caressing his cheek.

The third man, Ruth said, was Heinrich Sprieger. He was loud and bossy and he drank too much beer. Bregner was always trying to get him to behave. Then, she pointed to the last face: "That's Martin Specht, Bregner's assistant. You never saw one of them without the other," she said.

It was a faded photograph with several deep creases that obscured their faces, making it hard to see their eyes and noses. She had made the mistake of folding it when she hid it in her wallet. Susan took the photo from her and held it close. Sprieger was the shortest of the three men. The others were fairly tall, about the same height. They were wearing military-style peaked caps which dipped down on their foreheads, making it impossible to see their hairlines.

"You asked me once if I knew anyone else who might have known Bregner but I was afraid to tell you that I did," Ruth said. "If I did, then you'd know about Walter." Sprieger was too short. Kruck was Ruth's lover. If one of them were Bregner's lover, it had to be Specht.

"What did you know about him?" Susan asked Ruth, her finger resting on Specht's face. Her heart was racing, her hands were trembling, her knees were knocking together.

"Specht was always in the supply warehouse," Ruth said, admitting that she'd been in the warehouse more often than she'd said previously. "When I showed up early in the morning, he was already there, taking inventory in the back room. He ate his lunch there, too, since he was a civilian. He always kept to himself. I never saw him talking to anyone except Bregner," she said.

"The Allies were on the offensive," Ruth continued, "and in the barracks we heard rumors that the Germans were on the run. People were still disappearing and the smoke from the crematorium was white and thick. Anna, my best friend, had a bad cough and she was sent to the infirmary. One evening, the guard told us that Anna had died. A woman who returned from the infirmary reported that Anna's cough had gotten worse and they'd marched her off to the gas chambers.

"Death was still happening in the midst of our hope for liberation. One Thursday night, when we were lying in bed, Kruck surprised me," Ruth said. "We may have to surrender. Bregner says it could happen within four or five weeks." His face was very serious. He lit a cigarette and exhaled smoke rings, watching them dissipate in the air. "We will never let ourselves be taken prisoner," he told me.

"Evidently, the four of them had a plan. They would commit suicide. Bregner had a friend in the medical dispensary who'd given him cyanide capsules for the three of them: Bregner, Kruck, and Sprieger. But Martin Specht, ah, that was another story. That was the moment when Walter told me the truth about Specht. That was when I learned that Bregner and Specht were lovers. No one knew. Not even Sprieger. Walter told me that he found out by accident.

"Once, having left his helmet at the house, he drove back there to pick it up. It was almost midnight and he tiptoed in, not wanting to wake Bregner who'd told him that he was going there for the weekend.

"When he opened the bedroom door, Bregner sat up in bed, startled. Next to him, still sound asleep, was Specht. From what Walter could see, they were naked. Bregner put his fingers to his mouth, jumped out of bed, slid into his pants and motioned for Walter to move out to the porch.

"'You're not surprised, are you?' he asked Walter. 'You knew, right?'"

"'I just nodded. I didn't really know,' Walter told me, but he suspected something. Specht kept a low profile but Walter noticed that he blushed easily under Bregner's gaze. When the Allies were closing in on the camp, Bregner was worried. 'I can't let him die,' he told Walter. 'I have to save him.'

"Specht wanted to die with him. They would swallow the cyanide in unison and be found together, two lovers embracing each other. 'He is my soul,' Bregner said to Walter. 'He must live.'"

Ruth began to cry uncontrollably. "I can still feel his strong arms around me," she said. "He was hiding me in the bulrushes. Saving me from the Nazis. I was floating in the river, like baby Moses saved from the Egyptians." Ruth's eyes lit up when she said the name Moses, as if she was in prayer, a rapt child sitting in her Hebrew school class as her teacher recounted the story.

"And, there was Bregner, so handsome and so powerful," Ruth said. "In my dreams I danced with him. He held me close, lifting a stray curl of hair on my neck and whispering that I was beautiful. I kept my eyes steady on him, adoringly, but I was afraid. All he had to say was one word and I would be gassed."

Ruth reached for a cigarette and lit it, inhaling deeply. Suddenly, she sat up, startled. "I just remembered something," she said, barely able to spit the words out. "When Walter told me about the final plan to save Specht, he said that Bregner was giving him a new identity as a Jew. I feel so stupid. I forgot all about it until right now," Ruth said. "A new name." She paused for a moment and then continued. "He told me that Specht had chosen his own new name, Menachem Kreinen. It struck me as odd because I had a cousin named Menachem Kramer, almost the same."

Her confessions revealed, Ruth was eager to finish the story now. "When the allies liberated Mauthausen on May 5, 1945, they rounded up all of the Germans at the camp. I was told that they had found the bodies of Bregner, Sprieger, and Kruck. No one knew what happened to Specht." Ruth reached into her bag and took out a round metal pill box. Then, she swallowed two tiny white pills without water. "My heart pills," she said, patting her chest.

Susan's heart was racing now, faster and faster, thumping in her chest. Drumbeats. Loud. Louder. Loudest. Out of control. Impossible. Unbelievable. How could this be? Her sidekick Ruth, her sleuthing companion in the search for Yakov, providing her with the missing link. Meeting Ruth was *bashert*.

Bashert. That was the Yiddish word for something that is destined to happen, for people you are meant to meet, often a future husband or wife. They were preordained by God. Sent from above. All you had to do was lower your head, pay respect, follow the rules and your *Bashert* would appear. Everything that was meant to be, would be.

Susan and her father disagreed on this. She was sure that you shaped your own fate. He was sure that you did and you didn't. Above human will was God's will. God directing his chosen people. God giving the Jews Israel after the Holocaust.

"Do you believe in fate?" Susan asked after Ruth finished speaking. Susan thought that it was phony, an excuse for a contrived phenomenon—for things that were meant to be, for coincidences that weren't random.

"I'm not so sure, now," she said. "We met for a reason. It was no accident that I met you in the coffee shop. It was no accident that we became friends. There are thousands of survivors in Israel, and I met you. Together we were able to solve the puzzle."

Susan took out a blank piece of paper and she wrote three names on it: Yakov Reich, Martin Specht, and Menachem Kreinen. Then, she added arrows. "You knew him as Martin Specht, a German worker," she told Ruth. "But all of these men were the same man. He was a Jew who became a German who became a Jew. He was my Uncle Yakov. For most of his life, he kept a larger secret. He was a homosexual who didn't fit in the shtetl of Rozwadów and who may still be alive, somewhere, hiding from his past."

Ruth looked at her in amazement. "We were so close to each other," she said, "our secrets almost touched." She reached out her hand for Susan's. They sat there for a few moments in silence holding hands. An American girl and a Holocaust survivor, two Jewish women whose lives had been so different, yet connected by fate.

"What are you going to tell your father?" Ruth asked. "Will you tell him the truth?"

Susan hadn't yet decided what she was going to say to him. She was sure that he would call soon, having seen her photo with Ezra and Rachel outside Beit Ha'am. Her bold comments would have been perfect for a segment of the evening news wrap-up, one of his favorite shows. Who knows, she might have even made Page Ten of the *New York Post*. It didn't take much to imagine the headline to the story: *American Girl Spews Venom Outside of Eichmann Trial*. The opinion piece would be filled with the writer's venom. How dare these ignorant people pollute sacred ground?

When she got back to the apartment, she discovered she was right. There was a message from her father tacked to her bedroom door: "Call back," he said, "even if it's the middle of the night." She looked at her watch. It was morning in New York. She took the bus to the post office where she could make an international call and gave the operator his direct line. He picked up on the second ring.

"Are you crazy or something," he said, without saying hello. She knew that angry voice. His voice always moved up to a higher pitch when he was excited. "I didn't send you to Israel to get into trouble." His breathing was fast and she hadn't the faintest idea how she would appease him.

She decided that it was best to let him rant.

"What's going on?" he continued. In the background, she could hear the radio. It was faint but she heard the name Eichmann repeated several times.

"You deserve to go to jail," her father said. Then, as if reconsidering his own words, he added, "I would let you rot there if you weren't my own daughter! Maybe being in prison will set you straight."

While he was shouting at her, Susan rifled through her mail. She'd finally managed to get an appointment with a researcher from Yad Vashem. There had been a one-month wait list. The letter said that she should bring all documentation to their central office on Tuesday afternoon. She wasn't sure what help they could give her now, especially since she was convinced that Uncle Yakov had survived.

She shifted the phone closer to her ear and her father's

screaming became louder. "Are you still there? Are you listening to me?" he asked.

"I'm listening. I'm listening," she shouted. "Now, it's your turn to listen." She was determined to get him to stop. Her father could be stubborn but she could be stubborn, too. She remembered his harsh words about her red lipstick. *That's for whores,* he'd said, marching out of the kitchen.

But he was more than old-fashioned, and Susan understood that. He was principled in a sort of old-school way. There was no blurring right and wrong. There was no gray. There was black and white and just about nothing in between.

"Are you listening?" Susan asked her father this time. She could hear his breathing, so thankfully he hadn't hung up. She was thinking on her feet now, without really having a plan. He was so logical that one slip in the wrong direction would crush her argument.

"Dad," she said, "I know you love Israel but life here isn't easy, especially for new immigrants. I go to school with them in the ulpan and they're struggling. There's so much discrimination against them here. Their skin is dark and no matter how intelligent they are, they're considered inferior because they're not from Europe." Susan was surprised that he hadn't interrupted her.

"They work cleaning toilets and doing construction for almost no money. They live in apartments with black mold and missing windows. Israel is poor but, whatever wealth there is, it's not distributed evenly. I joined the Moroccans because you taught me to stand up for justice."

That was it. The word "justice" triggered a torrent of anger. "You're confusing justice with due process," he said, jumping into the conversation. "Of course, they deserve decent jobs and housing. But who said they should dare to raise their voices at the Eichmann trial? Thank God, you saw the light and backed down."

They'd come to the hard part, the Eichmann trial. That was sacred ground to him, a holy place. The words spoken there were never to be forgotten. He loved those moments: Lincoln delivering the Gettysburg address, FDR's first inaugural address to the American people in 1933. Whenever something frightened her, when she faced the bully down the street who threw rocks and commanded his black German Shepherd to growl at her as she made her way to the school bus, her father would always quote FDR's words: "The only thing we have to fear is fear itself."

She jumped into the fire. "Everyone is consumed with the Eichmann trial," she said. "The radio announcers blast the summaries on the news, the newspapers are filled with the testimony of guards and survivors. There's not one word about the immigrants. They're left out." There, she had finally said it. Strong words.

Her father stopped her. "I get it," he said. "But you chose the wrong time and place to make noise." Then, abruptly, he shifted the conversation to Yakov. "Have you found any new clues?"

Before she made the call, she'd debated what to tell him. Reporting that Yakov had a male Nazi lover would not go over well with her father. She didn't even think he would believe it. But if he did, he would be angry and sad and embarrassed.

Her father played golf with his buddies, bringing home white scorecards marked in pencil from their Saturday games and regaling her with stories about drives that landed in traps and holes in one. "Traps? Why put them there? Not fair," Susan would always say. Her dad and his friends were men who shared tips about the stock market and boasted about their wives and children. She couldn't imagine one of them having a male lover.

She decided to tell him that so far, she'd made no progress in finding Yakov. She'd interviewed a few survivors from Rozwadów and none of them knew what happened to him after the last roundup of Jews there. She was still pursuing new clues.

Her father sighed. "Keep at it," he said. "I loved him so much. Forget this immigrant protest business and keep looking into your uncle's story. That would make me happy."

They ended the conversation on a quiet note although after she hung up, Susan felt anxious. She'd lied to her father, not for the first time, of course. She'd lied about curfew when she was younger and about hanging out in the basements of friends whose parents were card-carrying Communists. Once, when she was careless, she brought home an issue of the *Daily Worker* and he'd challenged her: "Where did you get this?" he asked. She lied and said that she found it on a table in the library. If she'd told the truth, she would have been banished from her friend's house forever.

This lie though, felt different. He'd sent her there on a quest for the truth about his brother. How had he died and where? What was his life like after 1920? She didn't exactly know why but this lie felt huge, not merely a big lump in the throat but a paralysis of her entire body. Her legs were stiff. Her arms were heavy. She couldn't turn her head from side to side. It wasn't just about disappointing her father. It was, she felt, about betraying Yakov's memory. He'd kept his life a secret.

Later in the evening, she took a cold shower and stood before the broken mirror combing out the knots in her curly hair. She knew better than to tug at them. The best technique was holding your hair at the top with one hand, so that you didn't feel the pain. Instead, here she was causing pain, dragging the comb relentlessly downward through her tangled hair. The cold water and the pain in her head induced suffering, reminded her of the harsh life of Jews in the camps. It was suffering that Yakov, as a German camp worker, had most probably not experienced. His showers were always hot.

7

She wrapped a ragged towel around her hair and, shivering, returned to her bedroom. About ten minutes later, she heard Ezra's familiar double knock on her window: a soft tap followed by a loud knock. In English class, her teacher wrote lines of Robert Frost's verse on the blackboard and taught the students how to scan them. She remembered: "Whose woods these are, I think I know. His house is in the village though. He will not see me stopping here, To watch his woods fill up with snow." Why in heaven's name was the word *whose* unstressed? Susan thought that it was the most important. *Dah-dum-dah-dum-dah-dum.*

Ezra was still wearing the clothing that he had on earlier in the day. "I'm exhausted," he said, collapsing on her bed. He was angry with himself for backing down. "What a coward I turned out to be!" he said. "All of my words. They were just bluster."

Susan tried to comfort him. "We never know how we're going to act until we're actually in a situation," she said. "In my dreams, they grilled me over and over again. They wanted to know who was behind the event and what their ulterior motives were. I kept saying that you were just a group of Moroccan immigrants who wanted your voice to be heard, but they didn't believe me. They told me that I was covering up the truth and that they would not release me until I stopped lying. Then, I woke up."

The tomato in the face outside Beit Ha'am and the man's harsh words really stung her. He saw her as a misguided American college girl who'd found a cause without really understanding what was going on. "Who am I to speak for you?" Susan asked Ezra. "A spoiled American brat who gets pretty much everything she wants if she complains loud enough.

"When I realized that I'd left my handbag in Beit Ha'am, I called Ruth to retrieve it for me from the police station. It turned out to be a *big* event because the woman behind the counter recognized Ruth."

For a moment, Susan hesitated. She was reluctant to say more. Yakov and the Holocaust were not Ezra's favorite subjects. Swallowing a thick gob of saliva that felt stuck on her tongue, she forced herself to continue. Soon, the story was pouring out of her, water streaming from a deep well, unstoppable. "You're not going to believe this," Susan said, trying her best to prepare Ezra for what was coming. "But it turns out that Ruth was the mistress of a Nazi named Walter Kruck and Walter's boss was Karl Bregner. And"—Susan let out a big sigh—"Bregner's secret lover was Martin Specht, who worked at the camp as a German but was really my Uncle Yakov." By the time she finished speaking, Susan was out of breath.

If it had been a lecture, Susan would have made a list, just to get the facts straight. Who was with whom and why. A jumble of names and identities. But this was different.

Ezra put his hands on his head and he began to sigh. After a few seconds, his sigh became more of a wailing sound, a moan. "Our rabbi in Morocco warned us teenage boys to stay away from those men," he said. "They hung out in the doorways of little hotels, in the back alleyways. In the 1950s, Moroccan cities were a haven for homosexual men, especially tourists from America and Britain who fled harassment in their own countries."

Once, Ezra told Susan, his friend Sammy had been coming home late at night, walking through the Casbah, when he felt an arm on his shoulder. "You're a very handsome boy," the man said to him, flashing several francs in his face. Sammy ran, of course. "He never told his parents," Ezra said, "but he told me." He nodded his head up and down, for a moment looking like a young man in a prayer shawl davening for forgiveness on Yom Kippur evening.

"Are you sure?" he said. "It's probably just a rumor, a story made up to cover up some other story."

After a few seconds of silence, Ezra said, "Do you think he's still alive?"

"I don't know," Susan answered. "But I do know that he was liberated under the name Menachem Kreinen. Bregner committed suicide but he saved Yakov. Now, I have to search for Kreinen."

"We're so trapped by our past," Ezra said to Susan, trying to shift their talk to the future. His face was haggard and she could see that he was worn out. "There has to be something tangible to work for, beyond the Holocaust and the protests," he said. "The only way to get the Israelis to help us is if it makes sense for them to do so."

Ezra was back to his talk of founding a new kibbutz for the Moroccans. They had spoken about it often. The Moroccans would get a piece of barren land, like the old settlers in 1920s Palestine, and make it green. Susan spoke of her cousin up north and his decades of work there transforming the land. She didn't agree with Ezra about founding a new kibbutz. "Farming is brutal work," Susan said, picturing Cousin Hershel bent over his hoe in a field of weeds as he swatted mosquitos. It was 1960, not 1920, and already the bloom seemed to be off the rose as far as kibbutzim were concerned. "You need a life in a city," Susan said. "In Tel Aviv or Jerusalem. Why not start up an organization that would put pressure on the smaller political parties? It's the right time for the Moroccans to do this."

"Not possible yet," Ezra said. "Bringing together immigrants from different countries, especially the Yemenites and the

Moroccans, that would be tough," he said. He told Susan that many of them would still vote for the Herut party because they believed that it supported their protest against the racism they experienced when dealing with government institutions or quasi-public ones like The Jewish Agency. Others were more forgiving, deeming the discrimination more paternalism than racism. "My Moroccan friend Henri says that they think like the families they left behind," Ezra said.

"Organizing is a therapeutic enterprise," Susan said, her voice rising in passion. "It's a beginning, a way to share problems and, hopefully, bring about solutions." Then, throwing her arms up in the air in a kind of eureka gesture, she let out a sound that was halfway between a squeal and a cry. "I've got the perfect name for the group. Uru Marokayim, or UM, which in English would be *Wake Up Moroccans*. That name will force folks to think about your presence *and* your absence in Israeli society."

She was really getting into it now, not as an outsider but as someone with a future in Israel. Here was the old rebellious Susan. Argumentative Susan. The young woman who took on her father and rejected the path of her high school friends. She wasn't a Zionist, but she *was* sort of, increasingly feeling that the Holocaust had been her Holocaust, too, that being an American Jew didn't separate her entirely from Ruth or Ezra.

Ezra wasn't quite ready to give up the idea of physical confrontations, though. "There's nothing more satisfying," he said, "than punching the enemy in the eye. A one-two jab and they're down on the floor." Then, remembering how he'd started to stand up but instead sat down in Beit Ha'Am, he said, "*Wake Up Moroccans* sounds like a good idea. When we build a house, we always follow a construction drawing. But for now, we want to avoid physical confrontation. Moroccan Jews rioted in Wadi Salib just two years ago after a Moroccan Jew was shot and wounded by police during a brawl. The newspapers covered the Moroccans' economic plight but not much was accomplished. It's time to try political action."

"Right," Susan said. "Let's move on." Then, she offered to write up a little description that they would give out at the ulpan. They could meet in the social room of the Sephardi synagogue.

She lay on the bed next to Ezra, who threw one arm over her but who was too tired to do more. He fell asleep instantly, curling up in a fetal position and snoring. She rolled him over, shifting his position slightly, and the snoring stopped. Then, she was unable to fall asleep. She started to count people and that was a big mistake. There was Ruth, sitting on the bench weeping about Walter. There was her father, frustrated about her rebellious words outside the trial. There was Ezra shouting for justice. And there was Yakov, from the grave or from who-knows-where, pleading with her to stop looking for him.

She tried counting sheep but only made it to 20 before she became disinterested. She took out a blank sheet of writing paper and began a list. At the top of the paper, she wrote "UM." Beneath it, the words "Mission Statement." Organizations always had mission statements. She'd once seen papers on her father's office desk. He was editing the mission statement of the Rozwadówer *Landsmanshaft*, the immigrant society named after his birthplace. At one time, he'd even been their president. They had four goals and they spelled them out on the first page of the document:

1. To maintain close ties with *landsleit* in the U.S. and abroad
2. To help the needy through loans
3. To contribute to major Jewish charities
4. To participate in the financial efforts to sustain the Israeli economy by purchasing Israel bonds

Her dad had crossed out several of the verbs, replacing them with verbs of his own. He had x'd out "retain" and substituted "maintain," and deleted the verb "lead," replacing it with "participate in." That last change struck Susan as so typical of her father. He preferred taking a back seat instead of standing on a podium. Even when he was in charge, he was the puppeteer standing behind the scrim curtain.

UM's mission was much less clear. She began a draft and wrote six words in block letters:

Purpose

Promise

Potential

Power

Privilege

Prejudice

Then, she crossed out the last three. Who was *she* to tell the Moroccans what they needed or wanted? Ridiculous! An American girl writing a mission statement for Moroccans!

I: We would like to see the creation of a new Center for Moroccan Immigrants, completely separate from the Israeli Bureau of Immigration. This Center will have four divisions.

Division 1 will focus on jobs. It will authorize studies on job opportunities and investigate reports of job discrimination.

Division 2 will focus on housing. It will provide an up-to-date list of apartments that are for rent and sale, listing current rents. It will ensure that landlords cannot refuse to rent apartments to tenants because of the color of their skin or their economic status.

Division 3 will focus on education, providing special schools for immigrant children and adults.

Division 4 will handle all other social services, especially health-related issues.

Susan looked at her list and crumpled it up into a ball. It struck her as rigid and pompous. It was impossible for an outsider to write such a document. Ezra would have to draft it. She looked over and saw that Ezra was tossing in his sleep, shifting from side to side, his long body curled into an arc. Several times, he mumbled something. She moved closer to him to decipher the words but could not figure out what he was saying. Only one word was clear: mama. He said "mama" four or five times, like a bell tolling. Mama, where are you when I need you? Mama, why am I here so far from home?

She bent down and kissed his forehead, trying to console him and trying not to wake him. He opened his eyes and pulled her toward him, struggling to throw off the quilt. She put her index finger against his lips. "Sleep, *Motek*," she said. "Sleep." He closed his eyes again and shifted to his left side, his breathing heavy. She lay down on the bed, trying to keep a distance between them. Falling asleep was not easy. Her mind was like a movie projector with images jumping one after another: her father reading his newspaper at the kitchen table; Esther, chalk in hand, by the blackboard; the guard in the supermarket with his Uzi. She'd almost fallen asleep when he touched her shoulder, rolling her toward him. Without a word, she felt him hard against her, then inside her. What protest? There was only the sound of their moans in the darkness.

Before it was light, he left, whispering in her ear, *Motek, Motek*. It was the word of endearment that you heard on the street. Sweet one. Like a piece of candy unwrapped and savored.

Later that afternoon, they saw one another at the ulpan. Susan was dreading Esther's class. There would be a reprisal, she was sure. Hawk-like Esther had seen Ezra start to stand up. And even though nothing had happened, she would feel personally humiliated.

Susan was right. Esther's face was red and the skin around her eyes was puffy. Her nostrils were flared and she looked mean. Susan was sure that she'd come up with a harsh punishment. When the class was seated, she walked back and forth in the aisles, like an animal circling its prey.

"You can't imagine how I feel," she said, her voice stern and unrelenting. Rachel blew her nose several times loudly. To Susan it sounded like Joshua's trumpet marching around the City of Jericho. *Who would fall now?* she asked herself. *What walls would collapse?*

"I know what you were planning to do. The whole bunch of you. You're a disgrace!" Esther continued, "You should all be ashamed of yourselves. You do not deserve to be citizens of Israel!" She'd written down notes which she could barely hold, her fingers trembling. "If I had the power, I would revoke your citizenship. I thought about writing a letter of demerit to place in each of your files, but I realize that my power is limited. The truth is that you deserve to be sent back to where you came from. How would you like that?" Her eyes were focused on Ezra. "You're the worst of the lot," she said. "You deserve to rot in hell." Then she stuffed her notes into her briefcase. "I quit. I refuse to teach you anymore. They will be assigning a new teacher for you," she added. "I hope that he has better luck."

She slammed the door and left. Within a few seconds, the sound of her footsteps disappeared.

Rachel was worried. She wanted to know what a letter of demerit meant. If her boss saw such a letter, she would be fired. She hated her cleaning job, but was grateful to have work. Several of her friends were unemployed. "Don't worry," Ezra said to the class. "Nothing happened."

They sat in silence, afraid to move. After a few minutes, the classroom door opened and a gray-haired man entered. He had the posture of a soldier. Susan imagined him as a young man, with an Uzi slung over his shoulder, policing the border, wind ruffling through his military crew cut. He looked like a man who rarely smiled and never laughed.

There was no good morning. "I am Micha Herzog," he said, "Esther's replacement." He'd prepared his speech carefully, "In this class, you will all follow the rules. There will be no exceptions. If you are late twice, it will count as an absence. If you are absent three times, I will drop you from the class. If I drop you from the class, that notation will go on your employment record with The

Jewish Agency. To get work, you need a certificate to prove that you have passed." He looked up over his reading classes and asked, "Do you understand me?"

On the street below, an ambulance siren was wailing. Caught in traffic, it was stuck on the corner right below the ulpan. Its sound drowned out his words. Someone was fighting to live, strapped to a stretcher, face covered with an oxygen mask. Susan looked around her. Micha Herzog's stern words frightened the other students in the room. They were fighting for their lives too, for money, for jobs, for apartments in this strange new land where they found themselves on the bottom rung of the ladder.

He passed out an attendance sheet and began the lesson. Today's work was grammar, *deekduk*, and they were to conjugate reflexive verbs. He pointed to Ezra and said, "Conjugate the verb 'to embarrass.'" Ezra stumbled twice. Professor Herzog stopped him and called on Rachel, who conjugated it correctly. Then, he wrote five reflexive verbs on the blackboard and asked them to conjugate them.

He was rubbing salt in their wounds, this new soldier-teacher. Each verb had been carefully selected. Each assignment was designed to whip them into submission, like Pharaoh beating the backs of the Jewish slaves as they built the pyramids. "Take this! Take that! Behave! Or I will kill your firstborn!"

When they left the ulpan, Susan told Ezra about her attempt to write the UM mission statement. "I tried several times," she said. "I tore up three drafts."

Once, he told her, he'd tried to write an essay on the effects of the Holocaust but it, too, was a failure. "I just couldn't write about the consequences of the death camps and the psyches of survivors. They were foreign to me, a man who'd grown up in Casablanca, as foreign as heavy snow in the winter and dense forests of evergreen trees."

After class, Ezra told Susan he was convinced that forming UM was the right step. "The timing is right!" he said. A political pressure group with a social action platform was exactly what was needed. "Once we have the numbers we need—a couple thousand members—the Ashkenazim will have to collaborate with or, at the very least, listen to us." The plan was to create a sign-up sheet and give it to the women to circulate in the playgrounds, at the schools, and in the Machane Yehuda market. "It won't take long before people become passionate about *Wake Up Moroccans*," he said.

They were sitting in a run-down café near the ulpan, drinking tea from scratched glasses, listening to the radio. The news from the trial was especially grim. A survivor had fainted on the stand. The prosecutor had asked her to describe her family. She spoke of her parents and grandmother and of her husband and their two daughters, aged three and five. They'd been close-knit, always eating in each other's homes. The girls often sat on their grandmother's lap, stroking her soft skin.

One by one the Nazis killed them, the woman said. First, her grandmother was selected because she was old. Then her parents, who arrived in Auschwitz healthy, but caught bronchitis. Next to succumb was her husband, young and strong, nothing wrong with him. One day he fell and injured his leg. It wouldn't stop bleeding and it became infected. The doctors said that to save his life they'd have to amputate it. But they gassed him instead.

She was weeping now, barely able to finish relating the bitter end of her story. Since she worked in the nursery, taking care of Jewish children, she saw her daughters every day. One morning, a female guard showed up with the order to take all the kids on a hike. The kids cried. Her children tugged at her hands, reluctant to leave. They would be back in an hour, the guard said. When the woman asked if she should prepare lunch, she was told, no.

The children were all shot, their bodies dumped in a ditch, and she was left alone. "I wanted to kill myself," she told the prosecutor, "but I had no weapon. I prayed for a sharp knife or for poison." As she said the word "poison," there was a thumping sound, followed by commotion and many voices. She fainted, slipping off her chair and landing, a dead weight, on the floor. A soldier brought smelling salts; the announcer reported that they would call a 15-minute recess. Susan squeezed Ezra's hand hard. For once, he seemed moved by the testimony.

"Too much pain for one person," was all he said. He had tears in his eyes.

On Tuesday, Susan traveled to Yad Vashem for her appointment with a researcher. There were a million forms to fill out. She hated that. Especially daunting was the Shoah Survivors and Refugees Registration Form. There was a long list of questions to answer about the missing person:

What was your profession?
Where was your wartime residence before deportation?
Did you ever live in a ghetto?
Were you ever in a camp?
Where and when were you liberated?

Below these questions was an asterisk and a sentence in bold letters: "If the survivor/refugee is no longer alive, please fill in the following questions about his place and date of death, if known." An addendum asked her to list all relatives who had perished in the Holocaust.

Impossible! Susan couldn't begin to fill that out. She didn't really know relatives on her mother's side. They were such a small family. She'd been told, though, that most of them never made it to America, that they perished in the camps. A distant cousin, who hid out in Lvov and survived, had written a memoir, translated from Yiddish to English. At the back of the book, there were eight pages listing the names of those who perished. Susan hadn't recognized any of them.

Because they left in 1920, her father's immediate family survived, all except Yakov. Next to his name on the list, Susan wrote: He was born in Rozwadów. We believe that he was sent to Mauthausen. After that, I believe that he had two other names, Martin Specht and Menachem Kreinen. The second sheet asked for detailed family background information. Susan filled out what she could. When she looked over the paper, there were many blanks.

She was given a number and sent to a large waiting room filled with hard wooden benches, low to the ground as if one were sitting on a Shiva box in mourning. No one said the experience was going to be comfortable. There were no soft cushions, no boxes of tissues, and no couches on which to lie down and tell your story to a shrink. It was all about forms and facts. Things were cut and dry. If you were lucky, they would put your relative on their search list.

Just one hour later, a thin fellow with a few wisps of gray hair called her name. He told her to follow him. They walked down a long hall with identical doors and into a conference room. He had her sheets on his clipboard and he began reading the information aloud.

"We've checked all of the Yad Vashem records for Yakov Reich," he said, pausing to jot down a word on the paper before him. "There's nothing on him. Anywhere. There's nothing on Martin Specht, either. But we do have a record for Menachem Kreinen." He pulled out a sheet of paper.

Susan jumped up and clapped her hands. "Incredible. Just incredible!"

"He was liberated from Dachau at the end of April in 1945," the librarian said. "According to our records, he had no family." Then, running his finger on a line of print, he added. "I'm really happy to tell you that he is alive."

Yakov, alive? Susan closed her eyes and tried to imagine him. Did he still look like her father? He kept changing his appearance. Slender, stoop shouldered, grey-haired, walking with a cane. She blinked. Overweight, his hair dyed dark brown, his posture erect. Dressed in a plaid shirt and tan pants. Wearing a white shirt and navy trousers. A baseball cap on his head. A straw hat, tilted to one side.

Susan was thinking of Yakov, the man Bregner loved. How had

he altered his appearance? What had he done to prevent anyone from recognizing him? The questions began to pour out of her.

"What can you tell me about him?" she asked. "What does he look like? Where does he work? Where does he live?"

"According to our records, like many immigrants, he settled in the Vatikim neighborhood of Netanya, where he works in a stationery store and lives in a small apartment building. He lists this address for his survivor's check so he still should be living there." He handed her the address and telephone number. She was trembling as she took the paper and held it close to her heart.

Then, he showed her an ID photo of Kreinen. He had short dark hair and thick dark eyeglasses that obscured his eyes. *Too bad,* Susan thought. *The eyes would have been a giveaway.*

She decided to ask Ruth to come with her to Netanya. Ruth understood what it meant to be a survivor and Ruth had lived through the horrors of Mauthausen. Then, Susan had second thoughts. Maybe inviting Ruth was a bad idea. Maybe her presence would overwhelm Yakov. Maybe he would recognize Ruth instantly, and shut the door on Susan. After all, Ruth knew his secret and she could easily betray him. Susan debated back and forth for an hour, finally deciding to go alone.

As it turned out, Ruth agreed with the idea of Susan going by herself. "Walter is in my past," she said. "I don't want to revive his memory by even mentioning his name."

When Susan arrived the next day, Ruth was waiting tables in the café. It was very crowded and Ruth was hopping from table to table. She barely acknowledged Susan. The room was full of smokers and the minute Susan entered she had a coughing fit. She just couldn't stop. Ruth brought her a glass of cold water but said nothing. After she finished serving three tables, there was a lull. Ruth sat down and lit a cigarette.

"I've been thinking about meeting Yakov," she said. "It kept me awake for hours." She fumbled in a large shopping bag, finally finding what she was looking for, a blue book. "I kept a diary in the camp," she confessed to Susan. "I hid it in the wall by my bunk and prayed that no one would find it. Luckily no one did."

She hid the diary in the clothes that she was given in the DP camp and brought it with her to Israel. "I haven't read it in years," she said. There were dark rings under her eyes. She was shaking her head back and forth as if she was disagreeing with someone. She cradled the diary in her hands, rubbing her fingers against its frayed corners. The pages were rippled, clearly they'd suffered water damage over the years. She opened the book. On the inside flap, Susan could read three lines: *The Book of Ruth, Mauthausen, Of Life and Death*. Ruth's handwriting was elegant with small flourishes on the capital letters. Each entry was dated.

Susan kept her own diary for years. It was given to her as a birthday gift when she was ten and her initials were embossed in gold on the red leather cover. She loved the fact that it had a lock and a tiny key that she wore around her neck, even when she was sleeping. She was not particularly diligent and there were many days without entries. But there were breathtaking moments. A description of the long eyelashes of the first boy who'd caught her eye, trying on a training bra in a local lingerie store where the curtains did not adequately cover the try-on booths. "I saw him staring at me and I sort of liked it. I mean it was embarrassing but exciting, too." On the page, she'd drawn a training bra with pointy boobs. One year later, lying on the beach with a boy's head resting on her stomach and looking up at the stars, she wrote, "His head felt like a hot water bottle, the kind grandma puts on my stomach when it aches. His breathing was regular, like a pendulum in a cuckoo clock."

By the time she was 16, she'd put her diary away in the back of a dresser drawer after she found that the lock had been forced. She never knew who did it but it didn't matter. Her secrets were no longer safe.

Ruth clutched her diary and spoke softly. "I hated Walter and I loved him. I should have just hated him. He stole my innocence, violated me repeatedly, and yet I felt something for him." She exhaled a deep breath. "He was the only man I ever slept with," she said.

A woman at one of the front tables waved for a check and Ruth left to give it to her. Susan picked up the diary, flipping through its pages. Words she could not understand. Pain she could not comprehend. It was not like skinning your knee or bumping your elbow. Ruth's diary was like a dagger piercing her heart.

Ruth returned to reading her diary, biting her lip nervously as she turned the last few pages. She bit so hard that her lip started to bleed. Someone turned on the radio and the announcer was giving the roundup of the Eichmann trial news. Two guards had testified. Their answers were curt. Yes, I remember that long march in the hot sun. Yes, I ordered the prisoners to dig their own graves. Yes, I was following orders. Yes, we were all following orders.

"Let me go with you," Ruth said, suddenly slamming the diary shut.

Unable to speak, Susan nodded yes. Then, she leaned forward to give Ruth a hug. Something inside stopped her, though. Too intimate? Instead, she reached out and touched Ruth's shoulder. It was an act of comfort, however small.

A week passed. Twice, Susan had picked up the phone to call Menachem, putting it down when she decided that she hadn't the faintest idea what she would say to him. If he didn't want to be found or identified, he would probably hang up. She most certainly couldn't force him to talk to her. Maybe he had a new lover now. There were too many maybes.

From what she could see on the map, Menachem Kreinen lived only three blocks from the sea. Susan imagined him walking on the beach every evening, barefoot in the sand. Above him, seagulls fought the wind, as they swooped down to catch small fish and crabs. Yakov, who was now Menachem, the boy who skipped stones across the San River in Rozwadów. She thought of the stone that he'd given her father when they parted and in her fantasy, she saw him bend down and pick up a perfectly round white stone. He ran his fingers around it and then dropped it in his pants pocket. For two days, Susan had imaginary conversations with him. *Hello, Menachem.* Or should she say, *Hello, Yakov?* If she said Yakov, would he hang up? If she said Menachem, would she have to tell him about Yakov on the phone? Round and round, she spun. Every conversation ended in disaster. He hung up. He told her never to call again. He said: you have the wrong number.

In the end, she decided not to call. She and Ruth would travel to Netanya and visit him. If he were at work, they would wait for him to return home. They would ring his bell and he would open the door and, then, who knows what would happen next.

Ezra thought the plan was crazy. "You just can't show up there," he said. He was sure that Susan needed a better plan. Susan laughed when he said that. It was a strange comment from someone who'd failed at his plan for protesting at the Eichmann trial. They talked about the UM organizing session. Ezra expected nearly 200 people. The word had gone out on the street. It seemed that the Moroccans were eager to join. "They're tired of having no voice," he said.

He'd written their mission statement and come up with a plan of action, which was all about infiltrating the political system. "We may be immigrants," he said, "but we vote and our vote counts, especially in parliament." He'd done his research. The campaign for the election to the Knesset was heating up and the election was set for August. So far, David Ben Gurion's Mapai party was dominating the field and the prediction was that Mapai would receive more than one-third of the votes, earning more than 40 seats. The Sephardic vote would most probably be split among the parties, with a tiny group voting for the Religious Sephardi candidates. Even one Knesset member could make a difference.

"Imagine what we could accomplish if we were a presence there," he said. Ezra was determined to make a difference, either in the upcoming election or by the time the new government collapsed. He predicted that it would last, at most, for two years. The idea was to convert UM from a political pressure group into a political party. His followers would canvas from apartment to apartment, adding names to their membership list.

The plan sounded grandiose to Susan. She could not imagine the European Jews giving up real power. Everywhere she looked, the founding fathers of the state were in control. Zionist city dwellers who created new lives in Jerusalem, Tel Aviv, and Haifa. Zionist pioneers in the kibbutzim who turned the arid soil into rich loam. Everywhere, on the streets of the city, she saw Holocaust survivors, upon whose blood and suffering, they said, the Jewish State was officially created.

Still, spending time with Ezra and the Moroccans she'd become fully engaged with their cause. "I'm with you," she said, leaning over to kiss him.

The Netanya bus left from the Central Station every hour on the half hour for the two-hour ride. Susan and Ruth agreed to meet there at 10 a.m. on Sunday. Ruth was taking a day off from the café and Susan was playing hooky from the ulpan. Susan called Ruth to remind her to bring along the photo of the four friends. She called a second time to ask her to bring her diary. Ruth said that she was anxious about the visit. She hadn't slept since she'd decided to go. "Walter has been in my dreams. He told me how much he loved me. He told me that he never loved his wife that way. He said that he was not afraid of death but that he didn't want to swallow the cyanide and leave me."

In her dream, they were swinging in the starlight. He traced the constellations with his finger, placing her hand under his as he moved from star to star on the Big Dipper. As they touched the last star, she woke up.

Ruth hesitated and then spoke. "There's something else I want to tell you. Before Walter and I parted, I asked him for a keepsake. He cut off a lock of his hair and gave it to me. I wear it every day." Ruth sighed and Susan didn't respond. She wanted to be angry, to scream at her, to tell her that she was a traitor to the Jewish people. How could anyone love a Nazi? But no words came out. Her head felt like it was going to explode. Black spots floated before her eyes. A migraine was coming on. The light in the room faded. Suddenly, as if someone had turned the light switch back on, a spotlight illuminated Ruth's head. She loved him and she hated him too, Susan thought. *How can I judge her?*

"It's OK," Susan said, whispering. "You don't have to feel guilty. He saved your life."

On the bus to Netanya, Susan read the headline story in the newspaper that summarized the trial proceedings to date. The legal basis against Eichmann was the 1950 Nazi Collaborators (Punishment) Law. He'd been indicted on 15 criminal charges including crimes against humanity, war crimes, crimes against the Jewish people, and membership in a criminal organization. Since April 11 there had been nearly 60 witnesses and the introduction of hundreds of documents. The prosecution would be resting its case in two weeks.

A quote from Attorney General Gideon Hausner's opening address was featured in bold print: "It is not an individual that is in the dock at this historic trial and not the Nazi regime alone, but antisemitism throughout history," Hausner said. Defense attorney Robert Servatius was successful, the newspaper reported, in keeping out material not directly related to Eichmann.

Depositions by leading Nazis were submitted by the prosecution and a debate ensued. The defense demanded that they be brought to Israel so that they could be cross-examined. Hausner declared that if they arrived in Israel he would have to arrest them as war criminals. Susan tried to interest Ruth in the story, but she stared out the bus window and didn't seem to be paying any attention.

Ruth was dressed in black, as if in mourning, and she looked especially pale and gaunt. Without her bright red lipstick and silver hoop earrings, she looked old and tired. Suddenly, she seemed both frightened and forlorn.

"I was just thinking about my tenth birthday," she said, touching Susan's arm. "That was the happiest day of my life. My mother had baked an apple cake and there was real whipped cream. The table was covered with a pink cloth with white polka dots. Three of my friends arrived with gifts, all handmade, a wooden box decorated with painted flowers, a bracelet woven of grass, and a necklace made of shells. We sang songs and laughed for hours until it was dark."

The bus was pulling into Netanya's Central Station and the passengers started pushing their way to the front door. The temperature had already hit the 90s and Susan was perspiring heavily. Ruth kept mopping her forehead with a ragged handkerchief.

It was lunchtime and several of the outdoor cafés on Herzl Street were already crowded. Susan had read in the newspaper that the Hasharon Café at Herzl and Dizengoff was particularly popular with survivors. The owner, the story reported, who himself had survived three camps, said, "I let them run up the tabs. If they don't have the money, I feed them anyway." Squeezed between two women's clothing stores, the modest café, its painted green walls peeling, looked like it could use a complete renovation.

They sat down and ordered coffee. Ruth ordered hers strong and black. When the waitress arrived with the coffee, she drank it without waiting for it to cool.

"I've been thinking about Yakov," Ruth said. "Most of the time when I was sent for supplies, a worker at the front desk would stamp my request. Once, there was no one at the desk and Walter called me into the back room. That's where I saw Yakov, sitting behind a large oak desk. He was busy stapling papers together. When I handed him my form, he said 'thank you,' which was odd in the camp. 'Thank you' when I handed him a slip with a request for soap. 'Thank you' when I signed the form acknowledging my receipt of goods. No one else said thank you. That should have been a clue. He was reading a book, too. I was curious what he was reading, but of course never asked him. That would have been taboo. One only answered questions at Mauthausen.

"Bregner spoke to him in a soft voice. Their words were muffled and I could never hear what they were actually saying. When I dropped the soap, and two bars split, I thought that Bregner would reprimand me but Yakov gave him a stern look and Bregner was silent. Even then, I felt the powerful bond between them. Walter never intervened. When Bregner yelled out a command, Walter saluted him: 'Yes, sir. Yes, sir.' When Yakov spoke, it was different."

The woman at the next table was talking to herself. She was the two hundred tenth survivor Susan had seen with numbers on her arm. "My head is full of lice," she cried out. "There are black bugs floating in my soup. Lice are crawling all over me. There are black bugs floating in my soup." The manager of the café came over and touched her arm. "Shh, Rebecca, shhhh," he said. He handed her a cup of tea and patted her shoulder. It was easy to see that she was a regular there. "Bugs," she said. "Lice."

Ruth remembered the bed bugs at the camp. She often woke in the morning with tiny red bumps all over her body. She would scratch her skin until it bled. The tiny bumps would get larger and larger. On the second day, they would be unbearable. Then, they would start to fade just as new bumps appeared. Once, to avoid the bugs, she rolled up her thin mattress and hid it under her bunk, sleeping instead on the wooden board. There were no new bumps in the morning but her back ached and she could hardly walk.

Susan told the café manager that she was trying to find Menachem Kreinen, a survivor who had lived in Netanya since arriving in Israel. Perhaps he knew him? "I know most of the survivors here," the manager said, adding that he was himself a survivor. "I do my best to feed the ones who are struggling. It's a mitzvah!" There were three regulars, he said, who might be Menachem. One was a short man, slightly overweight. "Definitely not him," Susan said. "My uncle was tall." The other two were tall and thin with dark hair. He didn't remember their eye color but both wore glasses. Yes, they had numbers on their arms. No, he didn't know anything about their past. They were loners, preferring not to engage in conversation. Both were chain-smokers, one cigarette lit the next.

"They usually show up after the lunch crowd is gone," the manager told Susan. Then, looking at his watch, he signaled that she should wait. Ruth was on her third cup of coffee. She couldn't eat. She told Susan she wasn't hungry. Feeling anxious made Susan hungry. She ordered what she thought was an apple strudel. The waiter showed up with a dense, doughy cake that was almost flat. There was no sign of apples. Susan needed a knife to cut through the crust.

A man sat down at a corner table. He ordered coffee and took out his newspaper. Susan could see that he was reading the front-page story on the Eichmann trial. He took out a pen and wrote words on the margin of the paper. The radio came on with a summary of the morning's trial testimony. He stopped writing and listened. All around her, everyone had stopped what they were doing to listen. It was like an air raid siren. A startling, shrieking sound, the kind she heard at home—test warnings in case the Russians attacked and the children had to hide under their desks until they heard the all-clear sound. There was no all-clear sound here. Just the booming voice of the announcer over and over again.

A second man entered. He limped a little and he carried a cane. He sat down at the table just in front of them. He lit a cigarette and ordered coffee. He hung his worn leather briefcase, with its frayed buckled straps on the empty chair next to him. Susan could make out the initials "MK." Susan touched Ruth's arm and gestured toward the briefcase.

Neither of them could see his face. They hadn't planned to meet him in a café. Now, here he was, three feet away. Brave Susan suddenly felt not-so-brave and nauseated. A bitter acidic taste bubbled up in her mouth.

He took a paperback out of the briefcase and put it on the table. She could see the cover clearly. He was reading Elie Wiesel's *Night* in Yiddish. Her father was reading the English translation in America when she left New York. "This is the truth," her father said, as he read 12-year-old Elie Wiesel's account of being shipped with his family in a cattle car from the village of Sighet, Romania, to the Auschwitz-Birkenau complex. Wiesel wrote about babies being tossed into burning pits, the sight of huge ovens, and the stench of burning flesh. With the Russian forces closing in, Elie and his father, the only surviving members of their family, were evacuated to Buchenwald in central Germany. He was liberated there by American forces in April 1945. "I will never forget the ending of *Night*," her father said. "After having been sick with food poisoning, Wiesel looks into a mirror and sees a corpse gazing back at him. Do you hear that, Susan, a corpse!"

Susan decided not to interrupt the man with the MK briefcase while he was reading. So, they waited until he finished his second cup of coffee, left a few *agorot* on the table, and began walking down the street. Perhaps he was heading back to work after his coffee break. Or maybe he was heading home for a nap, a common Israeli practice as a way of coping with the afternoon heat. He stopped to buy a couple packs of cigarettes from a street vendor and then crossed the boulevard in the direction of the beach. Ruth and Susan followed at a distance.

When he arrived at the beach, he took out a small towel from his briefcase and spread it on the dry sand. Then, he sat down, contemplating the Mediterranean. There was a brisk breeze and the usually quiet waters were choppy.

Susan stared at the water. It was nothing like the raging Atlantic at home with its massive undertow. Don't fight it if it takes you, the kids were always told. The more you fight, the more you are in danger. Once, she'd been sucked out and then sucked in, suddenly finding herself dangerously near the rock jetty. That was a place to be avoided, with its slippery seaweed and sharp edges.

Float free, she told herself as she was propelled into danger. Miraculously, her body floated away from the rocks on the next wave. Within seconds, she was able to roll back onto the beach. Her father said that God had saved her. That was what he said whenever something good happened. When it was something bad, it was just bad luck.

The man on the beach lit a cigarette. There was no one near him. Susan walked over to him barefoot, her feet burning in the hot sand. Ruth trailed behind her. He didn't see them coming. When they were close, Susan took a deep breath and spoke. "Are you Menachem Kreinen?" she asked. He turned around, startled, and stood up.

He did have blue eyes, exactly the color of her father's eyes, blue with just the slightest tinge of violet in them. His hands, too, were just like her father's, broad hands with long fingers. She looked at his ears, which were prominent, standing out from his head. His hair was dark brown, probably dyed, unlike her father's gray. He had a moustache. There was a deep scar on his left cheek. She wondered how he got it. At first, no one spoke. Ruth stared at him. He stared at Ruth, his eyes squinting in the sunlight.

"Who are you?" he asked Susan, barely managing to get the words out of his pinched-together lips. He squinted as he tried to get Susan in focus. "Who are you?" he asked again. This time his voice was louder. He was standing now, one hand clenched into a fist. "What do you want from me?" His feet were apart as if he was about to pounce.

A jab to the left, a jab to the right. She would land in the sand, her nose bloody, her head spinning. *Who are you and why are you messing up my life? I'm sitting on the beach, watching the sea, far from Rozwadów, far from Mauthausen, far from my past.* A blow to the head. Watch out!

For a moment, Susan wanted to turn around. She took two steps backwards, almost tripping on Ruth, who was a couple of steps behind her. Maybe it was not too late to quit her assignment. Live her own life, not her father's. But somehow she couldn't. The quest was her quest now, not just his. Yakov was her uncle and her history.

"I'm Susan Reich, Yehudah's daughter," she said, holding the stone in her outstretched hand, as she took a slight step toward Yakov. For a moment, she feared that he was going to lunge at her. One hand was in his pocket. He was studying her face and then Ruth's, his eyes darting back and forth. After a few seconds, he turned slightly and stared at Ruth again. Ruth was fishing for something in her pocketbook. She took out the photo and waved it in the air. "You're here," she said, pointing to his face. "Right next to Bregner."

He squinted his eyes as he studied the photo, leaning into it. Then, touching Bregner's face. Still he didn't move. He didn't speak. *No,* his body was saying, *I won't break down. I won't admit that I am your uncle. No, too much time has passed. No to your stone and no to the old photograph. An emphatic no.* Yakov was shaking his head ferociously, from side to side.

Suddenly, he surprised her. He reached out his hand and took the stone. He rubbed it back and forth between his palms. It was just like rubbing a magic lamp. But there was no genie on the beach in Netanya. Just Yakov's hands rubbing the magic stone of memory.

He sank down on his knees, facing the sea, praying in the sand. They sat down beside him and waited. On a street nearby, Susan heard an ice cream truck driving by. Two girls skipped hand in hand at the waterline, stopping to splash one another and laugh.

Then, still holding the stone, he rose and walked to the water's edge, kneeling so that his forehead touched the sea. To Susan, it looked like he was bobbing up and down in the water, a piece of seaweed, riding the white foam on the crest of a wave, and then crashing to the blue-green sea below. Yakov, a piece of flotsam and jetsam, floating through a sad and stormy life.

He turned and faced them, his eyes wet with tears. "It's too much for me!" he said. "Go away! Leave me alone!" He picked up his towel and twisted it with his hands. He started to leave, walking quickly toward the ramp to the beach entrance. "Go away," he said again, stopping and falling to his knees. He was crying now, loud sobs, wailing sounds. For an instant, Susan's hands went to her ears, as if to block out the noise. A childish thing to do, Susan thought, trying to keep trouble out.

"You found me but I don't want to be found," he said, holding the stone tightly in his clenched fist. "Sometimes it's better to leave the past alone. If I'd wanted to find you, I would have done so." His face was flushed and he was struggling for words. "Turning your back on your life. Hiding from your past. Shutting down memories. Making a fresh start. Difficult! Impossible! So many times, I've wanted to run into the sea and drown myself. End my misery. End my troubles."

He turned to Ruth. "I remember you and Walter," he said. "How could I ever forget you?" Ruth swayed as he spoke. A strong gust of wind, off the sea, could have blown her over.

Yakov knelt down and, with his index finger, traced and retraced a circle in the sand. Inside, he wrote "Yakov and Yehudah." Then he smoothed the sand and wrote, "Karl and Yakov." "My story is complicated," he said.

Complicated. That was the word her father used when he wanted her to pay attention, when he was constructing an argument that she had to follow. Complicated meant challenging, difficult, often unpleasant, and sometimes harsh.

"At the Rozwadów yeshiva, I was not a diligent student," Yakov said. "I was not happy studying Torah and the rebbe often poked me in class to wake me up.

"My one salvation was the little job I had working after school as a clerk in a store on Rozwadów's main square. It wasn't much money but working there was freedom for me. My boss never yelled and he trusted me. I would unpack boxes of shirts and stack them on shelves. I knew where everything was and I never had to be told to do things twice. When my mother decided to immigrate to America, I didn't want to go. I cried. My boss took pity on me and offered to give me a room in his house. I jumped at the offer. If it didn't work out, I thought I could always join my family later. But I never did. In the decade that followed, there was a rise in antisemitism and the Jews faced new troubles. The Polish government's tax policy was particularly hard on Jews and many tried to gain admittance to medical, agricultural, and chemical institutes. There was a quota system in place. Some of the yeshiva boys left town for the gymnasium in the neighboring town of Nisko but I didn't even try. I just wanted to be left alone."

Yakov stuttered as continued. "Nnnnnot quite alone, though. I had one friend, Avram, who was also a loner. We used to lie on the riverbank and tell each other secrets. Once, Avram told me that he had a secret that was too much for him to keep inside, a secret that was bigger than his soul." He stopped speaking and took a deep breath. "Avram told me that he loved me."

Yakov paused and looked up at Ruth whose face was impassive. "Don't be shocked," he said. "Don't be disappointed. Don't be ashamed of me. The truth is, it made me happy. We sat there holding hands, not knowing how we were ever going to live in Rozwadów, where everyone knew everything. Of course, our happiness didn't last long. A few months later, Avram's neighbor saw us with our arms around each other by the San. He told the rebbe, who arranged for Avram to be sent to a yeshiva several hundred miles away. The rebbe called me in and he told me that he was giving me another chance. 'I will never tell anyone about this,' he said. 'Just get married.'"

As he spoke, Susan was twisting her curls around her index

finger, tighter and tighter. Yakov's face looked sad. "Not an easy solution," she said.

"But I didn't want to get married. I moved to Krakow, thinking that a big city would be better for me than a little shtetl." Yakov lit a cigarette and inhaled. He gasped. "When the economy got worse, I lost my job. I couldn't find another so I decided to return home to Rozwadów. It was June 1939. Not quite three months later, at the end of September, the Germans entered the city. That's when I met Karl Bregner for the second time." There. He'd said Bregner's name. Yakov shivered and looked up at Ruth.

Ruth looked down at the sand as he spoke.

"By that time, we had little stock and we were selling anything we could get our hands on. He came into the store to buy cigarettes," Yakov said, "and, of course, we recognized each other from the week we'd spent together in Berlin. We hadn't seen each other for almost ten years but that didn't matter. He introduced himself as if we didn't know each other, and put out his hand to shake mine. His skin was soft and his hand was warm."

Yakov's eyes were teary now. "After that," he said, "Bregner came to the store often. Jews were increasingly afraid and they were leaving, fleeing east across the San River. Nazi troops were everywhere. We heard that Jews were being shipped off and killed. No one knew exactly where or how. Some of us thought that maybe it was better to go off to one of their work camps. At least, we would have work there. Others said they were traps. That going to a work camp really meant going to prison.

"In October," Yakov continued, "when the Nazis began rounding up the remaining Jews in town, Bregner came to see me. There were no other customers in the store at the time since no one had any money and the shelves were almost empty of merchandise. He said that he'd received a transfer and a promotion. He was to be the head supervisor of the supply warehouse at Mauthausen. He offered me a job there, as his assistant. I wasn't sure what

Mauthausen was. It was all a rumor. By then, the camp was a year old and there already were some 1500 SAS guards working there.

"Bregner told me that he could *save me*. I would have to work there under an assumed name as a German. He would provide the ID papers. There would be no problem in my passing as a German. I would be working in a back room, where Jewish prisoners didn't go."

Susan interrupted him. "Weren't you terrified? How could you work in the den of the enemy? Eyes everywhere. Peering. Staring. Intense. If they caught you, they would have sent you to the gas chambers."

"It was not an easy decision but I loved him," Yakov said. He wiped away a few tears. He knocked his fist on his chest, over his heart like a penitent Jew asking forgiveness from God. "I agreed to go and was reborn as Martin Specht. Bregner arranged every detail. I lived in a house that Bregner leased for me, not far from the camp. The owner was a German friend of Bregner's and he asked no questions. We were two good friends spending time together as far as he was concerned. But he knew better. He washed our sheets and cleaned the house. He bought loaves of bread from the bakery and milk and cheese from a nearby farmer.

"We had two secrets," Yakov said. "So hard for both of us. Hiding me as a Jew was easy compared to hiding us as homosexuals. The Nazis saw us as deviants, men who were deformed and impure. We didn't fit their ideal image of the master race. It didn't matter whether you were Jewish or German. Even being a member of the Nazi party didn't give you protection. You were still the scum of the earth and you feared being locked up in prison or murdered. Bregner had bad dreams. Often, in the middle of the night, he would sit up and scream, 'Please, no! Don't shoot me.' Or he would hug me as we lay in bed awaiting the morning light. He'd heard about the violent purge of homosexual clubs in Berlin. They dragged the young men from the clubs. The lover of a close friend of his was beaten unconscious with a nightstick. He died two weeks later.

"In the camps, homosexuals wore pink triangles, pointed downwards. Bregner feared that we would be caught. I would end up with two badges, a yellow star as a Jew and a pink triangle as a homosexual. If we were discovered, we would be beaten by the Nazis and by other prisoners. If we lived, we would be given the most grueling work. Once, he said, he witnessed three homosexual men being used for target practice. He couldn't sleep for weeks after that, and I couldn't comfort him.

"We feared making eye contact with one another. We worked side by side without ever touching. I was not to speak to him unless he asked me a question."

"Sounds impossible," Susan said. "Working side by side and concealing your relationship. Too dangerous. I could never have done that!" Susan was having a difficult time listening to Yakov's story. He was supposed to sound like one of the survivors who spoke of starvation and beatings. But here he was telling them about his passionate love affair with Bregner, the man who was the love of his life.

She tried to imagine Yakov on the witness stand. The prosecutor was asking him to talk about his life in Mauthausen and Yakov was refusing to answer. "We understand that this is difficult for you." What could Yakov say? That he had a German lover. That he was hidden away and fed while his fellow Jews were hungry and dying?

Ruth was looking at the photo now. "There you are," she said, "next to Walter." She moved her index finger around his face, framing it in a circle. "I loved him. I've told myself a million times that he raped me, that I was forced to be his lover. But the truth is, I loved him." In the sunlight, Susan could see the crease lines on Ruth's face.

"You and I, Yakov," Ruth said, "we were in an impossible

situation. We didn't have any choice." She hesitated for a moment, then added, "Sometimes, I blame myself for being *weak*."

Yakov reacted to the word "weak" by shaking his head. Susan watched his cheeks tense up and his face stiffen. "You were not weak," he said. "I was not weak. We were crazy, perhaps, but we were brave, too. What we did was hard. We knew that we were taking a big risk.

"Things got worse at the end," Yakov said. "Bregner was trying to figure out what to do when the camp would be liberated. He wouldn't be taken prisoner. He was clear on that, but he wanted me to live. I argued with him.

"I think you know the rest, Ruth," he said. "Walter probably told you how things would end." Yakov's voice grew weaker and he couldn't finish the story. He was drawing Xs in the sand. Erasing them then drawing them again. "Now, I only have one request," he said. He took a deep breath, raising his shoulders as he inhaled. Raising them for a second time and, finally, speaking: "Leave me alone. Do not tell Yehudah that you found me. I do *not* want to be found."

"But we want to find you," Susan said. "It is not only up to you." After she said those words, she felt some remorse. Who was she to speak to her uncle that way?

Susan stared at her uncle, found now, but wishing to remain lost. What was he asking of her? How could she ever keep such a secret from her father? All her father had to do was look at her face or listen to her voice and he would know the truth. "Stop fooling me," he would say, waiting for her confession. "Stop lying and 'fess up."

Yakov was trembling, his eyes pleading with her: don't do it. Even his arms were shaking. Susan could see the numbers on his arm, dancing in the sunlight. "I've spent weeks looking for you," Susan said. "Running from survivor to survivor, prying them with questions. Did they ever meet you? Do they remember what you look like? Do they know anyone else I should talk to? Now, you're asking me to make an about-face, to forget about my promise to my father. I told him that I would find out what happened to you, that I would find out your fate, living or dead."

Promises are made to be kept. A ring made of woven grass slipped on the pinky finger of your best friend who will never disclose the secrets you whispered to her; the kiss in the dark on the balcony of the movie theater. Breaking a promise was like breaking a precious porcelain bowl, tiny, sharp pieces flying through the air.

Susan looked at his face, deeply creased but with not a hint of a smile. He was begging her to abandon her search. "I'm not sure I can do what you're asking me to do," she said. "You're asking me to break my promise to my father. He sent me on this journey. He deserves to know the truth." She thought of him at home, scouring the newspaper for stories on the Eichmann trial and sitting by the television riveted to the trial news. She was his personal reporter, sent to find out the truth.

But truth was an upside-down, inside-out messy construct. Whose truth? What truth? A list was running through her mind:

Do the right thing and tell your dad.
Do the right thing and don't tell your dad.
Just tell the truth.
Just tell a lie.

Sometimes, you just have to concede, to give in. Resistance only takes you so far. After a few minutes, Susan reached out to hold Yakov's hand. "I won't tell him," she said. "You have my word." Ruth was wringing her fingers, sitting almost in a trance. Suddenly, Ruth leaned forward and hugged Yakov. "This will be *our* secret, too," she said. "Yours and mine."

To seal their promise, they shook hands on the beach with the waves lapping the sand. Overhead, three seagulls flew in a V formation. *V is for victory*, Susan thought, although there was no clear winner. Then, she handed him a slip of paper with her father's office phone number and address in New York City. "Just in case you change your mind," she said.

"I don't need it," Yakov said. "I've known it for years."

Susan and Ruth headed back to the Central Bus Station. Yakov remained on the beach, staring at the water. He didn't invite them to his home. He didn't kiss Susan goodbye. There were no words of solace or comfort. They just parted.

Susan decided to wait to call her father. He had a way of grilling her and she wanted to be sure that she didn't trip up. Whom had she talked to and what had they told her, he would definitely ask. Then, in his lawyerly fashion, he would connect the dots. She had to figure out which dots to leave in and which to leave out.

When the bus pulled into Jerusalem, she could hear the radios blasting Eichmann trial news. It was now the fortieth day of the trial, the announcer said, and the defense had just begun to present their case. He interviewed three people on the street regarding their expectations. "The defense has no case," two of them said. The third, a woman, wasn't so sure. "When it involves Jews, there's always trouble. They'll come up with some wild story."

8

Susan found a note from Ezra taped to her bedroom window. He'd set the date for the first public UM meeting. Flyers had been given out in all of the immigrant neighborhoods and he expected a huge turnout. They had two days to decide on the meeting's agenda. He asked her to meet him at the Sephardi synagogue later that evening. All Israeli citizens had the right to vote but the percentage of Moroccans who voted was very low. Ezra had to convince them that voting was the best way to gain their civil rights.

He'd prepared a speech. If they got enough signatures, they would form the UM party and run a slate in the upcoming August election. If not, at the very least, they could vote as a bloc, trying to exert their influence. He was hoping they could convince Yemeni voters to join forces with them. They'd come to Israel a decade earlier on Operation Magic Carpet but were not active politically. He thought his group might be more effective if it were more inclusive—not just representing Moroccans.

Ezra was already rehearsing the speech when Susan arrived. Seated in the front row, on uncomfortable wooden folding chairs, were four of the Moroccans whom Susan recognized from the ulpan class. They were calling out suggestions to him. "Frustrated," one of them said, "that's not a very strong word. We're not frustrated, we're angry." Two others clapped in agreement. When Ezra spoke to his Yemeni brothers and sisters, urging them to join the fight, the Moroccans looked puzzled.

"It's about us, not them," Rachel said.

Ezra was quick to respond: "It's about more than us. We're all treated as inferior, second-class citizens."

Back home, Susan thought, you could hear this debate going on in the growing Civil Rights movement. *Who was discriminated against the most?* In her hometown, blacks and Puerto Ricans lived in separate neighborhoods. Even the Irish had their own place, separate from the Jews. You could live there, but inevitably you were an outsider. Christmas, on Susan's side of town, was much more important than Chanukah.

On the date of the big meeting, the room filled up fast. Susan noticed that there were many women there. Even though it was evening, they'd brought their babies with them. The women were angry about their lives, that was clear. They were sitting there cracking sunflower seeds with their teeth. At the entrance, Ezra had posted two women who were giving out flyers written in three languages, Hebrew, *Marokayit*, and French. They were not taking any chances.

At the top of the flyer, Ezra had written in large, printed Hebrew letters: FRIENDS, NOW IS THE TIME TO MAKE YOUR VOTE COUNT! He'd even drawn a logo for the new group: an olive branch with olives and the letters UM drawn in fancy, curved script on one leaf. Ezra's friend had secretly made copies of the flyer at work while his boss was away. The idea was to circulate thousands of them in Moroccan neighborhoods.

Ezra announced that he'd arranged a meeting with two politicians from Mapai. "We need to pressure them, too," he said. "This is a war on two fronts, from within and from without." There were a million opinions. One fellow stood up and argued that they should bribe the politicians. "Bribery," he said. "That's what works in this country. Trying to change the system is stupid."

The woman next to him disagreed. She'd tried to bribe the clerk in The Jewish Agency and he reported her to his supervisor. Only by getting down on her knees and weeping and wailing did they agree not to punish her. "I told them that I had babies to feed and I asked for forgiveness."

The young people were more outspoken. A slender woman, who kept twisting her dark curls around her fingers, spoke up. "We can't sit around and wait for things to change. If we get the politicians to depend on our vote, we will get what we want." She said that she was personally responsible for getting more than 500 names of neighbors on their petition.

A young man stood up. "I'm 18 years old," he said. "Old enough to vote. I'm here to tell you that you're doing the right thing." His speech was followed by spontaneous applause. Ezra fielded the questions and comments with grace, making sure that no one was left out.

The ceiling light shone on the three-week-old stubble that Ezra called his beard. Susan had tried to talk him out of growing it but he was convinced that it made him appear older and wiser. "All of the rabbis had beards," Ezra told Susan. "It was not just about the prohibition against cutting your hair. It was political, a way to keep their congregation in check."

Ezra was telling a joke now. "A Moroccan woman came to her rabbi to complain that her house was too crowded. 'What can I do?' she asked. The rabbi advised: 'Bring your goat inside and come back to me next week.' She came back the next week to tell him that the situation was worse. 'Bring your cow inside,' the rabbi said, 'and come back to me next week.' By the third week, the woman was frantic and pulling out her hair. 'Oy, rabbi,' she said. 'The house is so crowded that I cannot breathe. What should I do?' Her rabbi smiled. 'I have the solution,' he said: 'Put your goat and your cow out in the yard and come back next week.'

The next week the woman returned smiling, in her hands a freshly baked pie for the rabbi. 'Oh, rabbi, I am so happy. Life is perfect now. You are the wisest rabbi in the world.'"

The audience clapped their hands and laughed. Their apartments were small but they understood the joke. "Unlike the rabbi, I'm not telling you to be happy with your lot," Ezra said. "We can bring about change." Ezra winked at her twice, without interrupting his speech. After his remarks, he made his way through the crowd shaking the hand of everyone in the room.

Once, in Penn Station, Susan shook John F. Kennedy's hand. She remembered that his arm was suntanned. "Counting on your vote," he said to her. When he smiled, his teeth were white and even. He was wearing a white dress shirt, rolled-up at the elbows and no tie. Commuters were racing by but many of them stopped to talk to him. There was a buzz, a feeling of youth and strength. Even the homeless, sitting on the station floor, were staring at him. Bolting from his security entourage, Kennedy ran over to greet a homeless woman surrounded by her possessions which were stashed in red Macy's Department Store bags. He moved one bag to shake her hand.

Ezra reminded Susan of JFK. Sitting there, she forgot about Yakov and the Eichmann trial. Inside, they could not hear the news. They had other business. Rachel didn't want to clean toilets for the rest of her life. Ezra wanted to move out of construction work. Their homes were full of mold, their roofs leaked, and there was barely any hot water, although they did their best to keep their houses clean. Garbage lay strewn on the street for days before it was picked up. On Shabbos, the stench was unbearable.

Only the cats were happy. They tore into the leftovers, hissing and scratching their way through the mounds of garbage. Shabbos meant nothing to them. The Holocaust meant nothing to them. They knew how to survive.

Ezra was encouraged by the turnout. He had no time for the ulpan now and he was thinking of quitting. "This is the time for action, not learning," he told Susan. He was tired of the politics of the ulpan, too. "The education there is designed by European Jews," he said to her as they gathered up the extra flyers before leaving. "Every little bit of grammar there is stuffed with propaganda."

She laughed. "That's pretty dramatic," she said. There was no convincing Ezra, though. Susan already knew that. He was on a mission and she could go along with him or not.

After they left the meeting, they passed a green park bench on which someone had scribbled the word "Israel" in large Hebrew letters. "Let's talk," Ezra said, motioning that they should sit down. "When are you next going to the Eichmann trial?" Ezra asked, surprising Susan. "I've been thinking of going back," he said. "I know that I'm stubborn. What is that expression you Americans say? Pig-headed? Maybe I've been making too much noise," Ezra said. "Noise can get in the way of knowledge."

When he said the word "noise," he made a grimace, pursing his lips and scrunching his nose. She could see that he was struggling with his rejection of the Holocaust as a wholly European phenomenon. Something had clicked in his brain. He told her that it had happened a few days earlier when he sat next to a survivor on the Number 18 bus. "She was reading the Eichmann trial news in the paper and she began to cry. She told me that she and her aunt were the only survivors in her family. 'You wouldn't understand,' she said.

"Her words hurt," Ezra said. "I've started to read the trial news," he confessed. Ezra had boasted of never reading anything about the Eichmann trial. "Too many survivor stories," he said. "Not one story about the new immigrants." He'd complained about their coverage and he'd even left a phone message for one of the editors: "Call me for an inside look at the lives of the Moroccans in Jerusalem." But no one ever called him. He followed up with a long letter to the editor listing his grievances. Susan had read a draft and she'd given him some thoughts for editing it. "Tone down your language," Susan told Ezra. "Don't be negative. Tell them that they can improve their stories by weaving in interviews with Moroccans." He read her edits and tore up the draft.

Now, something had clearly happened inside Ezra's head. He was feeling guilty. "Sometimes, I'm too full of myself." He poked Susan to make sure that she was listening. "Did you hear what I said? The woman on the bus was shaking her finger at me. She was saying that everyone in Israel is a survivor, whether they survived the camps or not." Her words had affected him deeply. Ezra had decided to go back to the trial. "Not as a protestor this time," he said. He asked Susan to accompany him.

Like Ezra, Susan had tried to distance herself from the pain and the sorrow of the Holocaust. But she, too, felt increasingly uncomfortable. It was getting harder and harder to understand the Holocaust as simply her father's obsession, her father's history. She had argued with him about his Zionism. That was his dream, not hers, she told him over and over again. Living in Israel, though, she'd begun to understand his feelings. He was a proud Ashkenazi Jew who had settled in America, and he had never met Ezra or Rachel or any other Moroccan Jew.

She hadn't yet gotten up the courage to call her father with the lie. When she lay in bed at night, she rehearsed possible lines.

I really haven't found out anything about him.

I've found out so little about him.

In the beginning, I really was getting somewhere. I was on his trail. I was sure that I would find him alive.

No, that would seem too promising. It would be hard to pull back from there.

Her thoughts were like a rubber band, stretching and snapping back, swinging wildly and then collapsing. The room was revolving. It was the feeling she had when she had an attack of vertigo. Objects were spinning and it was impossible to hold on to them. The floor was shifting from side to side.

Ezra thought she should call her father before he called her.

That was always the best strategy.

Her father had started writing long letters once a week now. It was, he said, a diary of his childhood. He was putting on paper events that he might forget. At the top of this week's letter, he had printed one word: "Challah." "I can still see those twisted loaves of challah, balanced so carefully on one another on top of the tall wooden cabinet. They were there to cool and to keep them safe from the children," he wrote. "That didn't stop us, though. One day, I climbed on my brother Yakov's shoulders and stole a loaf. We put it in an old shirt and carried it down to the riverbank where we devoured it, feeding the crumbs to the fishes. Then, we fell asleep, our bellies full, on the damp grass, returning home just before Shabbos.

"Your grandmother greeted us with her wooden rolling pin in hand. She was a tall woman and very, very strong. 'Who stole the bread?' she screamed, looking at both of us. 'Which one of you did it?' When we each pointed a finger at the other, she whacked us both with her open hand."

His mother was a stern woman who rarely smiled and never laughed. Susan remembered her in America as a woman whose back was straight even when she was in her 80s. Her white hair was twisted on top of her head. Susan was never sure if she had teeth because her lips were always tightly shut.

He wrote about selling booze and cigarettes to the soldiers stationed in Rozwadów. He was afraid that they would arrest him but he was more afraid to come home to his mother without having earned money. "When we showed up without coins in our pockets," he wrote, "we didn't get dinner. She didn't shout or reprimand us. Instead, there was just no food."

He had vivid memories of life in Rozwadów. "Most of the soldiers spoke to us in Polish," he wrote. "A few spoke German. Once, I started to cry when a soldier grabbed the collar of my shirt. Yakov shook his head at me. He was telling me to stop crying, stop being a baby! When I stopped, the soldier let go."

Every other line in the letter was about Yakov. One memory crowded out another. One truth stretched out, maybe into a lie. He was burrowing into his past. Susan knew that he was anxiously awaiting her call. She was his surrogate in the Promised Land.

One winter, her father wrote, they built a fort made of snow in a small clearing in the forest. First, they made bricks of snow, carving them with branches. Then, they stacked them in rows. Yakov's bricks were precise. Each one was the same size as the other. Her father's were irregular, with chunks of ice and stones protruding. "We were so different," he wrote. "I worked fast and he worked slowly. His bricks were smooth and regular while mine were careless and rough."

In America, her father liked to build things out of wood in his spare time. There were cabinets where the doors didn't quite close and where the hinges didn't quite align. He filled their house with knotty pine creations that were clearly the work of an amateur. His cabinets resembled his snow bricks. Only his brother Yakov was perfect.

But the Yakov Susan had met on the beach was worn, even frail. His hair was disheveled. His eyeglasses were askew on the bridge of his nose. His fingers trembled. He was the older brother idolized in her father's letters but his life had been troubled and sad and, from what she could see, painful.

Susan thought of the photos of her parents on the steps of the United States Supreme Court. The young lawyer and his wife dressed stylishly, touring Washington, D.C. Her father in his pinstriped suit and straw hat, tilted rakishly to one side. They were holding hands.

He was wearing his I-made-it-in-America smile. He wore it at her high school graduation. He wore it when he whispered "find Yakov" in her ear just before she left for Israel.

Find Yakov. She had. And she hadn't.

9

Life in the ulpan without Ezra was boring. Their new teacher kept order but Susan was restless. During class, she doodled ominous heads with five eyes and three noses. They reminded her of the doodles that she saw on her father's yellow legal pads. Dybbuks from the shtetl. Demons to be vanquished.

Since she met Ezra, Susan had been fighting off an angry dybbuk. He kept appearing in her dreams, waking her several times each night. He was dressed in black, in the garb of an Eastern European cheder student. He had long peyos and black eyes. He kept shaking his long, thin finger at Susan. *You will be sorry for abandoning me*, he said. *Ezra never went to a cheder. He does not know his Talmud. He has never studied the fine points of Gemorah. Tsk, tsk, the granddaughter of a man from the shtetl of Rozwadów taking an ignorant Moroccan for her lover.* The dybbuk cursed her and Ezra, too. *You will not bear children*, he said. She woke up in a sweat. She couldn't imagine her life without a child.

The next week, he returned with another threat. *You will both be locked up in jail by the Israeli police for treason*, he screamed at her. *You and your Moroccan boyfriend will be handcuffed to the wall of a cell. Your life in the Promised Land will be spent in the dark. You will be fed stale bread and water. If you had married me,* said the spurned *dybbuk, your life would have been full of milk and honey.*

In the morning, she woke up feeling thirsty. As she sipped some water, she remembered the curse. At times, her dybbuk even accosted her during the daytime. Once, when she ordered shakshuka in a tiny restaurant that she'd been to many times, the spicy dish exploded in her mouth. She gulped water, unable to stop her tongue from burning. *You should give up this Moroccan thing,* the dybbuk whispered in her ear. *It is not healthy.*

She wondered whether her father was drawing his own dybbuks. The ominous black-inked heads that marked his store receipts and synagogue programs often had open mouths, words spewing out in the air. Sometimes, they looked like Yakov.

She imagined the dybbuk shouting at Yehudah. *You betrayed me. You should have stayed with me. You left me alone in Rozwadów.* Then, the dybbuk slapped her father hard across his cheek. The doodle reeked of pain. Perhaps her father had sent her on this quest because he felt that he had somehow betrayed his brother.

She kept on postponing calling him. Her doodles were beginning to look like the photos she saw of camp survivors in newspapers and magazines with bones sticking out of their jaws, shrunken heads, and hollowed-out cheeks. At times she drew dark, vertical lines through their faces, like prison bars. She gave each head a number. Once, she drew the head of a small girl with black, curly hair. Number 116. When she stared at the head, she realized she was looking at her own face, imagining herself in Mauthausen or Auschwitz, with a head full of lice and oozing sores on her emaciated arms and legs. "Help me," the girl cried. "Save me!"

The doodles were becoming nightmares. The words of the trial heard on every street corner had become louder and more shrill, the testimony of the witnesses in print in every newspaper were more anguished, and the phone call to her father, looming over it all, more frightening.

Her father answered on the first ring. It was well past midnight in New York. She had caught him reading the trial news. He'd been so busy during the week that the stories had piled up.

"You're calling with good news, right?" he said. His optimism surprised her. Most often he was somber, waiting for the boulder to land on his head.

Susan told him that Jerusalem was on edge as the trial was winding down. "We know how it all ended in the Shoah but the question here is what will the verdict be? Guilty, everyone knows he is guilty. No one here believes that he was just a cog in the wheel of the Nazi machine."

"Not so, here," her father interrupted. There were folks he knew who saw Eichmann as a petty functionary. A young lawyer with an office down the hall from her father was convinced that Eichmann was a scapegoat. "George says that the Nazi hunters are fools. They think that they can purge the world of evil through the execution of one man."

Her father strongly disagreed.

"That's the trouble with us Jews," he told Susan. "We're so damn tolerant. We forgive too easily. Not me, I don't forgive and I don't forget," he said. "The only right decision is guilty. Eichmann must lose his life." He exhaled heavily after the word "life."

Maybe this was a bad time to give him the news about her search for Yakov. This was the moment to tell him that she'd gotten a 100 on her physics exam or received the gold medal in the science fair. Once, when she received a 98 on a math test, he asked what had happened to the other two points. It was sort of a joke.

She had a plan, though. Susan had decided to recount the hunt for Yakov from the beginning, selectively including facts that would push her narrative in the right direction. Yakov had remained in Rozwadów after the family left. There was proof of that. But she would definitely not mention his friendship with a German soldier. Not one word on Bregner. The trail would just go cold. Like so many other shtetl Jews, there would be no trace of him. Not in the Yad Vashem records and not in the lists the Germans had so carefully made up in the camps.

She didn't want to disappoint him. He expected results. Her mission was to find out what happened to Yakov and, on the way, for her to become a Zionist, or at the very least to understand what it meant to be a Zionist. He didn't want her to become—like the rest of his friends' children—assimilated American Jews with little, if any, tie to their homeland. She knew that he'd bound together the quest for Yakov with love of her Jewish homeland.

"I know that you expected more of me," Susan said, speaking softly and slowly. "I know how much this means to you." She hoped that he would say something but he was only listening. There was an occasional sound, almost like a mechanical clicking, like the wheels of the train on the way to Auschwitz. She waited a few more seconds but he still did not speak.

She was trying to be composed. All of a sudden, though, she felt overwhelmed and started to cry. "This search has been stressful," she said. "Everywhere I've gone, I've found pain and grief. Old women and men, middle-aged women and men. Memories of being torn away from their parents and grandparents. Memories of sleeping on filthy bunks and drinking polluted water. One story slips into another. My heart is full. My head is full. I have no more room for such sadness."

Still, only breathing on the other end of the line. No words from her father.

Finally, she got up her courage. "I'm *sick* of the Holocaust," she said.

Enough of this Holocaust stuff. The Moroccans said it. Why couldn't she? Who said that she had to be the dutiful daughter of an immigrant from Poland who felt guilty that he'd escaped the

Holocaust and wanted his child to be passionate about remembering its every detail?

"You've put such a burden on me," she said. "Too heavy. Too distressing."

Now that she had begun to talk, her resentment poured out. "I've looked everywhere. I've spoken to everyone. All I'm doing is researching pain." Silence on the other end of the phone. Part of her was very angry; the other part felt immediate remorse for the harshness of her words.

"It's so emotional for me, Dad. I thought that I could be detached but when I arrived here I was no longer that spoiled American girl who had never once been hungry. The trial was like a beating, a repeated beating, wound upon wound of my psyche. I felt guilty for the life I've lived and resentful, too, that you sent me here to educate me."

"Educate," that was a funny word. It stuck in her throat. The whole family was built on education. Move up the ladder of life and get another degree, another credential. Her father had done it so his children had to do it, too. They were to be Americans who spoke English with no accent. Then, who knows why, he'd slipped back into memories of life in the shtetl. He'd decided that it was safe, even good, to be a Jew in America and he wanted her to become one, too.

Once, years back, he'd shown her a photo essay on America Day at the Educational Alliance Settlement House on the Lower East Side of Manhattan. The girls wore white blouses and the boys white shirts and they carried tiny American flags. On their heads, they wore paper crowns topped with replicas of the Statue of Liberty. The caption spoke of poor, Jewish immigrant children celebrating their new life in America. The second photo showed them sitting in a classroom, their hands raised to answer the teacher's question. On the board behind the teacher, Susan remembered, were words written in chalk in Yiddish and English: "*A Goldenah Medina* means: a land where the streets are paved of gold." Her father rested his finger on one of the boys in the front row: "That 12-year-old boy with the kippah, that was me," he said.

He prided himself on his perfect pronunciation and his perfect diction. When Susan said, "I ain't," he fumed. His face reddened and he waited for an immediate correction. When a waitress taking their order misspoke, he would wait until she was not within earshot and comment on her speech. In Susan's homework assignment, a missing semicolon was the occasion for a lecture. He'd learned English grammar in a class with other immigrants and he knew the reasons behind the punctuation. They were not just dots and dashes; they were signs that he was a true-blooded American.

She'd gained enough control now to tell him about all of the dead ends, the trip to Yad Vashem, the journey to the kibbutz in the north, meetings with Holocaust survivor researchers whose folders were fat and worn. "There are thousands of missing Jews," she told him. "Just like Yakov." As far as she could tell, he was rounded up with the last Jews from Rozwadów. "Where he was sent, after that, seems to be a mystery," she said. "So far, there is no record of him in any of the work or death camps."

Such a long interlude of silence. Maybe it was only a few seconds but it felt to Susan like days, the time it took for a green aerogram to cross the Atlantic Ocean. Finally, her father spoke, haltingly at first. "You can come home," he said. "There's really nothing more for you to do." Her usually loquacious father was struggling for words, a balloon without air. In a few seconds, he'd collapsed upon himself. She had only seen him this way once, at his father's funeral. He was the first to shovel dirt on the coffin. He stood there and said the prayer. Then, he turned to the family and said that he wanted to make a few remarks about his father. But he could not speak. A few words sputtered out, the last hiss of air from the balloon. "He was a good man," her father said of his father. Then, he wiped his eyes with a big white cotton handkerchief, his initials monogrammed in blue in one corner. She ironed seven of those handkerchiefs every week, folding them in thirds and then in thirds again, making sure that the monogram was visible on the outside. That was the way he liked them.

"There's no need for you to remain in Israel," he continued, emphasizing the word "remain." Susan had expected him to push her to do more. His caving in was a surprise. "Once the trial winds down, you can leave."

There it was again, the trial. For her father it was the line in the sand, the marker that would forever damn the Nazis. The world would condemn their evil and sweetness and light would prevail ever after. *Such utter naiveté,* Susan thought.

He'd stopped talking now, apparently waiting for her to speak. "I've made good friends here," Susan said. She'd wanted to tell him about Ezra for a long time. "I'm thinking of staying through the fall, at the very least. Maybe even staying for a year. My friend Ezra knows someone who hires English tutors." There, she'd finally done it. She'd said his name.

She could hear her father's breathing now, louder and more rapid. He wanted her to come back. Her assignment was over. The case was closed. She could see him tearing the yellow notes from the legal pad marked "Yakov" and filing them in a brown accordion folder.

Then, all of a sudden, he seemed to have heard her. "Ezra? Who exactly is Ezra?" he asked, back to his usual litigious behavior. "The guy from the protest?"

He had connected the dots. There was no fooling her father. He'd spent his adult life in a courtroom. He'd interrogated witness after witness. He boasted once of having won an accident case for a critically injured driver who opened up his car door, only to be struck by a bicycle, when he asked the rider: "Since you were riding your bike on the road, were you paying attention to parked cars?" The rider withered under his question and her father won several hundred thousand dollars for his client. There were dozens of these stories over the years, all recounting triumphant tales in the courtroom.

He asked again: "Who is Ezra?"

Susan hesitated before answering her father's question. "I met him at the ulpan. He's an artist who immigrated to Israel from Morocco."

"A Sephardi," her father interrupted. "That's not what I had in mind when I sent you to Israel. Our family is *pure* Ashkenazi."

Pure. What did he mean by pure? What a strange choice of a word from her father. Like pure German? Susan knew that the gulf between the Ashkenazim and the Sephardim was enormous, not only in Israel. A Jew from Poland married a Jew from Poland or Russia. A Jew from Poland worked at a firm with other Jews from the Pale of Settlement. There was absolutely no integration. They had their own synagogues and their own traditions.

"I didn't send you to Israel to *intermarry*," her father said. "Remember, we don't eat rice at our Pesach Seder." She knew that he wasn't making a joke. His understanding of what it meant to be Jewish was intertwined with the shtetl, with potatoes and gefilte fish, with matzo that he ran under warm water and ate sprinkled with kosher salt.

"I'm not ready to get married," Susan said. "He's just a good friend." She was afraid to say anything more. One careless phrase might lead to her talking about the UM party, another clue to her budding activism. He would definitely not approve.

He'd heard enough. Before she could respond, he was saying that he would speak to her next week. "Keep me posted on the trial," he said before hanging up without saying goodbye.

After their phone conversation, Susan tried to read a newspaper but she couldn't keep her eyes focused on one line. She thought about Yakov. He seemed to live such a lonely life, hidden away in Netanya. She thought of visiting him again. She fantasized that they would become friends. She would be the family that he had lost. She would give him photographs of his American family and fill in their narrative. He would learn of the successes of his American cousins and of their failures, too. She could tell him about his parents, now both dead. *Bubbe* and *Zayde* in their Brooklyn apartment with *Zayde* earning his living as a tailor.

But Yakov didn't want the connection. He wanted to be left alone.

Her father had said that she should leave after the trial was over. Newscasters were predicting that the trial would be adjourned in mid-August. Susan decided to attend a session at least one more time. She told Ezra about her conversation with her father when they met in the Central Bus station. "He asked who you were and he wasn't too happy that you're Moroccan. Looks like there's prejudice against you in America, too."

"There's prejudice against us everywhere," he said. "We have dark skin." He'd been reading about the African-Americans' struggles. "If I lived in America, I'd be joining with blacks there in their fight."

During high school, Susan had a black friend who lived by the railroad tracks, in the worst part of town. When they would drive her home after school, she asked them to leave her on the main avenue, three blocks from her house. She didn't want Susan to see the wooden building where she lived, which was more of a shack than a home. The shutters were broken and askew. The porch steps were collapsed and the garden was a field of weeds in mud.

No other white kid was friendly with her. Her name was Violet and she wrote wild poetry about black ravens picking at the eyes of white doves. She would never read the poems aloud but she shared them with Susan.

"Blacks in America are in pain," Susan said. "It is going to explode one day soon."

Ezra nodded. "It will explode here, too. For Moroccans, the UM is our only hope." They already had 8000 names on their sign-up list and the goal was to reach 20,000 before the August election. "The official parties, especially Herut, are becoming aware of our numbers," he said. "They have begun to woo us." That was, Ezra said, a sign of their growing power. UM was now distributing flyers at the Central Bus Station and near the Beit Ha'am building. The idea was to flood the city. Ezra had sent missionaries throughout Israel, to Tel Aviv and to Haifa to find friends wherever there were pockets of Moroccans.

For two hours, Susan and Ezra stood in the heat in the station. The fumes made Susan choke and every few seconds she had to take a deep breath to stop herself from coughing. Women were more receptive than men. "What are you making noise about now?" one man said to her, shaking his head no to the extended flyer. "That's the trouble with this country. Everyone has a gripe." An Orthodox man in a black hat walked around her, avoiding eye contact. A kibbutznik in boots and a sun hat told her to get a job. "This country needs workers, not protestors," he said. He took a flyer and tore it in half. "Take that," he said. Two children took flyers and folded them into paper airplanes. The planes whizzed through the air and landed in a green garbage pail.

Susan was discouraged by the reception. Ezra was not. He saw it as part of the process. "First, they will hate us for making noise," he said. "Then, they will like us for changing things for the better." It was the way the world worked. He smiled as he handed a flyer to a young man and then, still smiling, took it back when the man turned away. "Always with a smile," Ezra said.

They talked of the future. "I need you here," Ezra said, putting both of his arms around Susan. "I don't want you to go back to America. You belong with me." She looked into his eyes and thought of her father's tirade.

Her father was wrong. She was sure of that. Ezra and Susan were both Jews. They had different complexions and different traditions but they were both descendants of the 12 tribes. Whether they were expelled from Spain or rounded up in Polish ghettos, they were all Jews. She felt Ezra's arms around her, strong and confident. His world was hers now. She'd come to find Yakov and understand what it meant to live through the Holocaust. She'd tried to push it far away, as if Europe and the fate of the Jews was only her father's history, but she'd learned that it was hers, too. How else could she explain her obsession with counting the numbers of the survivors that she observed?

Recently, though, she'd stopped counting. There was no reason to count anymore. She was a survivor, too. They were all survivors. Yakov, Ruth, Ezra, and the Moroccans. The numbers were floating away in the sky, riding clouds. One minute, they were in her vision, the next they were gone. Cloud by cloud they disappeared, present but gone.

Like Yakov.

On Monday, August 14, 1961, Ezra, Ruth, and Susan arrived early at Beit Ha'am. Despite his having been nearly ejected previously, Ezra managed to get them seats in the main hall. Considering that this might be the final day of the trial, it was a sign of his growing political clout. A leading member of the Herut party had arranged all of the details.

"He is courting our vote," Ezra told her. They'd reserved seats right behind the reporters. This was the end and everyone was tired. The court officers looked like they'd been up all night. One of them kept rubbing his eyes, as if to keep them open. They were tired of the testimony, tired of listening to Eichmann's defense that he had no choice but to follow orders, that he was merely following his oath of allegiance. The decision to kill the Jews, Eichmann insisted, had been out of his hands. Repeatedly, he said that he was guilty of authorizing the transports but he was not guilty of the consequences. He'd said this over and over again, day after day. The audience could repeat the words by heart: he was only following orders. Ezra held her hand for the two hours that they were there. Every so often his eyes would tear up and he would wipe the tears away with his strong fingers. Susan saw Hannah Arendt sitting two rows in front of her, taking her last notes. Susan thought of her father back in New York with her family awaiting the final news roundup. Susan thought of Yakov in his Netanya apartment, listening alone to the news. Ruth sat beside her, wringing her hands together.

Suddenly, it was over. The judge declared that the testimonies were finished and his decision and the sentence would come later, probably in late November or early December. For those in the audience and for everyone listening on the radio, for everyone seeing the taped sessions around the world, the evidence was conclusive. They knew that the eventual verdict would be guilty. Guilty on all counts. That frail little man who looked innocent was guilty. Guilty in Hebrew, in Yiddish, in German, in English, in Arabic, in French, and in Spanish. Everywhere, a feeling of profound relief. Relief from the pain of listening to the testimonies of survivors. It was the start of a new mood in the cafés and on the streets.

When Susan returned to her apartment around 8 p.m., she found a note from a roommate taped to her bedroom door. "Your father called. He said that he will call you back every hour until he gets you." Susan crossed the street to the pension and waited for his call.

When she answered the phone, he didn't even say hello. "You won't believe what I'm holding in my hands," he said. "A letter from Yakov! Yakov!" His voice was trembling. "He's alive! I know that you know. He told me that you found him."

Susan was shocked. When she left Yakov, it had been with the clear understanding that he did not exist. She would keep his secret. He would live out his life in privacy. That was the way he wanted it to be. She couldn't imagine what had changed his mind.

"He's been hiding out since he was liberated," her father said. Susan listened, not sure how much Yakov had revealed to her father. Her father didn't give her a chance to speak, not that she wanted to.

Dear Yehudah.

Two weeks ago, your daughter Susan found me in Netanya. When she approached me on the beach, I had a strange feeling. I did not recognize her but somehow, from the very first moment I saw her, I saw you walking toward me. There was something in her gait, her hop, the way she landed on her left foot, that silly step that you make when you are moving forward, that made me think of you. She swung her hands as she walked, spreading her fingers slightly as she moved. It was a gesture that I remembered you doing as we walked the cobblestone streets of Rozwadów or when we played tag in the woods outside of town. You clenching and unclenching your fists, your hands flying in the air by your sides.

For the past few months, I have had the feeling that my life was about to change. Every day, when I listened to the testimony at the Eichmann trial, I found myself talking aloud. Whispering, mumbling, shouting. One confession after another. One lament after another. Just tell your story, Yakov, I said to myself. Don't be afraid. Go to Jerusalem, climb on the witness stand and testify. Tell the world the truth. Give up the secrets that have tormented you. Give up the memories, good and bad, that you have buried. You will be believed. You will be accepted. No one will call you a traitor or a collaborator.

Since the trial started, I have not been able to sleep. Every night I am awakened by nightmares and guilt. Boots marching before my eyes. Dogs sniffing at my feet. For decades, words have been dancing in my head. Words that I never said when we parted so long ago in Rozwadów and words that tormented me after I was liberated from Dachau and settled in Israel. I knew that I could find you but I didn't even try. If I found you, I would have to tell you the truth. I couldn't do that. I loved you too much.

Each year, on the Yom HaShoah holiday, I lit a candle and I said a prayer: Dear God, give me the strength to bare my soul. I am not a religious man, Yehudah. I was not exactly sure which God I was praying to, but I prayed to free myself from my secret and my silence.

Then, Susan appeared, an apparition come to life on the beach, a ghost who left footprints in the sand. To make matters worse, she was not alone. Beside her was Ruth, a woman whom I remembered from Mauthausen. It was almost two decades later but Ruth recognized me and I recognized her. My heartbeat sped up when I saw her, pounding as if my chest would burst, because ours was more than just a casual acquaintance. We knew each other's secrets. We were two souls trapped in the camps, each with a forbidden lover. Ruth with her Nazi lover and me with mine.

The truth is, Yehudah, that I lived in fear long before I was in the camps. Since I was a teenager, I would wake up in the middle of the night, sweat covering my body. I would stare at you, lying peacefully asleep next to me, nothing troubling you. I would reach over and tuck the thin blanket over your feet and you would sigh in your sleep. I loved protecting you. I was your big brother, the one who would make sure that no harm would ever befall you.

When we were boys at the yeshiva in Rozwadów, even then, I was afraid. You looked up to me. We confided in each other but there were things that I could not tell you. The rebbes taught us how to daven and we studied Torah. Neither of us, though, seemed destined to become a Torah scholar. We did our homework together, always at the last minute. We forgot to pray. We were more interested in skipping stones across the river.

It was not about strength, you always said. It was an art, a skill that we could master, just like the future ahead of us that we could mold.

But the truth was, in Rozwadów, at that moment in history, our lives were already planned for us. We were to study Torah until we settled down and got married. It would only be a few years until the matchmaker found our bashert, the beloved that God intended for us. The woman who would cook our meals, clean our homes and bear our children. Even then, I felt confused. I felt ashamed but I knew one thing. I did not want a bride.

One day in cheder, when I was almost 13, I looked across the room and could not take my eyes off of Avram. Do you remember him? He was so handsome. He had dark brown eyes, deeply set, and thick, curly black eyelashes. I looked at him and—please, Yehudah, do not tear this letter up—I fell in love. For days, I would sit in class, forcing myself not to stare at him. There was something wrong with me. A boy did not look at another boy that way. Has V'Hayil. God forbid! A boy did not have those feelings for another boy. When the rebbe spoke, I could not hear him. I could not hear or think of anything or anyone else except Avram.

All of the other boys were looking at the girls and their mothers were beginning to talk to the matchmakers. Almost every night, I dreamt of running away with Avram. When Mama decided to leave for America, I knew that I could not go with you. I would shame the family name. I would have to face Papa, who would never accept me. There was no place in our family for a boy who loved boys and certainly none for a boy who would grow up to become a man who loved men. No, it was better for me to remain hidden from view in Rozwadów. So, I lied. I said that I wanted to stay at my job. I said that I wanted to remain in the shtetl.

Susan interrupted her father's reading. "It was a hard decision," she said. "I could see the pain on his face when he spoke. I felt sorry for him." Her father continued reading.

After you left, I was very lonely. I worked all day long in the store and spent the nights by myself. Once, when I was 20, I traveled to Krakow. In a restaurant there was a man who invited me to join him for a meal. He was ten years older than me. He lived in Berlin but was in Krakow on business. I went back to his hotel room and we had sex. I had never been with anyone—a man or a woman—before, and I was afraid that someone would find out. His business brought him to Krakow every month and I met him there. I'm not sure if I loved him but I confess to you that I wanted to be with him.

No one knew about us. Back in Rozwadów, I was Yakov, the young man whose family had gone to America, a bachelor who was, as of yet, unmarried on the lists of the local matchmakers.

Nearly ten years after you left, I traveled to Berlin. I had heard that life for men like me was better there and I wanted to find out for myself. I was desperate to move out of the shadows and walk in the sunshine. One day, I saw an ad in the newspaper for Eldorado, a nightclub for men. When I was waiting in line at the entrance, I met Karl Bregner. He was so handsome. I was smitten by his violet eyes. He was smitten by mine. Bregner was on leave in the city and we spent a week together. Then, we parted. We kissed goodbye. I never expected to see him again.

After a while in Rozwadów the matchmakers gave up. They stopped sending me names. There were other things to worry about. The economy was in a downturn and the store was struggling to stay open. When Adolf Hitler was elected Chancellor, our lives changed dramatically. The Germans arrived in Rozwadów and the Jews who still lived there feared for their lives. One day, a German officer came into the store. I recognized him immediately. It was Bregner. Karl Bregner from Berlin. At first, I was afraid that he would say something personal. "So good to see you again." But he was careful. He wanted to buy some cigarettes. Then, keeping up the pretense of first meeting me, he asked my name. When I said Yakov Reich, he laughed. "With your blue eyes and blonde hair," he said, "you could pass for a German." The minute that I saw him I fell in love again. Please, Yehudah, forgive me, I truly loved him.

Her father paused in reading. He was crying. "Give me a minute to compose myself," he said. She could hear him blowing his nose, undoubtedly with one of his enormous handkerchiefs.

After that, Bregner came to the store often. He would bring me little gifts. A chocolate bar. An orange. A bottle of brandy. Each one was more precious. Our hands would touch when he gave them to me. Sometimes, when no one was watching, we would stand there holding hands, not wanting to let go.

One day he showed up early in the morning. I could tell that he was agitated. When I took his hand, it was cold and trembling. He had come to warn me. He told me that he had inside information that the Jews were going to be rounded up the next day. There was not much time. He said that I didn't have to be afraid because he'd made other plans for me. He squeezed my hand as he explained. He'd been reassigned to Mauthausen and he was going to take me with him. He'd already prepared new identity papers for me.

Yehudah, I know that this letter will shock you. Perhaps you will burn it. Perhaps you will decide to obliterate your brother Yakov from your memory. This is definitely not what you expected when you sent your daughter to find out what happened to me. Where is your joy in discovering that your beloved older brother, who vanished in the Holocaust, survived because he had a Nazi lover? I can see you now, my letter fluttering in the air. Your face flushed. Your fingers are trembling and your whole body faint. Forgive me, Yehudah. I cannot keep this secret any longer.

I packed my clothing and slipped out of town with him. I crammed everything I owned into that small, brown leather suitcase, the one that you left behind for me. The next day, almost all of the Jews remaining in Rozwadów were rounded up and sent to the work camp. Bregner and I traveled by train to Mauthausen where he'd made arrangements for me to have a room in a boarding house near the camp that was owned by his friend. Bregner had taken care of every detail. I was relieved and I was happy for the first time in my life. I was no longer Yakov Reich. I had become Martin Specht.

Yehudah, try to understand! I loved Bregner. It was not just because he saved my life. I loved him. We loved each other. Crazy, a Nazi and a Jew; crazy, two men loving each other when such love was a shandah. We were both taking a risk. The Nazi criminal code considered our relationship to be unnatural behavior. We were violating the Nazi Criminal Code (Paragraph 175) which made homosexual acts between males a crime. But some things are worth violating. Loving someone completely—how can there be a law against that?

For years, I worked in the supply warehouse at Mauthausen, taking the bus back and forth to the camp. I ate my meals with the Nazi officers. I kept to myself. I was not to socialize with anyone, Jew or German. I kept my answers short. I made little eye contact.

I worked side by side with Walter Kruck, a German friend of Bregner's who was Susan's friend Ruth's lover. Ruth knew me all right. When I saw her on the beach, of course, I knew her, too.

When the Nazis began to lose the war and liberation was imminent, Bregner knew that he was doomed. He was reconciled to his own death but he couldn't stand the thought of me dying. He said that he wanted me to have a life after him. His love for me went beyond our relationship: he wanted to save me. I wanted to die with him but he put his hand over my mouth when I said those words. "No, Yakov, you must live," he said, over and over again. Every night, he would come up with a different scheme for my survival. He would smuggle me out of the camp. He would ship me to somewhere safe and far away. But, always, he feared that I might be caught and killed.

One night, he came up with an idea that he thought would work. He would turn me back into a Jew. I would be transformed into a Jew with forged identity papers. Then, he would arrange to have me transferred to Dachau, where no one would recognize me. I would be liberated there as Menachem Kreinen. I wanted to swallow poison and be done with my life. We argued about what to do. That was the first time that we ever had a fight. But he won.

Bregner swallowed poison. I was liberated at Dachau and then, after spending time in a Displaced Persons Camp, I immigrated to Israel. I've lived in hiding in Netanya since then, collecting survivor's benefits and keeping to myself. When the Eichmann trial began, the wound festered and opened. I was a Jew who became a German who became a Jew. I was a survivor who had survived by *working in the death camps as a German. I was a homosexual whose lover was a Nazi.*

As I listened to the testimony, though, I realized how much I'd actually suffered. I'd been spared the gas chambers and the beatings. I'd been spared the long death marches. I ate three meals a day and slept in a warm bed. But I carried around the weight of my secrets: when I worked at Mauthausen I lived with a yellow star with the word "Jude" and a pink triangle, both hidden inside me. Now, with the end of the Eichmann trial and having met Susan, I no longer feel that I have to hide. I can wear the Jude and the pink triangle on the outside. I can write you the truth, Yehudah. I am a Jew. I am a homosexual. I am your brother. I can finally be all three. I pray that you will understand. May we see one another soon! Love, Yakov

Her father sighed. "I have read his letter a dozen times," he said. "Shocked at first, angry, in denial. Not my brother Yakov. Not my beloved Yakov. I sat outside on the porch looking up at the stars. The Big Dipper so clear in the sky. The North Star blinding me with its brightness. The same stars that we looked at when we were boys, on the banks of the San, the same stars that we counted and made wishes on, imagining what we would be when we were grown up. Where we would live—somewhere exciting, far from Rozwadów. How could I be angry at him? Such a heavy price he paid." She could hear him crying on the other end of the phone. She'd never heard her father cry like this before. "Yakov is alive," he kept saying. "Alive. Alive."

Susan could hear the shift in her father's tone as he repeated the word "alive," moving from shock to relief. He was feeling peace now. He wasn't angry at Yakov and he was not ashamed. He was grateful to have him back in his life, the precious, lost older brother who had not crossed the ocean to America. Now, her father would travel back to him. They would meet in a café in Netanya, smoking cigarette after cigarette. They would wade in the warm waters of the Mediterranean, arms around each other's shoulders, whispering secrets. Two brothers reunited.

The next morning Ezra voted. "The lines were long and the turnout high. For a few hours, no one on the street was talking about Eichmann or the *Shoah*," Ezra told Susan when they met at the café where the radio was blasting the election results. There were interviews with candidates from Mapai, Herut, the Liberal party, and the National Religious party, the parties who drew the highest votes, "as predicted," Ezra said. UM was not yet an official party, still Ezra felt encouraged. "The new reality is that Moroccans have come to understand the value of organizing and bloc voting. One day, we will be a party and fill many seats in the Knesset. Ashkenazim will promise us the world to gain our support."

Ezra was thinking about the future. Susan was still thinking about the past. Life in New York was easier. She didn't have to plan when she would take her hot showers.

Only a year ago, back in New York, she would spend hours at the Met Museum. She'd started to do that just before she left for Israel, seeking out little-known works that depicted Jerusalem. In Israel, she had no time to visit museums. Like everyone else in the land, she'd been consumed by the Eichmann trial. In the Holy City, spectators had been crowded into the Beit Ha'am building, watching and listening to the testimony. Returning home to New York would be simple.

But returning meant leaving Ezra. He loved his activism, that she knew, but she also knew that he loved her. He wanted her to remain, to join him in his fight. Her face would become suntanned, dark like his, her hair would be wild and curly. She would wear leather sandals on her feet, khaki walking shorts, and, on her head, a *kova tembel*, shielding her from the fierce Middle Eastern sun. Gradually, he would leave construction, moving on to become a professional organizer. She would earn a living as an English tutor for aspiring Israelis whose ultimate goal was to study or live abroad in the United States. They would move in together, renting an apartment near the Moroccans. On Friday nights, long after the

Shabbos meal, they would lie in each other's arms, making love until the morning. She would wake up, no longer frightened by the cats screeching in the alley outside of her new home.

Heading back to her apartment that evening, Susan made her decision. "I love you, *Motek*," she said, putting her arms around Ezra. "I love you and want to stay with you to build a new Israel."

10

The next day, when Susan and Ezra stopped by the café, coffee and dessert were on the house. "When we get the final verdict," Meir said, "I promise to treat you all to a whole meal! I've traveled a long, convoluted trail. From Vienna to Jerusalem, from Kristallnacht to this café, where we are all standing today, coffee in hand, toasting our future. We've lived through the trial. For some of us it was a catharsis, for others a step backward into despair and sadness. But we are all standing here today, citizens who have voted in the Jewish state, citizens who have just concluded the greatest trial in history."

For a moment, the audience hesitated, not sure if he was finished. Then, they clapped, beating their palms, loud and incessant, hard and defiant. Ruth clapped. Ezra clapped. Susan clapped.

Meir asked if anyone else wanted to speak. Ezra was eager to say a few words. He walked over to Susan and took her hand. "I've never been to Vienna. I cannot imagine Kristallnacht or the camps. But we Moroccan Jews, we've had our own sorrows and suffering, our own Shoah. This trial was our trial, too."

Everyone clapped again, several of the men, expressing their approval by slapping Ezra on the back. "You are one of us," said an old man with numbers on his arm. "We are one *mishpacha*."

Then, to Susan's surprise, Ruth stood up. "I've lived in the shadow of the camps since I was liberated," she said. "I've never had a day when I did not think about my life there, often feeling guilty because I managed to survive. My old decisions haunted me." She paused to catch her breath. "These past weeks, when I listened to survivors talk about what they had to do to survive, it freed me. I've begun to forgive myself. I was young. I was afraid. I made decisions, some I regret and some I don't.

"Last night was the first night that I didn't wake with a nightmare: always the same dream, of a vicious dog chasing me and me running into the outstretched arms of my lover, who vanishes as I approach him. The dog gets closer and closer but I wake before it bites. Last night, there was no dog. There was only the sound of the cats yowling in Jerusalem. A woman in a flowered dress handed me a handkerchief and said, 'Whatever you did, you are forgiven.'"

Instead of clapping, everyone in the café was nodding in agreement now. Susan could hear the word "forgiven" in English, in Hebrew, and in Yiddish. It's OK. Whatever choices you made to survive, you are forgiven.

Ruth wasn't quite finished. "I've made a big decision," she said. "I'm leaving my life as a waitress. I applied to a counseling program at Hebrew University and they've accepted me with a scholarship." She turned to Ezra. "Israel is not an easy place. I know how difficult life can be when you first arrive. I struggled for years. Now, I want to help new immigrants assimilate. People like you."

Ezra walked Susan back to her apartment. On the way, they talked about Ruth's remarks. Susan was surprised by her candor. "She's been so guarded, so private. I never expected her to make a public speech. The trial, finding Yakov, telling me about her Nazi lover Walter—one secret after another has been revealed. She does not have to hide anymore."

People were gathered on street corners talking and smoking.

"Thank God, the testimonies are over," a woman said.

"We have to get back to life."

"Enough with sadness and death."

Two girls were jumping rope. Three boys raced their bicycles down the street. A grocery store owner was pulling down the grates and locking up for the night. Electric lights were being turned on in apartments as people sat down for dinner.

Susan felt free now, too. Her quest for Yakov was over. In Israel she had discovered what being Jewish meant to her and she now understood her father's Zionism. She didn't have to follow his route. Israel was the Promised Land but it was also a land of challenges and inequalities. She dreamt of a future with Ezra where they would build a life together, not as farmers on a kibbutz but as activists. They would lobby for the rights of women and children and for better jobs for workers. They would spend their days distributing flyers and marching in protests, and their nights making love.

For once, there were no radios booming. They walked through the quiet streets, like two children, swinging their clasped hands in the air. Higher and higher.

GLOSSARY

All words are Hebrew or Yiddish unless otherwise noted. Hebrew words in the book use the Ashkenazic pronunciation except when spoken by a Moroccan when the Sephardic pronunciation is used.

afikoman - matzo hidden at Passover Seder

agorot - Israeli coins

aliyah - to settle in Israel

bashert - divinely ordained, meant to happen, the person you are meant to marry

Beit Ha'Am - "House of the Nation," Jerusalem cultural center now the Gerard Behar Center

B'ezras Hashem - with God's help

bimah - reader's platform in a synagogue

bubbe - grandmother

charissa - Moroccan hot sauce

chuppah - wedding canopy

dai - enough, stop it

dybbuk - a malevolent, wandering spirit that enters the body of a living being

Eretz Yisrael - Land of Israel

falafel - fried chickpea balls

Forverts - The Forward, a Yiddish language newspaper

gadol - big, large, important

gevinah levinah - white cheese

Goldene Medina - the golden land, America land of opportunity

gut glik - good happiness

Haaretz - The Land, Hebrew newspaper

Haggadah - booklet which recounts the Exodus from Egypt and details the rituals of the Passover Seder

jawohl - yes, sir (German)

kippah - Jewish skullcap

landsleit - fellow countrymen

landsmanshaft - Jewish fraternal and mutual aid society

libe - love

lo - no

maher - quickly

Marokayit - Moroccan Arabic language

mechitzah - divider between men's and women's sections in a synagogue

mitzvah - meritorious act

mishpacha - family

motek - sweetie

nachon - correct

non - no (French)

parfaite - perfect (French)

petit - little (French)

peyos - side locks worn by religious boys and men

rebbe/rebbes - rabbi/rabbis

retzach - murder

Rozhinkes mit Mandlen - Raisins and Almonds (Yiddish song)

sabra - native-born Israeli

Shabbos/Shabbat - Sabbath, Saturday

shalom - hello, goodbye, peace

shandah - scandal

Shema - key prayer declaring that the One God is the essence of everything. Lit. hear

shidduch - an arranged marriage

Shoah - The Holocaust

shtetl - Jewish village of old

shuk - market

shul - synagogue

Shulchan Aruch - code of Jewish law

siddur - Jewish prayer book

tahini - dip made from sesame seeds

taleisim - prayer shawls

tefillin - phylacteries, a set of small black cubes containing Torah verses on parchment

todah - thank you

tzedakah - charity (root means justice)

tzitzis - fringes on corners of prayer shawl or other four-cornered garment

ulpan - Hebrew language school in Israel

vinkyl - corner (German)

vrai - true (French)

Zayde - grandfather

ACKNOWLEDGMENTS

In the course of this writing project, many friends, family members, and colleagues read drafts and excerpts from the manuscript. Below is an incomplete list of those who made it possible for me to finish this novel. For his meticulous critique of the book, thank you to Bert Hansen, a former Baruch colleague. For his help in shaping early chapters of the novel in the Sackett Street Fiction Writers workshop, thanks to Josh Rolnick, author, editor, and teacher. For a stimulating creative environment where I began the novel, thanks to the Virginia Center for the Creative Arts.

Thank you to colleagues and friends from Baruch College, CUNY, New York City, and the Buffalo Colony in the Catskills for their perceptive comments including Glenda Hydler, Dov Schlein, Bridgett Davis, Karlan Sick, Laura Limonic, and Kate Crehan, with whom I drank many cups of coffee as we exchanged drafts of our books-in-progress.

I am grateful for author and editor Wayne Hoffman's shrewd advice on characters and plot, always perceptive and always sharp. I am in debt to many people who were quick to answer my myriad questions relating to accuracies of time, place, and language: Donna Robinson Divine, Michael Wolff (and his late wife Carol), Deborah and Oded Shmueli, Boaz Adler, Sylvan Cappell, and my daughter Sara Miriam Gross who deftly edited the glossary.

I want to express my very special thanks to Liesbeth Heenk, Amsterdam Publishers, for welcoming my manuscript to her imprint and for believing in this novel.

I could not have written this book without the enthusiastic encouragement of my family in New York and Israel, my children and grandchildren, all of whom listened to endless questions and issues that floated through my mind, especially Malka Gross, my oldest grandchild, always quick to suggest changes large and small.

Most of all, though, I could not have researched and written this book without the loving support of my husband Shael Shapiro, who read and critiqued the novel as it evolved. Indeed, Shael has the perfect name. He is my rock.

ABOUT THE AUTHOR

Roslyn Bernstein has been a storyteller all her life, sometimes working for a true account in the narrow sense as a journalist when it's reporting or history, and sometimes in a wider, more resonant sense when composing poetry, short stories, or a novel.

As a journalist, she has reported in-depth cultural stories for venues including *Guernica, Tablet, Arterritory,* and *Huffington Post*. Sixty of her online pieces were reprinted in an anthology, *Engaging Art: Essays and Interviews From Around the Globe*. While reporting on all forms of art and architecture, documentary photography has been a major subject of Bernstein's writing and teaching since the 1970s.

She is the author of a collection of linked fictional tales, *Boardwalk Stories,* set in a seaside community during the 1950s, and the co-author with Shael Shapiro of *Illegal Living: 80 Wooster Street and the Evolution of SoHo,* which focuses on one building to tell the story of SoHo's transformation from a manufacturing district to a live-work arts community.

For most of her career, she taught journalism and creative writing at Baruch College, CUNY where she was the founding director of The Sidney Harman Writer-in-Residence Program.

The Girl Who Counted Numbers was inspired by the seven months that Roslyn Bernstein spent in Jerusalem in 1961. She has tried to be attentive to historical details although the story of Susan Reich, her family, and friends is fictional.

www.roslynbernstein.com

AMSTERDAM PUBLISHERS HOLOCAUST LIBRARY

The series **Holocaust Survivor Memoirs World War II** consists of the following autobiographies of survivors:

Outcry. Holocaust Memoirs, by Manny Steinberg

Hank Brodt Holocaust Memoirs. A Candle and a Promise, by Deborah Donnelly

The Dead Years. Holocaust Memoirs, by Joseph Schupack

Rescued from the Ashes. The Diary of Leokadia Schmidt, Survivor of the Warsaw Ghetto, by Leokadia Schmidt

My Lvov. Holocaust Memoir of a twelve-year-old Girl, by Janina Hescheles

Remembering Ravensbrück. From Holocaust to Healing, by Natalie Hess

Wolf. A Story of Hate, by Zeev Scheinwald with Ella Scheinwald

Save my Children. An Astonishing Tale of Survival and its Unlikely Hero, by Leon Kleiner with Edwin Stepp

Holocaust Memoirs of a Bergen-Belsen Survivor & Classmate of Anne Frank, by Nanette Blitz Konig

Defiant German - Defiant Jew. A Holocaust Memoir from inside the Third Reich, by Walter Leopold with Les Leopold

In a Land of Forest and Darkness. The Holocaust Story of two Jewish Partisans, by Sara Lustigman Omelinski

Holocaust Memories. Annihilation and Survival in Slovakia, by Paul Davidovits

From Auschwitz with Love. The Inspiring Memoir of Two Sisters' Survival, Devotion and Triumph Told by Manci Grunberger Beran & Ruth Grunberger Mermelstein, by Daniel Seymour

Remetz. Resistance Fighter and Survivor of the Warsaw Ghetto, by Jan Yohay Remetz

My March Through Hell. A Young Girl's Terrifying Journey to Survival, by Halina Kleiner with Edwin Stepp

Roman's Journey, by Roman Halter

Beyond Borders. Escaping the Holocaust and Fighting the Nazis. 1938-1948, by Rudi Haymann

The Engineers. A memoir of survival through World War II in Poland and Hungary, by Henry Reiss

Memoirs by Elmar Rivosh, Sculptor (1906-1967). Riga Ghetto and Beyond, by Elmar Rivosh

The series **Holocaust Survivor True Stories** consists of the following biographies:

Among the Reeds. The true story of how a family survived the Holocaust, by Tammy Bottner

A Holocaust Memoir of Love & Resilience. Mama's Survival from Lithuania to America, by Ettie Zilber

Living among the Dead. My Grandmother's Holocaust Survival Story of Love and Strength, by Adena Bernstein Astrowsky

Heart Songs. A Holocaust Memoir, by Barbara Gilford

Shoes of the Shoah. The Tomorrow of Yesterday, by Dorothy Pierce

Hidden in Berlin. A Holocaust Memoir, by Evelyn Joseph Grossman

Separated Together. The Incredible True WWII Story of Soulmates Stranded an Ocean Apart, by Kenneth P. Price, Ph.D.

The Man Across the River. The incredible story of one man's will to survive the Holocaust, by Zvi Wiesenfeld

If Anyone Calls, Tell Them I Died. A Memoir, by Emanuel (Manu) Rosen

The House on Thrömerstrasse. A Story of Rebirth and Renewal in the Wake of the Holocaust, by Ron Vincent

Dancing with my Father. His hidden past. Her quest for truth. How Nazi Vienna shaped a family's identity, by Jo Sorochinsky

The Story Keeper. Weaving the Threads of Time and Memory - A Memoir, by Fred Feldman

Krisia's Silence. The Girl who was not on Schindler's List, by Ronny Hein

Defying Death on the Danube. A Holocaust Survival Story, by Debbie J. Callahan with Henry Stern

A Doorway to Heroism. A decorated German-Jewish Soldier who became an American Hero, by Rabbi W. Jack Romberg

The Shoemaker's Son. The Life of a Holocaust Resister, by Laura Beth Bakst

The Redhead of Auschwitz. A True Story, by Nechama Birnbaum

Land of Many Bridges. My Father's Story, by Bela Ruth Samuel Tenenholtz

Creating Beauty from the Abyss. The Amazing Story of Sam Herciger, Auschwitz Survivor and Artist, by Lesley Ann Richardson

On Sunny Days We Sang. A Holocaust Story of Survival and Resilience, by Jeannette Grunhaus de Gelman

Painful Joy. A Holocaust Family Memoir, by Max J. Friedman

I Give You My Heart. A True Story of Courage and Survival, by Wendy Holden

In the Time of Madmen, by Mark A. Prelas

Monsters and Miracles. Horror, Heroes and the Holocaust, by Ira Wesley Kitmacher

Flower of Vlora. Growing up Jewish in Communist Albania, by Anna Kohen

Aftermath: Coming of Age on Three Continents. A Memoir, by Annette Libeskind Berkovits

Not a real Enemy. The True Story of a Hungarian Jewish Man's Fight for Freedom, by Robert Wolf

Zaidy's War. Four Armies, Three Continents, Two Brothers. One Man's Impossible Story of Endurance, by Martin Bodek

The Glassmaker's Son. Looking for the World my Father left behind in Nazi Germany, by Peter Kupfer

The Apprentice of Buchenwald. The True Story of the Teenage Boy Who Sabotaged Hitler's War Machine, by Oren Schneider

Good for a Single Journey, by Helen Joyce

Burying the Ghosts. She escaped Nazi Germany only to have her life torn apart by the woman she saved from the camps: her mother, by Sonia Case

American Wolf. From Nazi Refugee to American Spy. A True Story, by Audrey Birnbaum

Bipolar Refugee. A Saga of Survival and Resilience, by Peter Wiesner

Before the Beginning and After the End, by Hymie Anisman

Malka Owsiany recounts, by Mark Turkow (editor)

I Will Give Them an Everlasting Name. Jacksonville's Stories of the Holocaust, by Samuel P. Cox

The series **Jewish Children in the Holocaust** consists of the
following autobiographies of Jewish children
hidden during WWII in the Netherlands:

Searching for Home. The Impact of WWII on a Hidden Child, by
Joseph Gosler

See You Tonight and Promise to be a Good Boy! War memories, by
Salo Muller

Sounds from Silence. Reflections of a Child Holocaust Survivor,
Psychiatrist and Teacher, by Robert Krell

Sabine's Odyssey. A Hidden Child and her Dutch Rescuers, by
Agnes Schipper

The Journey of a Hidden Child, by Harry Pila and Robin Black

The series **New Jewish Fiction** consists of the following novels, written by Jewish authors. All novels are set in the time during or after the Holocaust.

The Corset Maker. A Novel, by Annette Libeskind Berkovits

Escaping the Whale. The Holocaust is over. But is it ever over for the next generation? by Ruth Rotkowitz

When the Music Stopped. Willy Rosen's Holocaust, by Casey Hayes

Hands of Gold. One Man's Quest to Find the Silver Lining in Misfortune, by Roni Robbins

The Girl Who Counted Numbers. A Novel, by Roslyn Bernstein

There was a garden in Nuremberg. A Novel, by Navina Michal Clemerson

The Butterfly and the Axe, by Omer Bartov

To Live Another Day. A Novel, Elizabeth Rosenberg

A Worthy Life. Based on a True Story, by Dahlia Moore

The series **Holocaust Heritage** consists of the following memoirs by 2G:

The Cello Still Sings. A Generational Story of the Holocaust and of the Transformative Power of Music, by Janet Horvath

The Fire and the Bonfire. A Journey into Memory, by Ardyn Halter

The Silk Factory: Finding Threads of My Family's True Holocaust Story, by Michael Hickins

Hidden in Plain Sight. A Journey into Memory and Place, by Julie Brill

Against All Odds. A Memoir, by Grace Feuerverger

The series **Holocaust Books for Young Adults** consists of the following novels, based on true stories:

The Boy behind the Door. How Salomon Kool Escaped the Nazis. Inspired by a True Story, by David Tabatsky

Running for Shelter. A True Story, by Suzette Sheft

The Precious Few. An Inspirational Saga of Courage based on True Stories, by David Twain with Art Twain

The series **WWII Historical Fiction** consists of the following novels, some of which are based on true stories:

Mendelevski's Box. A Heartwarming and Heartbreaking Jewish Survivor's Story, by Roger Swindells

A Quiet Genocide. The Untold Holocaust of Disabled Children in WWII Germany, by Glenn Bryant

The Knife-Edge Path, by Patrick T. Leahy

Brave Face. The Inspiring WWII Memoir of a Dutch/German Child, by I. Caroline Crocker and Meta A. Evenbly

When We Had Wings. The Gripping Story of an Orphan in Janusz Korczak's Orphanage. A Historical Novel, by Tami Shem-Tov

Jacob's Courage. Romance and Survival amidst the Horrors of War, by Charles S. Weinblatt

Join the AP Review Team

Reviews are very important in a world dominated by the social media. Feedback for Holocaust books is more than just a customer review; it also shows the relevance and importance of such books in today's society.

Please go over to the AmsterdamPublishers.com website (top of page) if you want to join the *AP review team*, showing **at least one review on Amazon** for one of our books. You will get updates about new releases and will get the chance to read and review.

www.ingramcontent.com/pod-product-compliance
Lightning Source LLC
LaVergne TN
LVHW091548070526
838199LV00024B/577/J